Application Integration: EAI, B2B, BPM and SOA

Application Integration: EAI, B2B, BPM and SOA

Bernard Manouvrier
Laurent Ménard

iSTE

WILEY

First published in France in 2007 by Hermes Science/Lavoisier entitled "Intégration applicative EAI, B2B, BPM et SOA"
First published in Great Britain and the United States in 2008 by ISTE Ltd and John Wiley & Sons, Inc.
Translated from the French by Marc Swanson

ISTE Ltd
6 Fitzroy Square
London W1T 5DX
UK

www.iste.co.uk

John Wiley & Sons, Inc.
111 River Street
Hoboken, NJ 07030
USA

www.wiley.com

Library of Congress Cataloging-in-Publication Data

Manouvrier, Bernard.
[Intégration applicative EAI, B2B, BPM et SOA. English]
Application integration : EAI, B2B, BPM and SOA / Bernard Manouvrier, Laurent Ménard.
p. cm.
"First published in France in 2007 by Hermes Science/Lavoisier entitled "Integration applicative EAI, B2B, BPM et SOA."
"Translated from the French by Marc Swanson."
Includes bibliographical references and index.
ISBN 978-1-84821-088-2
1. Enterprise application integration (Computer systems) 2. Application software. 3. Management information systems. 4. Systems integration. I. Ménard, Laurent. II. Title.
QA76.76.A65M3337 2008
620.001'1--dc22

2008014999

British Library Cataloguing-in-Publication Data
A CIP record for this book is available from the British Library
ISBN: 978-1-84821-088-2

Printed and bound in Great Britain by CPI Antony Rowe, Chippenham, Wiltshire.

To the memory of Jacques Roy, expert in professional action

Table of Contents

Acknowledgments

The authors extend their particular thanks to Nicolas Manson, collection director, Aline Bec, manager for Information Systems and Technologie Groupe in Crédit Agricole SA and author of the foreword, the teams from Axway and Sopra Group in charge of the management of projects and products of Application Integration, and most particularly Claude Pagnier for his friendly and exacting companionship, Bernard Debauche, Jean-Luc Giraud, Jean-Paul Leydier, Sébastien Vugier, and Gilles Wu for their contributions and their sound advice.

The authors would equally like to thank their spouses and their families, whose patience and support during the writing of this book, often at unusual hours, is much appreciated.

Finally our thanks go most particularly to Monsieur Pierre Pasquier, without whom none of this would have been possible.

Foreword

Managers of information systems in enterprises are confronted by a cluster of major constraints, all of which they need to integrate in a balanced way.

First of all, the quality of the service supplied to both clients and employees of the enterprise. In two respects, this factor is fundamental: first, clients compare notes on their various suppliers; and second, clients expect flawless service to be available seven days a week, 24 hours a day. To stay competitive, the enterprise constantly has to raise its standards of quality and the level of commitment to customers. Computing services must be able to deliver on commitments of rates of availability and dependability of deliverables. Operational managers pursue automation to eliminate human intervention, so often a source of error and interruptions in executing processes. They need to understand the critical nature of the services that they deliver, well beyond technical components, in an end-to-end vision that links different applications, technologies, and, in very large enterprises, partners. That understanding requires close collaboration with services from research & development and from business specialists, charged with the tasks of production in the enterprise and marketing the offerings.

The enterprise is placed under tension by all of these players, who define performance indicators for the global process.

Quality of service is fundamental, not because it is a differentiating element from the competition, for the client sees that service as natural, but because it is indispensable to the functioning and to the development of the enterprise. Internally, it is the guarantee of professional credibility for information systems managers, ensuring that they will be listened to on the subject of the ongoing investments necessary to maintain functioning at the best level.

We arrive then at the constraint of costs. The ongoing optimization of operating costs, favored by best governance practices and the drop in technology costs, is an obsession that must not sacrifice investments in tools and internal methods.

An enterprise will put into place decision mechanisms for investments linked to its own business, but should rely on IT staff for specialized investments. This explains why the trust of the General Management team is imperative; the quality of service provided is the master component here.

However, technical environments are heterogenous, with multiple actors in the enterprise and sometimes multiple partners among the subsidiaries of a group. In certain cases, the dispositions are common to different enterprises or groups, which in addition, require control over development quality, and thus end-to-end control over exchanges between applications. This requires the definition of technical architectures and communication modes, but also involves supervising exchanges: what data in what transmission delay, what restart parameters in case of incidents, what solutions for maintaining the continuity of activities?

Enterprises assemble applications developed by their own IT with commercial software packages, on varied hardware, and use high-performance networks for communication, which in turn necessitates acquiring tools to supervise services.

This is not an easy message to convey to General Management, and an economic approach is expected to justify such investments: increased control in exchange for fewer incidents. To succeed here, a certain maturity in tracking quality and measuring the financial and client consequences of incidents is required.

Finally – time. Everything gets faster, technological evolution occurs at ever greater speeds, clients want information about their order in real time, and want to be able to approach distributors via different channels such as telephone, Internet and their point-of-sale. For employees of the enterprise, as well as for clients and partners, all this gives rise to a need for knowledge that is practically simultaneous with the information.

All these actors are in direct contact with system operations, which explains the extreme demands placed on IT staff. The operational supervision systems of the enterprise are for the same reasons submitted to a daily rhythm, or even more frequently. This is without counting the inevitable search for reactivity to respond in the shortest timeframes with a new product offering, which calls on the performance of all teams and brings to light difficulties of integrating new elements in existing systems.

Even the production of the financial information required for general supervision is experiencing new requirements, with delays in accounting settlements reduced to days – an imposed constraint on supervising results and communicating financial data.

The characteristics and qualities of information systems required by this context are generally known: the system must be well urbanized, with standardized data access, process-oriented access services, limited synchronous exchanges, and well ordered asynchronous exchanges.

The periods of top-down reconstructions are the occasion for building according to these principles, but most often, managers of information systems are confronted with systems of different origins, which respond precisely to defined architectural targets, with older portions poorly oriented towards customer service. And even then, they put into operation sets of systems that are dictated by strategic and economic considerations in the case of mergers and acquisitions.

This is a genuinely baffling problem, and one that requires a cool head and perseverance, and when confronting general management, the force of conviction for investing in domains such as urbanization, process supervision and tools for technical supervision of the extended enterprise, communicating with the partner base.

Managers of computing, research and development, and IT production are often the only players with a vision of the whole and an understanding of all the issues. Beside them, in the best of cases, are application architects, little versed in technical specialties, and technical architects, specialists in infrastructural components but far from the vision of the business processes. Parameters for exchanges – vital programming for operations – contain management rules which are, however, not as documented and secured as the rest of the application resources.

Suppliers who propose their support in these approaches are unfortunately too often biased to the sale of one product or another, without a wide knowledge of other products. Caution is required, even if only because while the concerns are permanent, suppliers are often followers of fashion.

It is with particular pleasure that I invite you to read this work, in the first place, because its authors, whom I have encountered at different junctures in my professional life, escape the criticism of suppliers I just made, and who have always, with me, demonstrated wide expertise and sound advice. But above all because you will find here a complete and realistic panorama of integration topics, conforming to the preoccupations and the roadmaps of IT managers.

This book is therefore your chance to focus on the different concepts and the solutions provided in each particular context, and you can thus measure the path to be traveled to reach a reasonably consistent and accomplished target. It also serves as a reference document for computing services, and provides, with pedagogy and precision, a fascinating light on the techniques and competencies that may not often be shared by IT management, and yet, are essential for their performance.

Aline Bec

Chapter 1

Introduction

Recently, a friend and colleague who is also an expert in complex systems integration related the following real-life experience to us:

"I was mandated to assess the adaptability of the information system for a large French high technology company, because any modification, even a minor one, was turning out to be impracticable. My conclusion was that neither people nor technologies were the cause. It was only the confusion reigning between the business, technical and organizational models of the information system that made evolution impossible. A revolution was necessary."

This anecdote illustrates the importance of application integration. The growing inter-connectivity between information systems that underlie the business of enterprises leads the "web" of application integration to become a more important issue than the technical and business content of the applications themselves.

For all of that, this network of exchanges between applications is often poorly visible and little known to decision-makers. Its existence is often diluted and dispersed owing to the departmental segmentation of operating budgets and of the interfaces between applications developed "at the end of the project when deadlines are tight". Nonetheless, as we will show, the financial and business consequences of application integration can be immense.

The paradox then is that the computing community is usually more interested in technical architectures for development than in mechanisms for integration between applications. It is as if in international commerce, exchanges of goods and services were only considered at the level of the rules and procedures of the member countries, with no attention paid to common rules for exchanges.

Nevertheless, when issues of application integration do come to light,[1] the few successful implementations of integration solutions can barely conceal the resounding failures.

How does it happen that this clear awareness of the interest in sustainable integration of applications has not led to a plethora of successful projects? Is this a problem whose solution lies in technique, in implementation – in organization perhaps?

For a number of years, it has been our privilege to work at the heart of the practice of application integration, designing software packages and successfully implementing integration projects. This field experience has allowed us to draw some key lessons, resulting today in a practical guide that can sharply increase the chances of success in this domain and that constitutes a follow-up to the work *EAI Intégration des applications d'entreprise* ("EAI – Enterprise Application Integration") [MAN 01]. The present work returns to a certain number of themes broached in that work, while bringing others up to date and presenting new aspects of application integration.

The objective of the present work then is to help the reader to:

– understand what is involved in application integration;

– become acquainted with integration services and how to use them advisedly;

– map out an integration specifications document that conforms to reader needs;

– avoid common errors in application integration projects;

– succeed the deployment of integration solutions inside the enterprise;

– put into practice methods for calculating return on investment (ROI) and implementation costs.

Depending on what you want from this book, we can suggest several "paths" to reading it.

1 Which is, in addition, beginning to be shared by representatives of the computing community.

Chapter \ Profiles	"Discovery"	General Manager	Business user	IT user
1. What is application integration	X	X	X	X
2. Levels in application integration				X
4. Types of integration projects	X	X	X	X
5. Application integration	X	X		X
6. Understanding integration failures	X	X	X	X
7. Application integration tools			X	X
8. Integration and IT urbanization		X	X	X
9. Choosing an application integration solution		X	X	X
10. Deployment methodology		X	X	X
11. Operational examples of implementation	X	X	X	X

Table 1.1. *Reading paths*

Chapter 2

What is Application Integration?

2.1. The economy: the "engine" of integration

The liberalization of the rules for international commerce over the last 30 years has disrupted the rules for producing and exchanging goods and services.

Markets have gone global, as large enterprises have become increasingly international in their culture and their mode of production.

Faced with the continuous development of computing technologies (Moore's Law doubling machine power every 18 months is constantly validated) and with the explosion of bandwidths on networks that are now standardized around Internet protocols, information systems in enterprises have paralleled developments in the real world, becoming extended, dispersed and continuously interconnected with other information systems.

The conjunction of this mass market coupled with technological development has caused a fundamental transformation of the economy, whose principal effects are the following:

– *Globalization:* that allows any enterprise to sell anything anywhere in the world, based on its cost of production. The competition is also globalizing, and enterprises that are accustomed to operating in protected markets must from now on confront competitors from anywhere in the world. Is anything easier for a consumer than using an Internet connection to compare offerings?

– *Mergers and acquisitions*: to attain the economic weight indispensable for keeping up in this new environment, enterprises are also seeking size and power, particularly through the national and international mergers and acquisitions that routinely make headlines in the financial pages.

– *The multiplication of exchanges*: in such a context, to leapfrog the competition and increase market share, the enterprise must show greater reactivity, becoming the first to present a new product to the market. Inevitably, this reactivity involves multiplying information exchanges, first inside the enterprise, but also with the outside world. However, the exchange chain is no longer limited to the classic and well defined channels of communication with suppliers and clients. Through the new channels and new protocols on the Internet, this chain must also start integrating subsidiaries, partners, banks and government agencies. It is in this context that sector-based exchange networks (RosettaNet, SWIFT, FIX, etc.) or multi-sector networks (such as Bolero.net) are proliferating.

Today it appears certain that the success of an enterprise is closely linked to its capacity to respond to new requirements:

– increase reactivity and adaptability (becoming what Gartner Inc. refers to as a "Zero Latency Enterprise");

– accelerate time-to-market;

– manage external exchanges optimally;

– etc.

However, is the information system – and more specifically, are intra- and inter-enterprise information exchanges – ready for this kind of positioning?

The history of business computing allows us to understand the state of information systems of today in terms of application integration.

2.2. The history and the issues of application integration

In the beginning[2] was ... the IT island.

Each enterprise or department that had been computerized lived serenely in its own universe, with its specific applications and with no interaction with the outside world. The ocean was vast and limitless, and ships never met other ships (Figure 2.1). When information did reach the ears of the inhabitants, borne by birds or

2 That is, the beginning of the 1960s ...

bottles drifting on the sea, there was no particular problem treating it "by hand" – in the form of computing data entries – in data files of the enterprise.

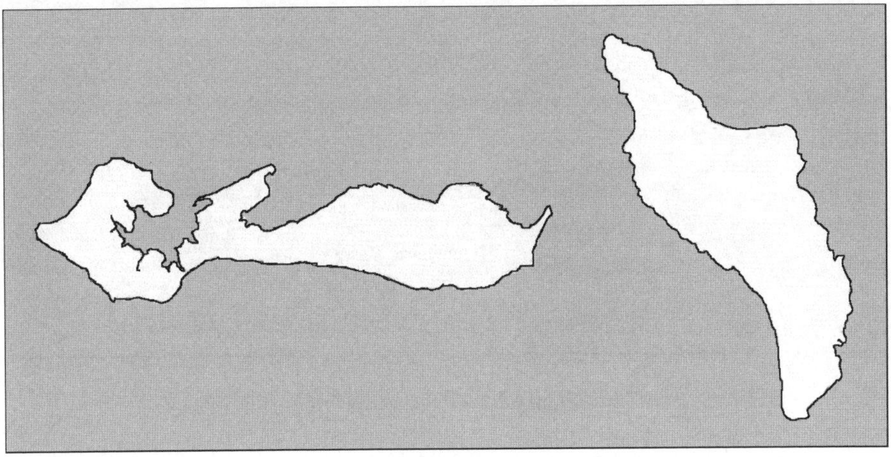

Figure 2.1. *Islands*

With the increase in economic exchanges and the continued progress of computing technologies, each island started growing, little by little, to serve much larger needs. From the computerization of payroll or accounting, applications appeared on the island for managing clients or production, as we might put it in this metaphor, forts, dungeons and castles were added. Applications had to be put into communication with each other, to avoid re-entering data "by hand"; thus integration between applications (EAI[3] and A2A[4]) was born. It came first in small steps, without greatly altering the landscape. Paths were "dug" between different applications but there was no map, no overall rule of conduct (Figure 2.2). The number of vehicles circulating was increasing, and at rush hour, it was not unusual to see all the vehicles stopped at the side of the road. Resolve was needed to increase the roadways and create avenues and other routes, to assign right-of-way – in short, to begin "urbanizing" the applications.[5]

3 EAI: Enterprise Application Integration.

4 A2A: Application to (two) Application.

5 *Translator's note:* "Urbanization", a term which occurs frequently in this book, refers to a set of principles for applying ideas and insights taken from the discipline of urban or city planning to the design of computerized information systems. A staple of computer science discussions in France, the idea of urbanization is less well known elsewhere. Section 4.2.1 provides a slightly more extended discussion of the concept of "urbanized IT".

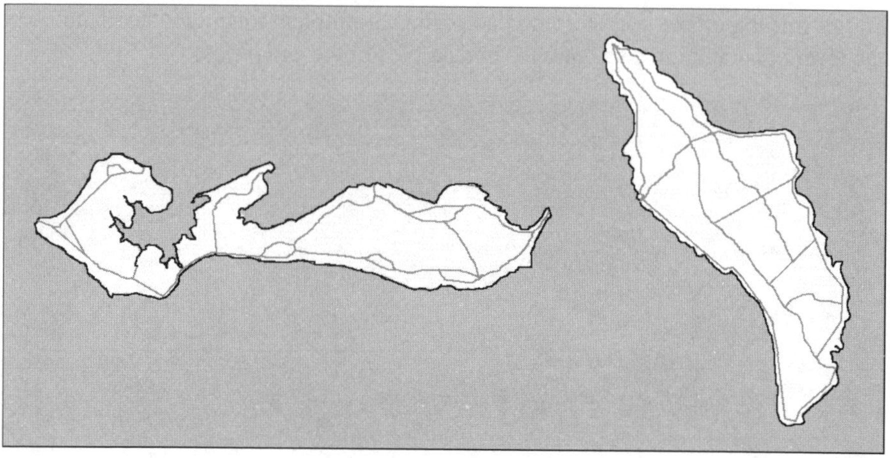

Figure 2.2. *Island roadways*

The ocean did its part by bringing information from the outside directly to the beach. At first, boats did not dock together; there was no port yet. Only little dinghies run ashore on the beach – in the form of diskettes or magnetic tape. Their content was transported on mule-back to the concerned computing domains. Sometimes the cargo was not "digestible" by an application, which tended to reject it collectively. The frequency of arrival of boats accelerated, because food from the open sea was also necessary to the native computing population. Ports had to be constructed, with rules of the road for ships, for checking the quality of merchandise, and for dispatching it to the different computing domains, sometimes repackaging it in the process. B2B[6] was born. Maritime routes prospered, and with them, the risks of collision or (information) piracy. All this had to be regulated, which helps explain the appearance of network protocols, file transfer managers and the means to encrypt the information. However, sometimes this was not enough. Since islands tend to become continents, and boats tend to block up ports, it also became necessary to construct bridges to drain off information in real-time (Figure 2.3). MOM[7] was created.

6 B2B: Business to (or "two") Business.

7 MOM: Message-Oriented Middleware.

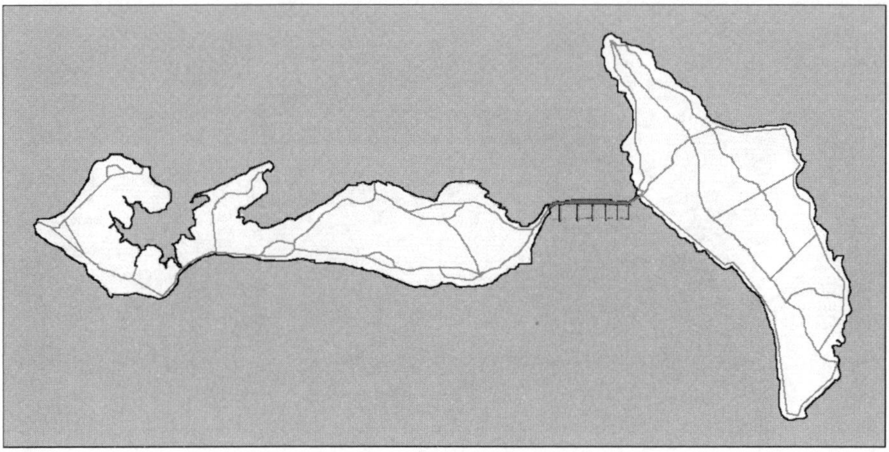

Figure 2.3. *Island communication*

Not only did the islands or continents of business computing need high-performance intra- and inter-enterprise infrastructures for information exchange, but they also had to check that the information they were producing and taking into account actually conformed to what was expected to advance the business.

Observation satellites were then required (Figure 2.4) because with the wrong priority in the timing of transporting and processing information by the applications, a significant part of the activity of the enterprise could find itself blocked with a "head cold", leading to loss of revenues and lowered profitability.

It then became necessary to check first that everything happened correctly and second (as in Star Wars) that a "bad shot" could be corrected quickly. Thus, BAM[8] was born.

8 BAM: Business Activity Monitoring.

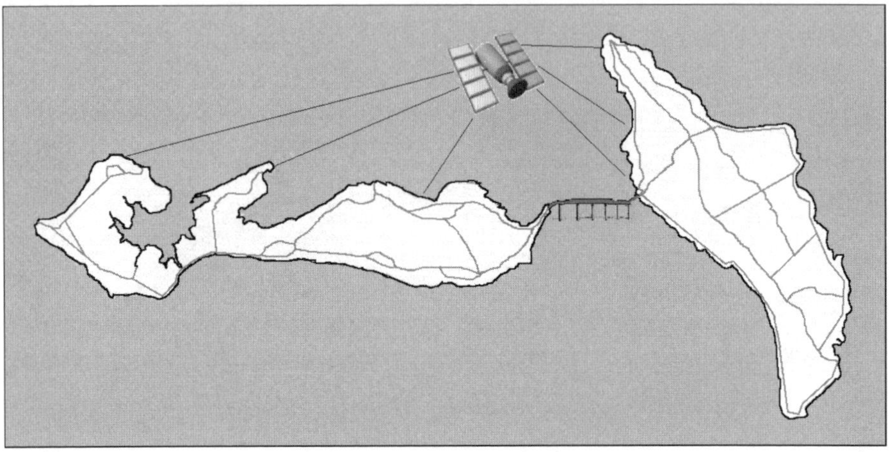

Figure 2.4. *Island supervision*

A complete set of technologies reinforce the reactivity and harmony that must reign on the islands, continents, and oceans of computing: urbanization, dataflow management, secured transport, transformation and storage of information between applications, technical and business supervision of the dataflows. These technologies make the applications reactive, by taking account of the business events that arise in the information system, "just-in-time".

Most of the range of application integration problems is situated at precisely this level.

At the same time, when what is at stake is the complete "subjection" of IT to business logic, it is sometimes necessary to go further still.

This is notably the case when goods and services must be produced on request, such as when processing a request for a high-speed phone connection, coupled with a rate for fixed line, the whole may be associated with a digital television offering.

In classic (often mass) application processing, for each order, a set of elementary tasks could be overlaid for processing the demand from one end to the other. We can speak of processes that activate tasks, or "activities" on the various IT islands and continents involved, thus transcending the boundaries of countries.

This new need is added to the application integration technologies mentioned above, but it does not replace them. Instead, it imposes two supplemental elements:

– Provide standardized services inside applications which can still be accessed from outside the application: SOA[9]. This presupposes bringing down the ramparts of those application citadels, opening up to others as soon as their intentions are peaceful, and being "always ready" to provide the requested service.

– Using BPM[10] technologies, model and orchestrate the tasks required to execute the demand. Modeling is required to handle frequent modification of the business offerings, which is particularly true for high-tech offerings such as for connecting telecoms operators. Orchestration is imperative since we want to subjugate – though we could just as well say *align* – the information system to the business.

Abandoning these rather medieval and geographical metaphors for a more musical one, services (SOA) are like a group of concert artists each playing their own solo musical scores, but under the direction of an orchestra conductor (BPM) who coordinates and tunes them, smoothing over their sour notes, allowing them to catch up at the next bar to move their playing towards harmony for the greater pleasure of "spectators", i.e., clients (Figure 2.5).

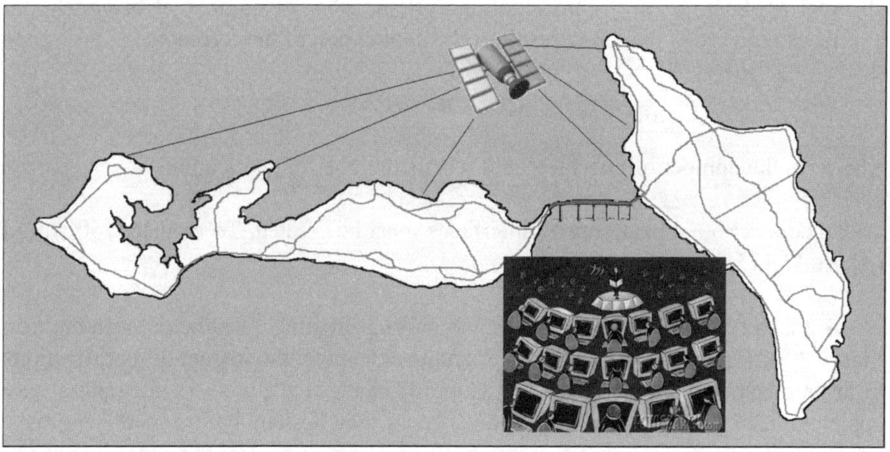

Figure 2.5. *Orchestrated islands*

Organizing the application territory and the communications between applications renders business process "music" audible and harmonious. Metaphorically but genuinely, then, these are the issues in application integration.

9 SOA: Service Oriented Architecture.
10 BPM: Business Process Management.

2.3. Consequences for IT

Current information systems are therefore composed of applications that were developed in different periods, by different development teams, most of the time without real coordination, and using different technologies. In the majority of cases, new applications were created using the most recent technology at the time, often without genuinely questioning the necessity of implementing such a technology, and forgetting that a "modern" technology becomes obsolete in an instant of time.

In addition, as we have seen, these applications were not originally designed to communicate with each other. The links and interfaces that allow them to cooperate had to be created between each application. The introduction of commercial software packages in information systems has only reinforced this problem, since they were designed to respond to a particular problem without being preoccupied about communicating with the existing system.

If we consider the extreme case where all applications must communicate with all other applications in the information system, then the number of bi-directional interfaces required is the direct result of the application of the formula:

$$i = n\,(n - 1)/2$$

where i is the number of interfaces and n is the number of applications.

To connect 6 applications, 15 interfaces must be created. To connect 150 would require 11,175!

In this way, and quite inevitably, we end up creating "spaghetti" systems (see Figure 2.6), where it is very difficult to analyze the potential impact of modifications to an application or to measure the scope of changes required to integrate a new application. IT managers reach the point where they hesitate before modifying their information systems, because they are no longer able to control the consequences of their own changes. The system itself starts to resist change, and the result could be termed the *fossilization* of the information system.

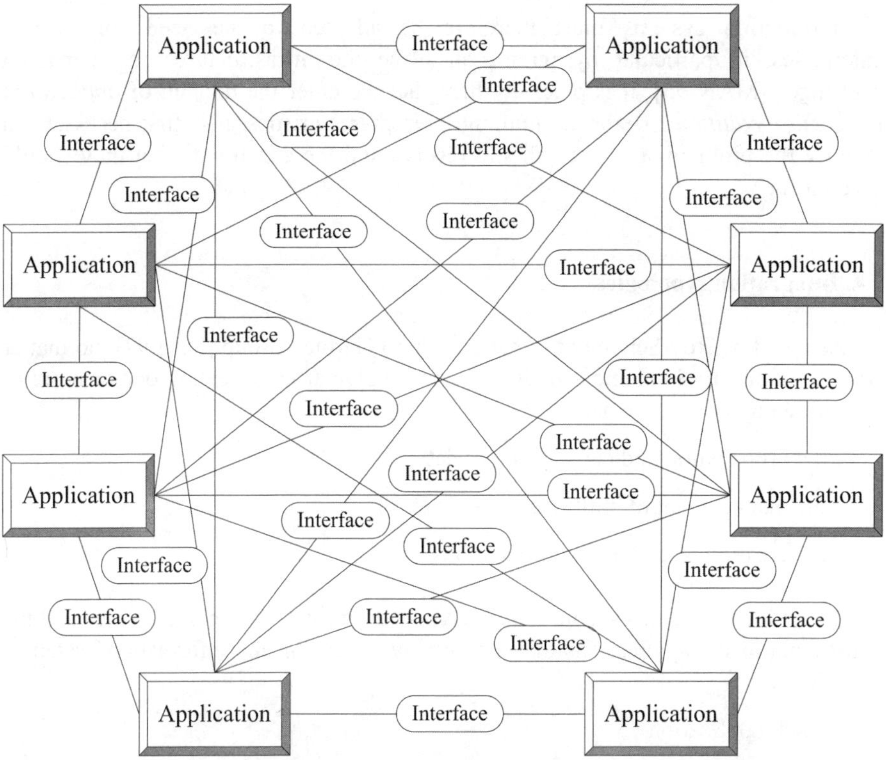

Figure 2.6. *A "spaghetti" system*

Enterprise information systems are largely characterized by:

– heterogenity in the hardware platforms and the applications;

– multiplication of the interfaces between the applications;

– a well known incapacity to easily exchange information, either internally or with the outside world.

In terms of speed of evolution and communication, such systems are thus absolutely poorly adapted, but as we have seen, it is precisely those qualities that are indispensable to the survival of enterprises in today's economic context. Indeed, it must today be possible to – for example – delocalize a portion of the information system or to pool back-offices so as to optimize costs and concentrate investments in areas that add value and help differentiate the enterprise from its competition.

Information systems must therefore be adapted to the needs of today's enterprises, in particular by putting in place the infrastructures for managing exchanges [MAN 95]. It is precisely here that we enter the domain of *application integration solutions.* Before examining their characteristics, it is first necessary to identify the problems that they should resolve and the constraints that they should account for.

2.4. Integration typologies

As noted by Roy Schulte of (what was then) Gartner Group [SCH 97], no matter what solutions are implemented, all of them revolve around treating one or more of the following problem areas:

– the propagation and consistency of data;

– the management of multi-step processes;

– the creation of composite applications.

To achieve these goals, solutions must take account of the characteristics and the constraints of the applications that are already present in the information system,[11] including:

– batch applications;

– transactional applications;

– client/server applications;

– Web applications;

– real-time applications;

– commercial software packages.

2.4.1. *Classifying the integration problem types*

2.4.1.1. *Data propagation and data fidelity*

The principal reason for implementing an application integration solution is typically propagating data and imposing consistency on it. This involves ensuring the consistency of data stored redundantly by different applications for geographical, technical or organizational reasons. This type of integration impacts multiple

11 For definitions of the different types of applications, refer to section 2.4.2.

business processes, comprising multiple steps with asynchronous and uni-directional interactions which function on independent platforms.

For example, consider three applications, one to take an order, one for managing customers, and one for managing sales. Each application operates on different platforms and uses technologies appropriate to those platforms, and each uses information about enterprise customers. Consistency of information among these three applications must be ensured.

Two methods can be used:

– The *repository* approach: *copy the data directly* from the database (or from files) used by the original (order-taking) application to the databases (or files) used by the other two applications (Figure 2.7). This approach goes through the *data*. It presupposes that the semantic and data models used by the applications are compatible. Furthermore, it does not preserve the integrity of the data from the recipient applications since it does not make it possible to apply the update logic and management rules of those other applications.

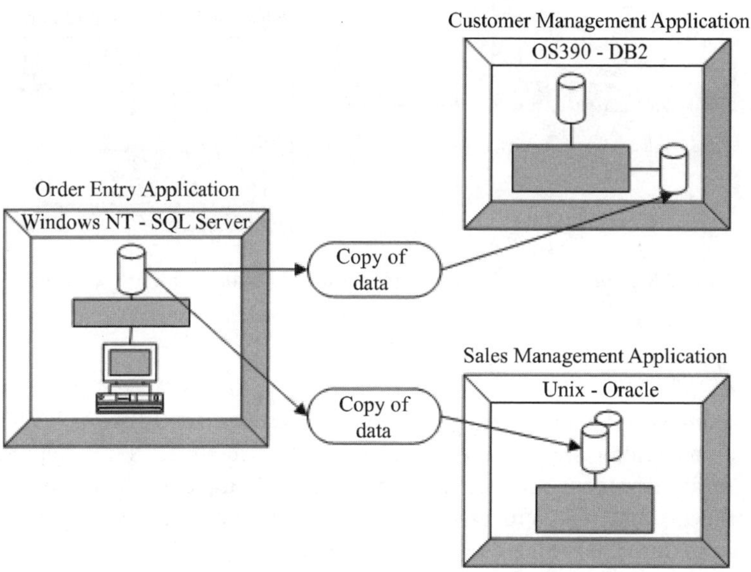

Figure 2.7. *Propagate data and impose consistency: going through the data*

– The *event-based* approach: *transmit an event* from the original application to the other two applications, which will then ensure its processing, updating their own information themselves (Figure 2.8).

No matter which method is used, data can be copied or events transmitted in *sessions* (batches to copy information or send events) or *in real time* (copy or send each process performed in the original application).

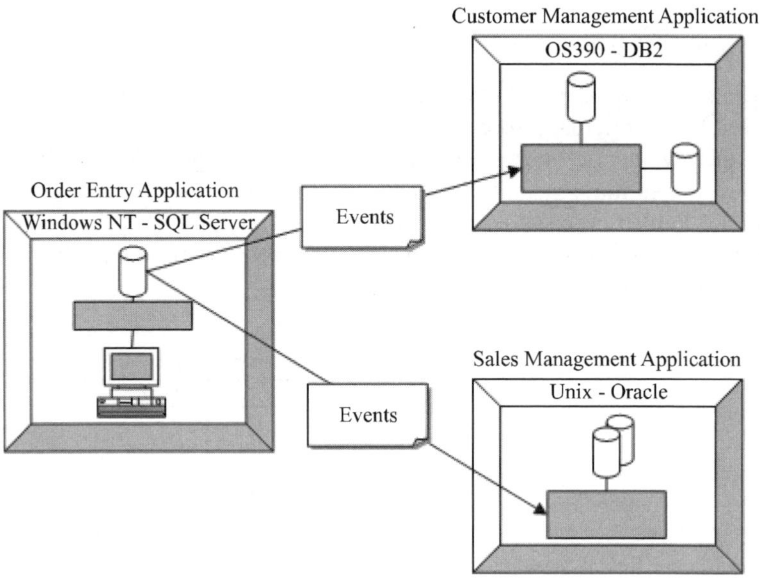

Figure 2.8. *Propagate data and impose consistency: going through the events*

2.4.1.2. *The management of multi-step processes*

The management of multi-step processes addresses the business processes in the enterprise. Integration enables a business process that comprises several application steps with asynchronous and uni-directional interactions, but which are logically interdependent, and with processing performed by each step dependent on the processing performed upstream by the other steps. These applications can of course function on independent platforms. Such a process can involve human interventions, but most of the time, it is entirely automated, exhibiting what we could term express processing, or "straight-through processing" (STP):

– As an example, consider three other applications: one for taking orders, one to manage production, and another to handle billing. Again, they all run on different platforms and use technologies appropriate to those platforms. The objective is the integration of the complete process in an STP approach: take the order – manufacture the article – invoice it. This integration will require automatic sequencing of the three applications by also managing the transmission of the associated management events, for example manufacturing order and request to output the invoice.

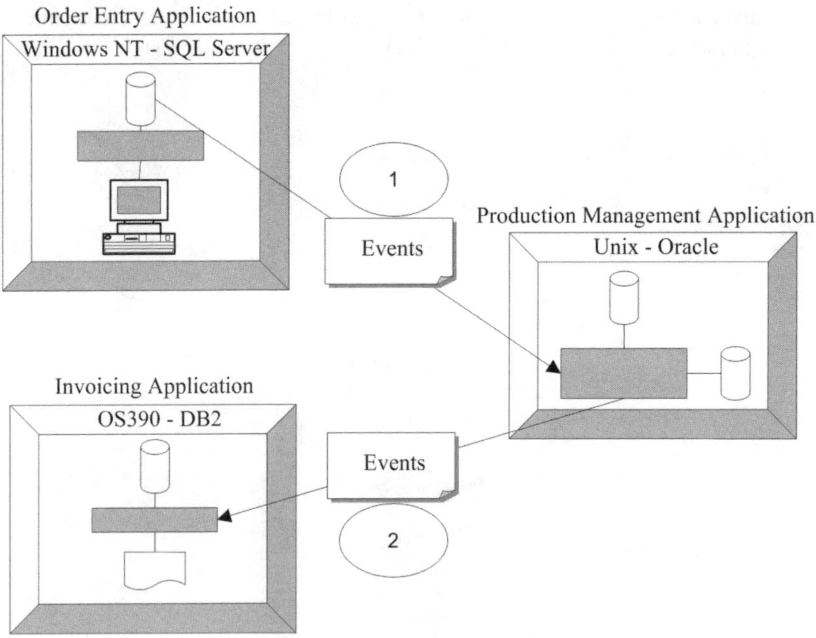

Figure 2.9. *Management of multi-step processes: event-based approach*

– Events can be transmitted in batches (copy the information or send the events) or in real time (copy or send as and when the original application executes). Real-time transmission is, of course, more appropriate for achieving STP.

2.4.1.3. *Creating composite applications*

Here it is a question of creating a new application by using the data or the services available in the existing applications, which explains its denomination of "composite application". This is the type of integration found most often at the basis for implementing a client application on the Web. This application will, for example, request one or more transactions on a central computer, and will call software packages on Unix or NT.

As an example, consider an application for handling orders on the Web. The application is developed by calling data stored in the database of the client applications on an MVS platform under DB2; it will call a service in the sales management package (operating on Unix); and it will interrogate the inventory database (on another Unix platform).

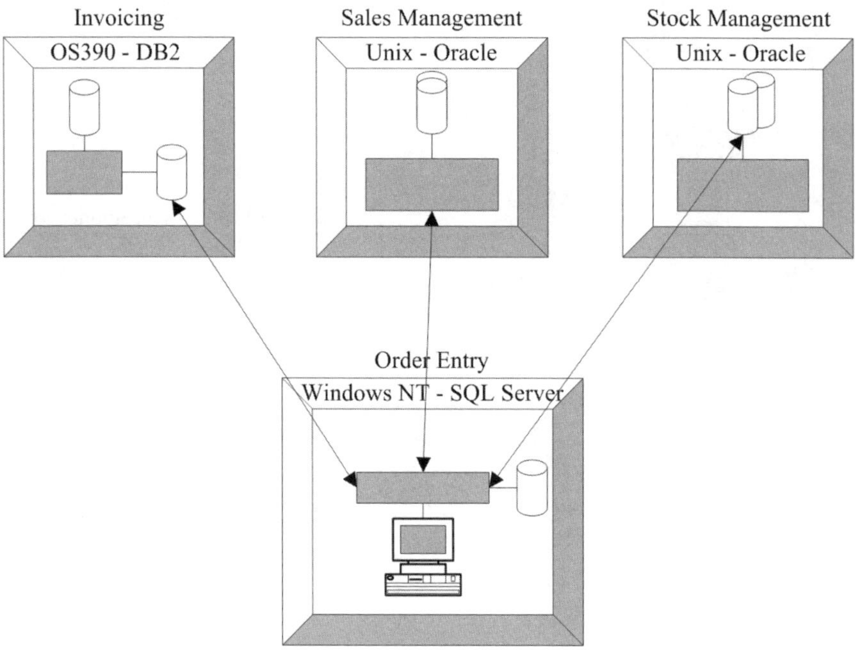

Figure 2.10. *Creation of a composite application*

This integration example concerns a single, mono-step business process, necessitating synchronous and bi-directional interactions, through unitary exchanges in real time. Most often, it will use an approach that mixes data and events.

To put an application integration solution in place then involves first determining the problem(s) to resolve (data propagation, straight-through processing, or composite applications), then the method for solving it (integration through the data, or through events), but it is also necessary to know the characteristics and constraints of the applications to be integrated.

2.4.2. *Classifying the applications*

The examination of the applications to be integrated makes it possible to determine the constraints that follow from the characteristics intrinsic to each of the integration types to which we can attach them. For example, putting a Web application in relation with a batch application could only be performed under certain conditions, because the philosophies of those types of applications are so different.

The characteristics that we will examine concern the operating rhythm or *pace* of the applications, the *format* of the events or data that they process, the *volume* of these events, and application *connectivity* or *exchange capacity* with other applications.

2.4.2.1. *Batch applications*

This is the oldest type of application in the information system. Batch applications are characterized according to our criteria in the following way:

– *Pace:* as their name indicates, batch applications do not process events as and when they occur: instead they take charge of sets (batches) of events grouped into files or in databases for batch processing. The periodicity of such applications can depend on very different elements, or on a combination of elements, such as:

- the volume of the events to be processed: this can impose frequent executions so as to be able to integrate them more easily when scheduling production at the processing center;

- dependencies with other applications;

- inability of other applications to coexist with batch applications (batch and transactional, for example);

- the way departments in the enterprise are organized (a factor which should in fact be the first element that sets the pace for the rhythm of exchanges);

- etc.

– *Format:* the formats processed by these applications are typically fairly simple ("flat" formats – see section 3.2.1.1), since a significant number of these applications were developed using languages such as COBOL that provide little support for complex structures. In general, "old" applications do not create events, creating instead as many reports and formats as there are receiving applications and with as many business rules for interpreting them, thus reinforcing the "spaghetti" system.

– *Volume:* for the most part, batch applications can support extremely significant volumes; a single batch can contain millions of events.

– *Connectivity:* these applications communicate using files or databases only.

2.4.2.2. *Transactional applications*

We can characterize transactional applications applying the same categories as above, with very different results:

– *Pace:* transactional applications process events as and when they occur in production. Further, since most of the time they also manage the interface with users, it is critical for them to be available during the working timeslots for these users. However, this can sometimes lead to problems of coexistence with other applications (as mentioned above for batch vs. transactional).

– *Format*: the formats processed by these applications depend on the technologies that are implemented and the development languages that are used. Generally these applications handle more complex data structures than traditional batch applications (hierarchical formats, for example – see section 3.2.1.1).

– *Volume:* what is important for these applications is their capacity to absorb a large number of events simultaneously.

– *Connectivity:* These applications typically communicate using databases (or files), and via the screen interface itself.

2.4.2.3. *Client/server applications*

We can consider client/server applications as a more advanced form of transactional applications, which means that they exhibit quite similar characteristics:

– *Pace:* as with transactional applications, client/server applications process events as and when they occur in production and, in the same way, the availability of these events is of paramount importance.

– *Format:* since they use relatively recent technologies, these applications can handle complex data structures.

– *Volume:* simultaneity remains a significant characteristic, even if part of processing is performed on the client workstation.

– *Connectivity:* these applications also communicate using the database and the screen interface.

2.4.2.4. *Web applications*

Web applications constitute a particular form of transactional application and therefore retain similar characteristics:

– *Pace:* events are processed as and when they occur in production. Availability and ergonomy remain key characteristics.

– *Format:* the processed data structures are complex (for example, XML).

– *Volume:* since access is performed via the Internet, the potential number of connected users cannot be controlled and can be extremely large. Simultaneity remains critical.

– *Connectivity:* more recent, these applications are often much better able to communicate than traditional applications. In addition to databases, they can communicate using Internet technologies (HTTP, SMTP) in particular.

2.4.2.5. *Real-time applications*

These applications made their appearance at the end of the 1990s with the emergence of technologies in inter-application messaging (MOM – Message-Oriented Middleware – see section 3.1.2.3). They function according to logics that can operate in both batch and transactional modes. As a result, their characteristics are hybrid:

– *Pace:* these applications handle events in real time, at the same rhythm as their production.

– *Format:* the processed data structures can be complex.

– *Volume:* as with batch applications, they are designed to support significant volumes, though with lesser performance.[12]

– *Connectivity:* these applications communicate essentially through APIs (Application Programming Interfaces) relying on MOM queues.

2.4.2.6. *Software packages*

Depending on their destination, commercial software packages exhibit characteristics of one type or another, and for Enterprise Resource Planning (ERP), which by definition covers numerous functions in business IT, practically the sum of these characteristics.

At the same time, connectivity – long a weak point in software packages – has become for most of them a differentiating factor. This is why it is now possible to

12 Because the integrity constraints at the event/message level are more fine-grained than at the level of batch processing.

exchange with these software packages through multiple access points: files, queues, databases, APIs, HTTP, Web-Services, etc.

This constitutes an important point concerning the capacity to connect these software packages to the rest of the system.

2.5. EAI: integrating enterprise applications (A2A)

The term EAI first appeared in the USA around 1996-1997 with the publication of articles or research notes by large analyst firms, including studies from Roy Schulte (then) of Gartner Group [SCH 97] or those of Mike Gilpin of Giga Group [GIL 99]. These studies analyzed the approaches encountered at a certain number of large enterprises to explain the emergence of a range of problems in integration, which they predicted would become one of the most important problems of the next ten years.

However, if the term “EAI” was invented, conceptualized, and brought to market by North Americans, the precursors in this matter were French.

2.5.1. *Accounting interpretation: EAI precursor*

The concepts and the first operational implementations appeared from 1975, driven by regulatory accounting reforms in banking establishments in France.

The pioneers were Jacques Sassoon [SAS 98] and Jean-Paul Leydier. While working on an accounting interpreter based on events and rules, they solidified the principles of event-based transformation of information between operational systems and the accounting system of the “Banque de Paris et des Pays-Bas”.[13]

This first implementation opened the way in France to the development of software packages for accounting interpretation (no longer commercially available) such as STEGEC from the Stéria corporation and ROCADE from Arthur Andersen.

Only the software package Règles du Jeu (RDJ)[14] from Sopra Group/Axway, worthy successor to that 1975 accounting interpreter, is still going strong today, with several hundred references in the banking and financial world.

---

13 Now part of the banking group BNP Paribas – *translator's note.*

14 Now marketed under the name “Synchrony AccountingIntegrator”, and for which one of the authors of the current work ensured the design and implementation.

2.5.2. *EAI today*

Today, from reading the articles appearing in specialized journals or viewing the publications from consulting firms, it seems that defining EAI is anything but simple, so different are the various positions staked out by different players in this domain. Still, we would put forward the following definition, which seems to us to accurately reflect various facets of the question:

EAI is a collection of methods, tools, and services that work together to bring heterogenous applications into communication, as part of the traditional, distributed or extended enterprise.

In other words, the essential problem to resolve is the exchange of information between the applications in the information system, and more specifically, to respond to the question: how can we make sure that *heterogenous* applications, designed at different periods, by different teams and using different technologies, can communicate, without needing to "know" each other, or take account of their respective constraints?

To us, it also seems necessary to insist on what is not in the domain of EAI, because confusion often arises: *EAI is in no way concerned with communication inside an application.* The problem of communication between the components of one client/server application does not fall in the domain of EAI. That is a problem of application architecture. However, the way in which that client/server application communicates with other applications in the information system constitutes a genuine EAI problem.

Moreover, EAI concerns communication between *heterogenous* applications. Applications that share common repositories and use common semantics and identical technologies do not pose a problem of integration with each other. In other words, *homogenous* applications are *already integrated.* Deploying the methods and development tools for creating these integrated applications (for example: application objects integrated around CORBA) *does not fall within the domain of EAI.* An EAI approach results in applications coexisting with other applications that were built around different technologies, and which are therefore incapable of communicating naturally with each other.

EAI therefore deals with the oldest domain in integration: the domain of business applications – Application to Application (often shortened to "AtoA" or "A2A"). This is typically the domain of ERP integration, or the integration of front-office applications with the back-office applications, or the integration of software for Customer Relationship Management (CRM), Supply Chain Management (SCM), etc.

The projects that implement EAI solutions are examined in sections 4.1 and 4.2.

2.6. Integrating inter-enterprise exchanges (B2B)

Inter-enterprise exchanges (Business-to-Business – BtoB or B2B) concern exchanges of goods or services between two commercial entities (partners, clients, suppliers), as opposed to exchanges with the end consumer (see section 2.9).

Exchanges between enterprises only really got started when they involved automating the exchanges of commercial transactions (purchase order, invoice, etc.) through EDI (see section 4.3.1).

The technical support for these exchanges takes the form of implementing automated functions for file exchanges (see section 3.1.2.2). Once again, the precursors in this matter were French corporations, such as NETSYS with Inter.Pel (formerly known under the name of PELICAN),[15] Crédintrans with CFT,[16] as well as the American software provider Sterling Commerce.

To draw a parallel with the definition of EAI, we can say that *B2B integration* is a *collection of methods, tools and services that work together to bring heterogenous IT applications in multiple enterprises into inter-communication, with the goal of carrying out commercial transactions between them.*

The integration of inter-enterprise exchanges is therefore an extension of the set of problems in EAI, and therefore remains fundamentally attached to the capacity to exchange information between heterogenous applications that do not belong to the same information systems, since they are in different enterprises.

We can therefore say that *B2B integration corresponds to inter-enterprise A2A integration*. The differences flow essentially out of what the enterprise cannot control:

– the communication network;

– the exchange format;

– the exchange process.

Projects that implement inter-enterprise exchange solutions will be examined in section 4.3.

---

15 For which the other author of the current work participated in the design and implementation.

16 These two products have since been acquired by Sopra/Axway.

2.7. Coupling A2A and B2B: A2B (or Business Collaboration)

In today's world, the range of problems linked to A2A and B2B not only coexist but tend, for business reasons, to interpenetrate:

– exchanges between domains in very large enterprises sometimes belong more to the range of problems in B2B;

– providing a service to the client helps to federate both the applications inside the enterprise and the applications inside suppliers and sub-contractors;

– the domains of responsibility are becoming increasingly more horizontal, thus both *intra*- and *inter*-enterprise.

Awareness of the coupling of the two approaches is relatively new and involves certain specific points. We refer to it as *A2B* ("Application to Business"), though increasingly, it is known under the term Business Collaboration.

2.8. Managing business processes (BPM)

Business Process Management, or BPM, groups the complete set of activities carried out by enterprises to optimize and adapt their business processes. In other words: "*the engineering of business processes, integrating both automatic and manual tasks with the help of information technologies*" (see the work by Bernard Debauche and Patrick Megard [DEB 04]).

Following the definition formula used previously in this work, we could write: *BPM is an approach that groups the complete set of methods, tools and services for modeling, executing and optimizing business processes in the enterprise, i.e., the processes in the value chain that are horizontal to the organizations in the enterprise, and that further extend to the partners of the enterprise, including suppliers, clients, banks, etc.*

BPM thus involves dealing with problems that concern the management of multi-step processes (one of the integration types classified in section 2.4.1.2). Projects that implement BPM solutions will be examined in section 4.4.

The ultimate goal of BPM is to be able to optimize the business processes of an enterprise to bring about a more effective and better performing enterprise. In turn, this goal implies that the enterprise must be able to measure its effectiveness and performance. Here, we enter the domain of Business Activity Monitoring (BAM) often – but not always – indivisible from BPM.

The term BAM was introduced by Gartner analysts in July 2001 and defined as "*providing real-time access to critical business performance indicators to improve the speed and effectiveness of business operations*."

Setting up a Business Activity Monitoring solution will therefore often – but not always – go hand in hand with the implementation of BPM. BAM then handles supervision, using dashboards, indicators and alerts to supply real-time analysis of the business events produced by multiple sources that are independent from each other, or originating in the business events themselves when they are managed by a BPM tool.

2.9. Service-oriented architectures (SOA)

The implementation of a services architecture is not directly associated with a particular type of integration, though it often traces its origins to the problem of integrating composite applications (see section 2.4.1.3), or in other cases, follows and helps support a BPM approach.

This type of integration was strongly accelerated by the development of exchanges between enterprises and end consumers: Business to Consumer – "B to C" or "B2C".

B2C is probably the domain that has provoked the most discussion around integration in recent years. Indeed, with the Internet explosion, B2C exchanges with consumers have multiplied, requiring the implementation of new applications that use Web technologies: browsers, HTML (Hyper Text Markup Language) presentations, HTTP (Hyper Text Transport Protocol) servers, SMTP (Simple Mail Transfer Protocol) servers, Java applications, etc.

The need to integrate these applications in the existing information system appears as a crucial element in the capacity of the enterprise to respond rapidly to consumer demands in online access to the catalog, prices, sales conditions, delivery delays and the possibility of ordering, paying, etc. In short, a consumer who always wants better, faster, cheaper.

A typical example of this range of problems is the implementation of Internet sales portals, which requires, for example, real-time inventory consultation and update, as well as interaction with a client management application (Figure 2.11).

To stay within the lines of our definitions to this point, we could write that *B2C integration is a set of methods, tools and services that work together to put heterogenous applications in an enterprise into communication with each other, with the goal of giving clients direct access to the services offered by that enterprise.*

The points to resolve in integrating exchanges with consumers are similar to those mentioned for integrating applications in the enterprise: in both A2A and B2C, applications must be able to exchange information with each other. However, in B2C, one of those applications is constructed from data or services in existing applications, and it is *that* application which manages the interface with the consumer.

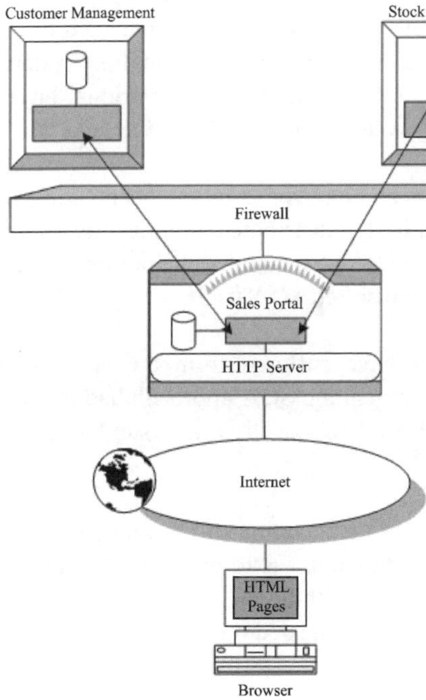

Figure 2.11. *Example of integrating exchanges with the consumer*

B2C integration is therefore a special case of A2A integration. The essential difference is that in B2C, the enterprise must confront the problem of a consumer who can consult the site of a competitor at any moment, for example, if response times are not fast enough or if the ergonomy of the site does not show whatever the consumer was looking for. Paramount here is first the quality of the application which ensures the exchange with the consumer and, as a result, the quality of its integration with the applications it uses.

Unfortunately, since the existing applications were not originally designed to respond to this type of request, then either the applications must be adapted, or integration solutions must be implemented. Here, we enter the domain of *service-oriented architecture*, or SOA.

In the document "Reference Model for Service Oriented Architecture 1.0" [ORM 06], OASIS defines SOA as "*a paradigm to organize and use distributed means that can be the property and under the control of different domains*". SOA provides a uniform way to offer, discover, interact with and use these means to produce the anticipated results with regards to expectations and measurable conditions.

A service-oriented architecture is an approach intended to confer greater agility and reactivity on distributed, heterogenous information systems, by presenting a "new" way to integrate and manipulate the various bricks and application components in a computing system, and to manage the links that they support.

This approach is not new and has, for example, been widely used in the design of client/server software. Similarly, distributed architectures and remote invocation methods such as DCE or CORBA also handled the notion of "service". In fact, those last two technologies largely inspired SOA itself.

However, these models have suffered from the lack of exchange standards, which in turn explains why a genuine SOA approach had to await the emergence of technologies linked to Web services. Section 4.5 examines projects that implement SOA solutions.

This concludes the general presentation of the range of problems in application integration. What remains at this point is to examine the various functions that this solution must provide in order to handle the needs and constraints identified in this chapter. These functions can be delineated on three levels:

– transport and connectivity;

– adaptation of the information;

– automation of the processes.

It is also necessary to determine whether the best adapted exchange architecture is centralized or distributed.

In the next chapter, we turn our attention to these questions.

Chapter 3

Levels in Integration Services

The various needs to which the integration infrastructure must respond can be grouped into three major service levels:

– transport and connectivity;

– information adaptation;

– automation of business processes.

Each level can in turn be divided into three subsets:

– modeling;

– execution;

– supervision.

These levels and subsets are summarized in Figure 3.1. Subsequent sections explore them in detail.

An application integration solution will always incorporate a portion of the service levels presented.

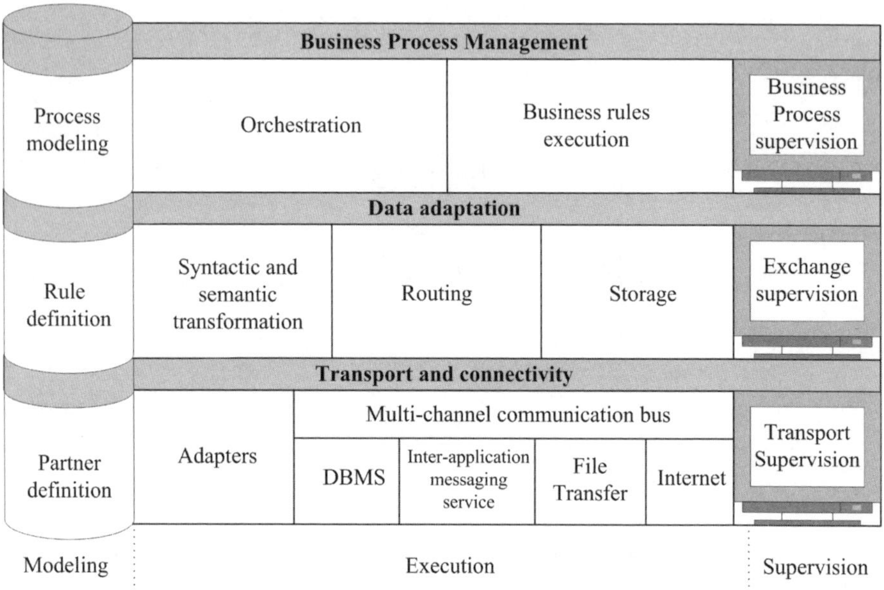

Figure 3.1. *Components in the integration infrastructure*

3.1. Transport and connectivity

The transport and connectivity level a) captures information or events generated by source applications, b) transports them to the receiving applications, then c) delivers the data or events that those applications expect.

As indicated, this level comprises three parts:

– *modeling* and therefore in this case the definition of data exchange partners and the rules for routing data between them;

– *execution*, or the capture, routing and passing of data or events;

– *supervision* of both these operations.

3.1.1. *Defining partners*

In order to separate the applications from technical exchange parameters, those parameters must be externalized and centralized in a global repository that describes the complete set of elements for making sure that data or events can pass from one application to another.

This repository must contain the following information:

– the topography of the applications to be integrated, i.e., all the information for accessing these applications, such as:

- location (application inside the enterprise or, in the case of a B2B integration, in the partner's system);

- platform to connect to;

- communication channel to use (inter-application messaging system, file transfer, DBMS, HTTP, SMTP, etc.);

- protocols to use;

- network address;

- identifier of the database manager;

- identifier for tables in the DBMS;

- identifier for files;

- name of the queues;

- messaging system address;

- etc.;

– the possible conditions for capturing data or events, and for delivering data or events, for example:

- a timeslot for capture or delivery;

- application triggering on reception of data or events;

- etc.;

– information concerning security levels:

- authentication;

- encryption;

- hashing;

- non-repudiation.

The complete set of information contained in this repository can then be distributed for operation to the execution components, i.e., the multi-channel communication bus and the adapters.

3.1.2. *Data transport*

The transport of the data or the events requires a multi-channel communication bus. The exchange must be able to adapt to the different supports used, without imposing the privileged use of any one of them, which in this case would necessitate costly conversions. Below, we take a brief look at the principal channels that can comprise such a bus.

3.1.2.1. *Database management systems*

The DBMS (database management system) constitutes a way to transport data between applications, since it offers basic replication mechanisms or inter-DBMS access bridges (gateways). For the most part, they are used in projects that require integration through the data (refer to section 2.4.1.1), essentially projects of integration through data propagation or integration of composite applications. In most cases, the semantics and the data models used by the applications to be integrated are compatible.

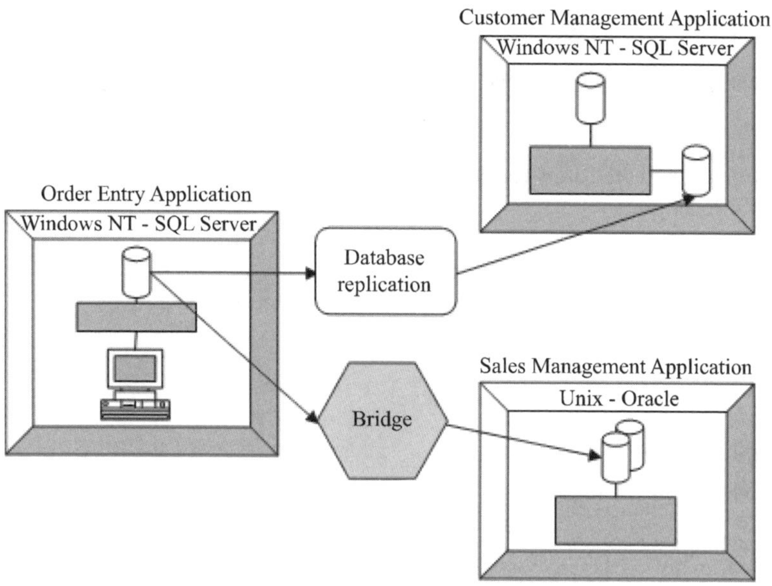

Figure 3.2. *Using DBMS for transport*

3.1.2.2. *File transfer*

This is the oldest data transport mode implemented in network technologies. The development of Unix and PC platforms led to the extension of its usage through the FTP (File Transfer Protocol) standard.

This standard has the advantage of being simple to implement. It is basic to most of the operating systems on the market. However, it has the drawbacks of being poorly secured and, above all, unsuited to heavy and voluminous operation of file exchanges. Indeed, it necessitates manual actions by the operators.

This explains why, at the beginning of the 1980s, the *file transfer managers* that appeared on the market were much more elaborate than simple tools for implementing FTP, offering the set of functionalities required for secure, entirely automated transfers (Managed File Transfer – MFT).

Figure 3.3 presents the various services integrated in these managers.

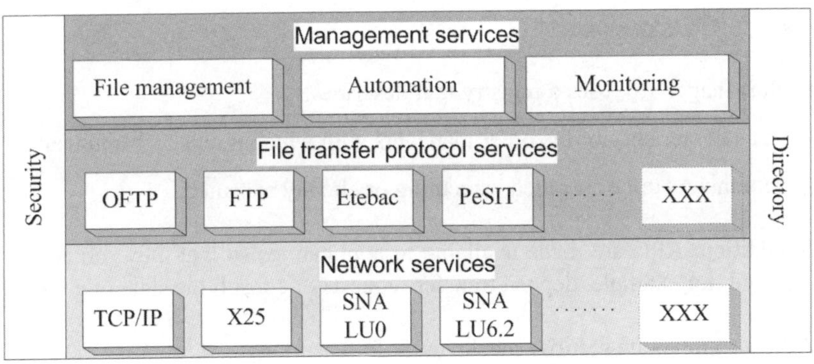

Figure 3.3. *Services of a file transfer manager*

Network services authorize:

– support for different types of networks (TCP/IP, X.25, SNA, DSA, DNA, etc.);

– commutation of networks (example: TCP/IP to X.25);

– capacity to initiate a connection (*requester*), or wait for the connection from another manager (*server*), as required.

File transfer protocol services allow:

– support for different file exchange protocols (PeSIT and ETEBAC in banking, OFTP in automotive, FTAM, etc.);

– commutation of transfer protocols (example: ETEBAC to PeSIT);

– data compression;

– the designation of synchronization points to avoid having to restart an interrupted transfer from the beginning;

– the guarantee of delivery.

Management services provide in particular:

– the capacity to route files to other destinations (*store-and-forward* mechanism);

– automatic handling of restarts in case of interruption of transfer;

– taking account of priorities in transfers;

– scheduling of transfers;

– automatic launch of procedures at the end of transfer;

– logging of operations.

Each manager also uses a registry that describes:

– the characteristics of the other managers with which it must communicate;

– the transfers to be executed, executing or already executed.

In addition, APIs are made available to applications so that they can access the registry and, for example, deposit transfer requests or consult the state of a transfer.

APIs also integrate security mechanisms for ensuring:

– partner authentication;

– data encryption;

– data hashing;

– non-repudiation of transfers.

Finally, these managers offer all these service levels on most of the platforms used in large information systems.

Figure 3.4 provides an example of implementing a file transfer protocol in a file transfer manager, illustrating the exchange possibilities that the protocol offers.

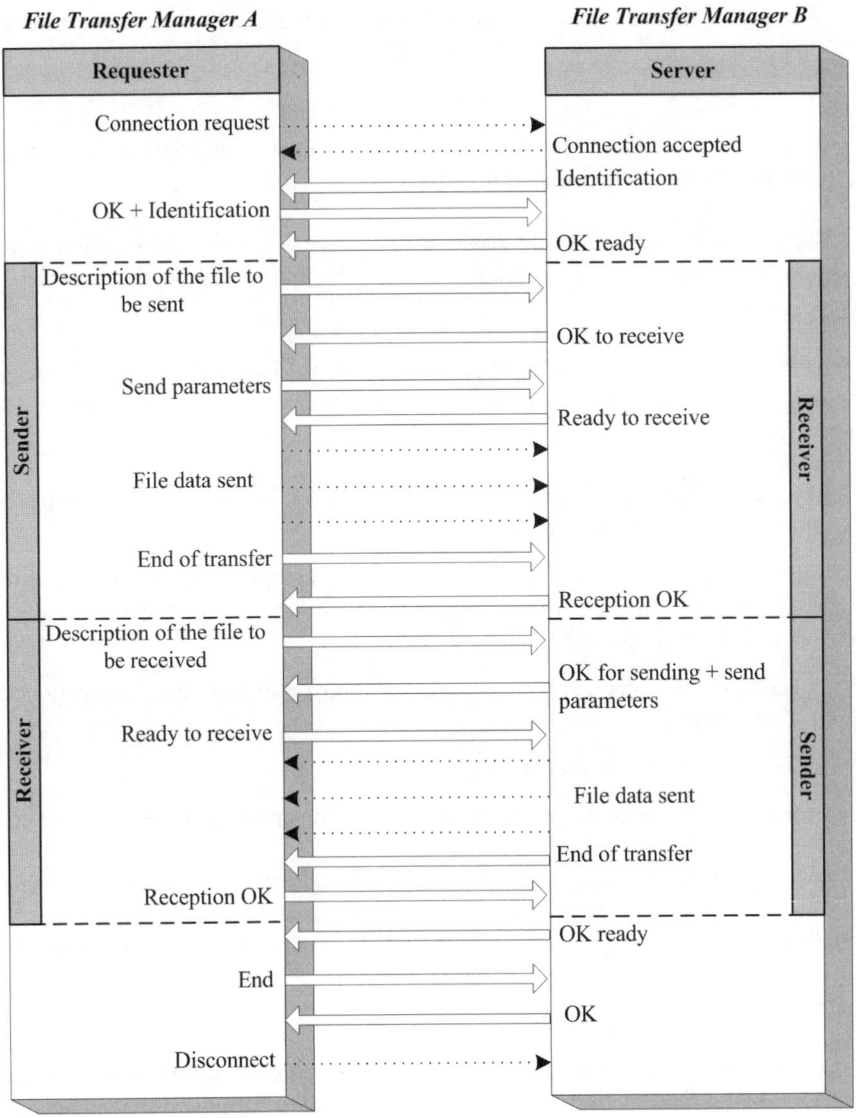

Figure 3.4. *Example of file transfer protocol*

File Transfer Manager A takes the initiative in the connection and therefore, for the transfer session that is being established, becomes the *requester*. For this session, File Transfer Manager B, which accepts the connection from Manager A, becomes the *server*.

Manager A first requests sending a file to Manager B. It switches then to the position of *requester-sender*, with Manager B finding itself in the position of *server-receiver.*

At the end of the file transfer, Manager B sends an acknowledgment to Manager A to signal the correct reception of the file.

Then, Manager A calls on Manager B to receive a file. It then switches to the position of *requester-receiver*, while Manager B finds itself in the position of *server-sender.*

At the end of the file transfer, Manager A sends an acknowledgment to Manager B to signal the correct reception of the file. Manager A then ends the session and disconnects.

Beyond the advantages previously noted, the basic versions of these products nevertheless exhibit certain limitations:

– the requirement at each site in the exchange for transfer managers from the same vendor, or managers from different vendors that support the same type of network and the same protocol;

– handling the manager-to-manager relation, but not the application-to-application relation;

– an exclusively batch orientation;

– for small structures, the inertia in implementation and operation.

In many countries, these drawbacks have held up the use of transfer managers for inter-enterprise exchanges (it is very difficult to impose on a partner the acquisition of the manager that is used in-house). On the other hand, they are currently extremely widespread in large enterprises, where they handle internal exchanges.

A recent development in these managers overcomes these limitations. They now integrate the FTP protocol for exchanges with the standard tools provided on most platforms. In addition, for secured file transfers over the Internet, they also offer solutions that are light but still high-performance. *This makes them one of the preferred tools for exchanging files over the Internet, and allows them to enter fully into the constitution of a B2B integration infrastructure.*

Figure 3.5 provides a simplified example of a transfer which uses the services of a file transfer manager:

1. an application on platform A is executed, creating a file;

2. the application deposits a transfer request with the file transfer manager, specifying in particular the name of the file to be transferred;

3. the file transfer manager verifies the existence of the file to be transferred and its associated rights, then determines the file transfer manager for receiving the file;

4. to initialize the transfer, the manager establishes a session with that receiving manager, and implements the file transfer protocol appropriate to this exchange;

5. the receiving manager creates the envelope for the file to be received, and writes the data received into the envelope;

6. at the conclusion of the transfer, using an end-of-transfer procedure, the receiving manager triggers the application that will consume the received file;

7. the application on platform B consumes the received file.

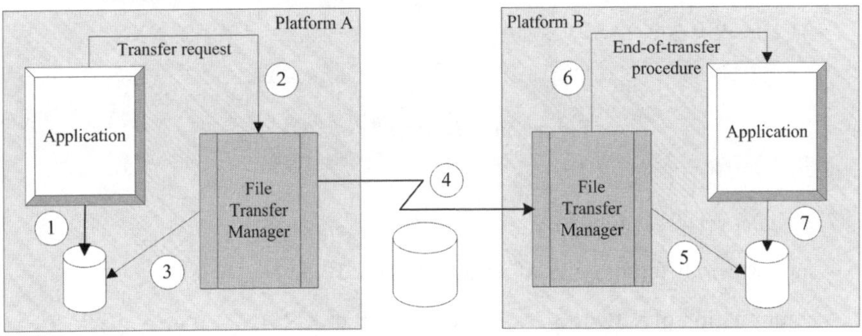

Figure 3.5. *File transfer manager*

3.1.2.3. *Inter-application messaging systems*

Inter-application messaging systems referred to as "Message-Oriented Middleware" (MOM) made their appearance at the beginning of the 1990s but only became widespread beginning from 1996-1997. The major difference with file transfer managers is that MOMs allow an *application-to-application* exchange of unitary events in the form of messages, adapting to the operating rhythms of those applications through the use of a system of *queues*.

The MOM can put applications on the same machine, or applications hosted on different machines, into contact with each other. In the latter case, a MOM must generally be installed on each machine to retain the complete set of available functionalities. The transition of messages on the network is performed using exchanges between the MOMs installed on each of the platforms.

Figure 3.6 illustrates the different services integrated in MOM.

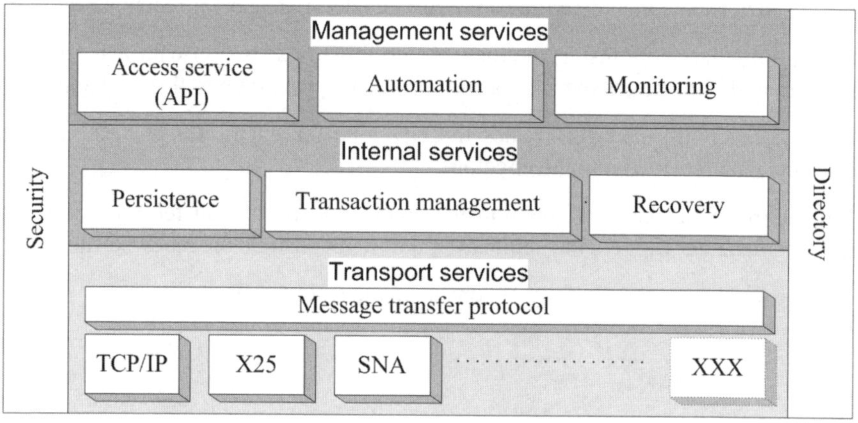

Figure 3.6. *The services of MOM*

Transport services authorize:

– support for different types of networks (TCP/IP, SNA, etc.);

– commutation of networks (example: TCP/IP to X.25);

– capacity to manage bi-directional connections with another MOM;

– message compression;

– message grouping;

– data integrity;

– the guarantee of delivery once and only once for messages.

Internal services include:

– message persistence;

– multiple types of access to queues (FIFO, direct access, etc.);

– sending messages in transactional units appropriate to the applications;

– restart on incidents;

– commutation of messages;

– notification of receipt.

Management services notably provide:

– automatic launch of an application on receipt of a message;

– APIs for the applications;

– logging or supervision of the operations.

In addition, each MOM relies on a registry that describes:

– the characteristics of the other MOMs with which it must communicate;

– the queues that it must manage, and their characteristics.

Moreover, MOMs integrate security mechanisms which they use to ensure:

– partner authentication;

– data encryption.

Finally, they offer all of these levels of service on most of the platforms used in large information systems.

At the same time, the use of these tools presents certain drawbacks:

– They have an intrusive aspect, since an existing application must be modified to exchange using MOM queues. In this case, of course, the partner application(s) must also be modified to use MOM.

– An application must know the applications with which it exchanges, since during the call to the MOM, it must provide the name of the receiving queues for the message that it wants to send. It must be said that this point tends to disappear with the implementation of publication/subscription mechanisms in MOMs, making it possible for applications to "publish" a message without knowing the applications that will make use of the message. The applications interested in this type of message "subscribe" to receive it (refer to section 3.2.2).

– In persistent mode (i.e., secured to each message), intrinsic performance is less relevant than the performance of the file transfer managers owing to management constraints on the transactional integrity of the message.

The use of MOM is today encountered essentially in multi-step process integration projects and, sometimes in B2C, in certain composite application integration projects. Taking account of the importance of these integration projects, MOMs now constitute an indispensable component in most tools of the "integration broker" or "message broker" types (see section 5.1.1).

Figure 3.7 provides an example of using a MOM:

– an application on platform A is executed, creating a message;

– the application deposits this message in the MOM, specifying in particular the name of the queue for the receiving application on platform B;

– the MOM on platform A determines the location of the indicated queue. Since that queue is not defined on platform A, it addresses the message to the MOM concerned (on platform B);

– once the message is received, the MOM on platform B places it in the receiving queue;

– it triggers the application that will consume the received message;

– the application on platform B consumes the message.

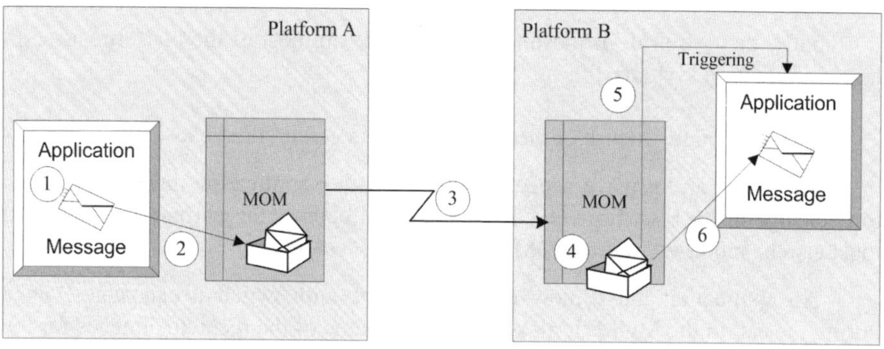

Figure 3.7. *Inter-application messaging system*

3.1.2.4. *Internet*

The Internet has brought about the emergence of new means of communication which can be used in application integration: HTTP, SMTP and FTP. On the basis of these standards, a certain number of other, more complex protocols were created for exchanging dependably and securely over the Internet.

HTTP

HTTP (Hypertext Transfer Protocol) is a client/server communication protocol developed by the W3C (World Wide Web Consortium) that is used for exchanging all types of data between HTTP client and HTTP server. The primary usage of HTTP is the implementation of Web applications that manage exchanges with browsers through HTML pages (Hypertext Markup Language), another W3C standard that makes it possible to describe Web pages.

HTTPS is the variant of HTTP that is secured with one of the protocols SSL (Secure Sockets Layer) or TLS (Transport Layer Security).

SMTP

SMTP (Simple Mail Transfer Protocol) is a protocol for sending messages between servers over the Internet. Messaging systems use this protocol to send messages. Then the receiver uses a messaging client and either POP3 (Post Office Protocol 3) or IMAP (Internet Message Access Protocol) to recover the messages from the server.

SOAP

SOAP (Simple Object Access Protocol) is a protocol for information exchange in decentralized, distributed environments. This protocol uses the XML standard (see section 3.2.1.1) and defines three portions: an envelope that constitutes a framework for describing the content of a message and how to process it; a collection of coding rules for expressing instances of application data types; and a convention for representing remote procedure calls and the associated responses. SOAP can potentially be used in conjunction with a wide variety of other standards. At the same time, its specifications only describe how to implement it on HTTP communications. SOAP is one of the standards on which the definitions of Web services rely (see section 4.5.3).

ebMS

ebMS (ebXML Messaging Service) is the ebXML (Electronic Business using eXtensible Markup Language – see section 4.3.2) specification that defines a dependable and secure transport standard for messages. This protocol presents the following technical characteristics:

– it uses SOAP syntax with attachments;

– no communication protocol is imposed, even if HTTP and SMTP are the most widely used;

– transported messages (useful load) are not necessarily expressed in XML. Traditional EDI formats, as well as messages based on XML, can be transported by an ebMS service;

– it uses existing security techniques, such as XML digital signatures (XMLDSIG), and public key encryption.

RNIF

RNIF (RosettaNet Implementation Framework – see section 4.3.2) provides the layer for packaging, routing and transporting messages for the execution of RosettaNet PIPs (Partner Interface Processes). This protocol uses the two standards MIME and S/MIME, but imposes no communication protocol, even if it favors HTTP and SMTP.

EDIINT

The EDIINT protocols (EDI over INTernet), defined by workgroups of the IETF (Internet Engineering Task Force), are exchange protocols available in three versions, each defined by an "Applicability Statement" (AS):

– AS1, which uses SMTP communications;

– AS2, which uses HTTP communications;

– AS3, which uses FTP communications.

The EDIINT protocols were designed by EDI users for transporting the data over the Internet. They use the two standards MIME and S/MIME (for encryption and signature) and integrate functions indispensable to the electronic exchange of documents (notice of receipt/non-receipt, receipt of non-repudiation). The sender receives a notice of receipt and of correct decryption, referred to as a Message Disposition Notification (MDN). This acknowledgment guarantees that the transaction progresses correctly from end to end, and that it is also signed and encrypted.

3.1.3. *Connectivity*

The multi-channel communication bus will therefore ensure the transport of data or of events. Upstream, in the application environment, the data or the events that applications produce must be captured to transmit the data or events expected by the downstream applications: this is the role of the adapters.

3.1.3.1. *General approach*

The first concern for integrating an IT application consists of *non-intrusiveness* with respect to the application itself on the one hand, and on the other hand, to the other applications of the information system.

One of the major problems with existing applications is their "knowledge" of the receiving applications, of their needs, even of their business rules, which are often hard-coded in the programs. In this context, the desirability of non-intrusiveness can be sharply reduced by trying to remain non-intrusive before the existing applications start respecting the rules of urbanization (see section 4.2.1 and Chapter 8). Nevertheless, if we presuppose that efforts have been conducted in this domain, then non-intrusiveness becomes perfectly relevant.

It is expressed under different aspects:

– the information must be recovered from the application:

- in the form under which it was produced: file, message in a queue, element in a DBMS table, etc.,

- while respecting the structure and the format of data,

- on the hardware platform where it was created;

– the information must be made available to the application:

- in the expected form: file, message in a queue, element in a DBMS table, etc.,

- while respecting the structure and the format of expected data,

- on the expected hardware platform;

– it should not be necessary to modify the existing applications in the information system in order to communicate with the new application.

To respect this principle of non-intrusiveness, we turn to a technique that is well known from many domains: the implementation of *adapters*.

3.1.3.2. *Adapters*

The objective of adapters (sometimes named "connectors") is to physically link the application to the exchange infrastructure. An adapter should therefore implement two elements: on the one hand, the link to the application, and on the other hand, the link to the infrastructure.

The nature of the adapter is directly linked to the capacity of the application to open up to the outside world, and more specifically, to the means that the adapter provides for communicating with the outside: APIs (Application Programming Interface), interfaces with communication middleware packages (MOM, file transfer managers), etc.

For example, an application or software package that produces or reads files does not provide a specific means of communication. The adapter should therefore detect when the application creates a file (most of the time via a mechanism for monitoring catalogs or directories), then generate an event that indicates this creation to the infrastructure (Figure 3.8). Conversely, the adapter should be capable of generating a file for the application, and ensuring that the application can process this file, either by direct triggering, or by posting an event to a scheduler that will handle launching the application.

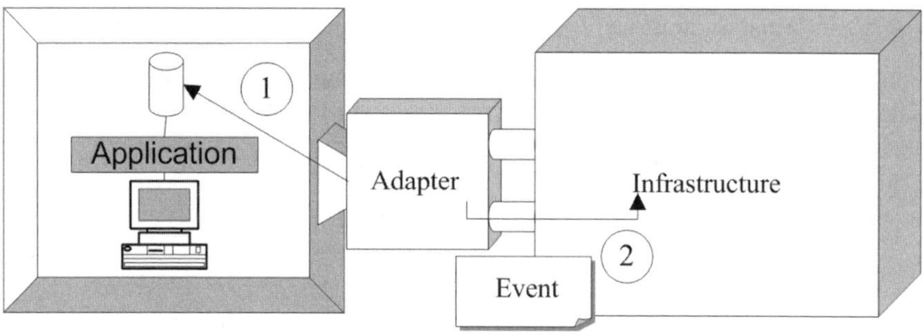

Figure 3.8. *Example of mechanism for a file adapter*

In exactly the same way, a transactional or client/server application which uses a DBMS will probably not provide other means of communication. The adapter should therefore detect the events occurring in the database, relying in particular on triggering mechanisms supplied by the DBMS or by examining the modifications to the database, and should generate an event indicating this modification to the infrastructure. Conversely, it should be able to update the database directly.

A near-real-time application only knows to exchange through a MOM to which it is connected. For this application to be able to, for example, receive events from a batch application which generates them in a file, without having to modify this batch application, a file/message adapter is required (Figure 3.9). This adapter can read the events in the file produced by the batch application, and generate messages or groups of messages in the queue where the near-real-time application can then consume them.

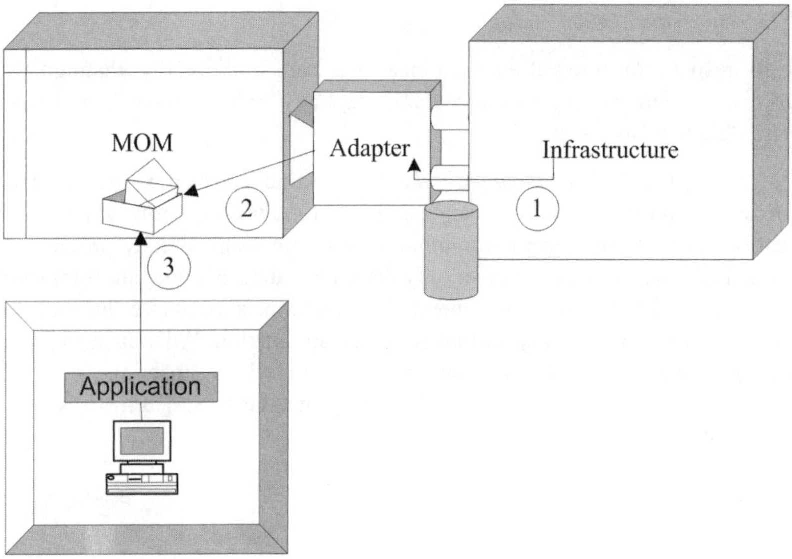

Figure 3.9. *Example of mechanism for a file/message adapter*

On the other hand, an application or software package that provides multiple communication points would facilitate the development of this adapter.

This is the case for certain ERP, notably of the most widespread, R3 from SAP. Indeed, SAP offers several methods for exchanging information with the modules that compose it: API (BAPIs), communication in batch mode (BTCI), communication in conversational mode (ALE), etc.

However, these communication modes do not all present the same coverage or the same technical capacities (notably in terms of volume to be processed). In most cases then, with this type of software package, several adapters are required, each using a method of communication and, in certain cases, a single adapter that covers all of these methods.

Further, an adapter must whenever possible allow the application to recover the description of the data that it manipulates (the *metadata*). This data can be used to input the dictionary where transformation rules are defined (see section 3.2.4) with the structures of events or data. For example, this could be done by having the application extract the description of the tables that it uses directly from the database.

3.1.3.3. *"Thin" and "thick" adapters*

With respect to integration solutions, we can traditionally distinguish two categories of adapters: light or technical adapters ("thin adapters") and business adapters ("thick adapters"):

– *Light (Figure 3.10) or technical adapters* are characterized by the fact that they do not require the installation of any component on the platform which hosts the application, because they use the communication functions already present on that platform. They therefore accomplish only communication between the application to be integrated and the core of the integration solution, and ensure the transport of information in the proprietary format for each application. All transformation and routing processes are performed on the platform which hosts the core of the integration solution. Below, we provide some advantages and drawbacks for this type of adapter.

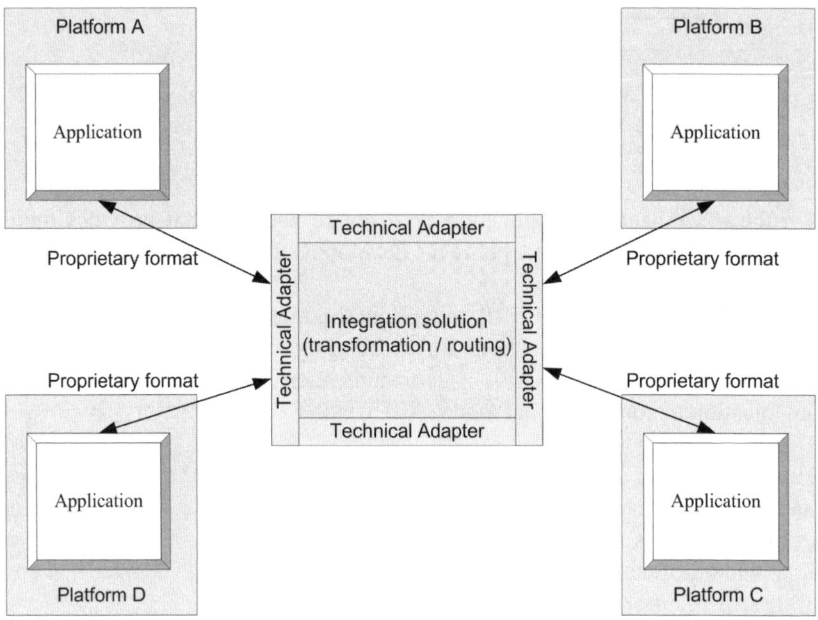

Figure 3.10. *Light (technical) adapter*

Advantages

- Transformation solely on the platform which hosts the core of the integration solution.

- Easy deployment, since no special component is to be installed on the platforms that host the applications to be integrated.

- Significant lack of sensitivity to the development of the software packages, since this type of adapter is independent of the format of data and linked solely to the type of communication used by the software packages to be integrated.

- Entirely adaptable solution, whatever the context (loose coupling with applications).

- Capacity to manage complex transformation rules, since those are centralized at the core of the integration solution.

- Affordable price.

Drawbacks

- No direct, automatic loading of the descriptions of the structures already defined in the ERP system, which means difficulties in delivering both the complete pre-set parameters for standard use of the software packages, and the transformation rules that can be defined between proprietary formats.

- No automatic processing of the statuses for taking account of dataflows by the ERP.

- Point-to-point links among the applications via transformation rules (often recreating a spaghetti architecture in the integration solution). *This drawback can easily be worked around using a pivot format in the transformation sequence on the platform which hosts the integration solution.*[17]

- Complexity of certain transformation rules.

- Potential bottleneck, because all transformations are performed in the core of the solution. In general however, the possibilities of scalability in the transformation function help to mitigate this drawback.

– *Thick (or business) adapters (Figure 3.11)* can be used to ensure decentralized transformation functions on the information. To carry out their task of transforming the sending application's proprietary format into a pivot or canonical format, or of

17 In the case of centralized transformation function with thin adapters, the use of a pivot or canonical format is carried out by implementing two transformation phases on the platform which hosts the integration solution: proprietary format 1 ⇒ canonical format ⇒ proprietary format 2.

transforming the canonical format to the receiving application's proprietary format, these adapters require components to be installed on the platform which hosts both the application to be integrated and the core of the integration solution. Below, we provide some advantages and drawbacks for this type of adapter.

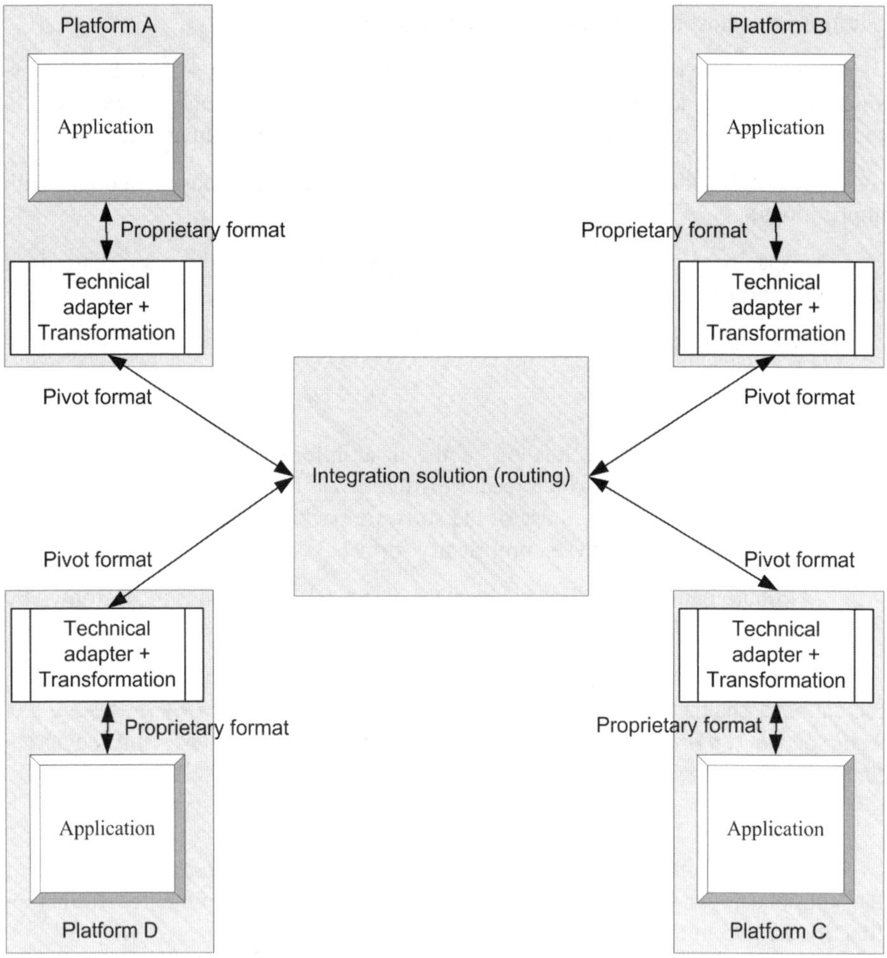

Figure 3.11. *Thick (business) adapter*

Advantages

- The systematic use of a pivot or canonical format for constituting a repository of standardized business events.

- The possibility of a complete set of parameters delivered with the integration solution (plug-and-play) for the standard use of certain software packages, again through the use of a canonical format.

- The allocation of the transformation workload between the platforms that support the adapters.

Drawbacks

- Need for double transformations, increasing the global processing workload, and therefore potentially impacting solution performance.

- Predefined parameters for connecting the software packages are not usable if the enterprise does not use standard formats of those packages (i.e., if it adapts them, which is the case most of the time).

- Increased sensitivity from the development of software packages, since the adapter is very often closely linked to the version of the software package used.

- Need to deploy components on the application platforms with frequent updates of the main parameter settings.

- Legacy applications in the enterprise not taken into account by these adapters.

- High price of these adapters since they may incorporate advanced transformation functions.

As so often, when we compare different possibilities, there is no absolute truth. In most cases, the right solution consists of finding a balance between the use of thin adapters and thick adapters.

3.1.3.4. *Tools for developing adapters*

Since it is unlikely that the standard solutions on the market will supply the complete set of adapters required to integrate all the types of applications that can be found in different information systems, it is strongly recommended to acquire a tool set for developing the missing adapters.

At a minimum, this tool set must comprise a core to ensure communication with the infrastructure, and an API that developers can use to call the different functions in this core. Developers can then develop the necessary code to interface the application to be integrated. This code will implement the algorithm required to chain accesses to the application and calls to the core services in such a way as to generate the set of corresponding events in the infrastructure. Together, the executable program that comprises the user code, the API and the core will make up the adapter.

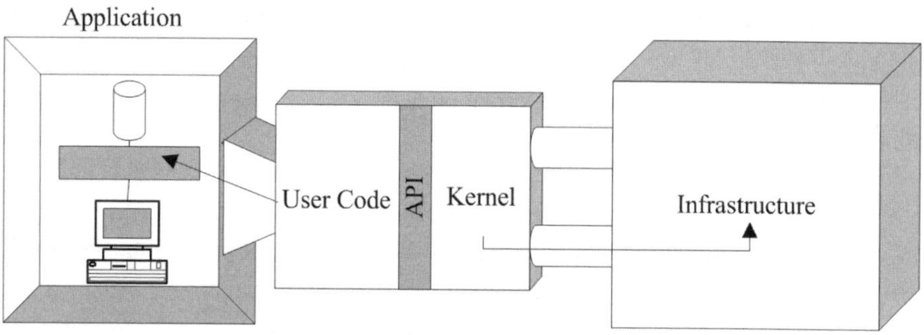

Figure 3.12. *Constituting an adapter with development tool*

3.1.4. *Supervising transport*

The events or the data transmitted between applications can comprise information critical for the enterprise. At all times, it must be possible to determine where they can be found. This is even more important because the implemented exchange mechanisms are most often asynchronous.

When two applications exchange information in synchronous mode, they are connected to each other. If one of them becomes unavailable, the other immediately detects that fact, and executes the instructions planned for such a case. For example, it posts an error or alert message informing on the non-response from the application partner.

In an asynchronous exchange mode, applications are not informed of problems that can arise during the exchange. In addition, this is precisely the objective to be achieved through implementing the integration infrastructure: applications must remain independent of the technical conditions of the exchange. Incidents must be detected by the tools themselves.

Transport tools as well as adapters used must therefore make it possible to send information about the progress of routing operations to a supervision system. These tools should in particular provide indications as soon as an incident occurs:

– problems of connection between file transfer managers, between MOMs, or with the application;

– restarts that could be carried out to transmit the information;

– problems of environment encountered, such as: lack of disk space for creating a file, the absence of a queue or its saturation;

– etc.

In case of serious incidents, these tools should of course post the alerts that allow operations staff to intervene to correct the problem and relaunch interrupted operations.

To do this requires a global supervision system that will centralize the complete set of supervision information and events, and provide a graphical interface where operators can consult tracking information and perform interventions. This interface will present dashboards that allow a geographical visualization of the transport infrastructure and of the exchanged dataflows (Figure 3.13), as well as indicators that allow global activity (Figure 3.14) to be assessed.

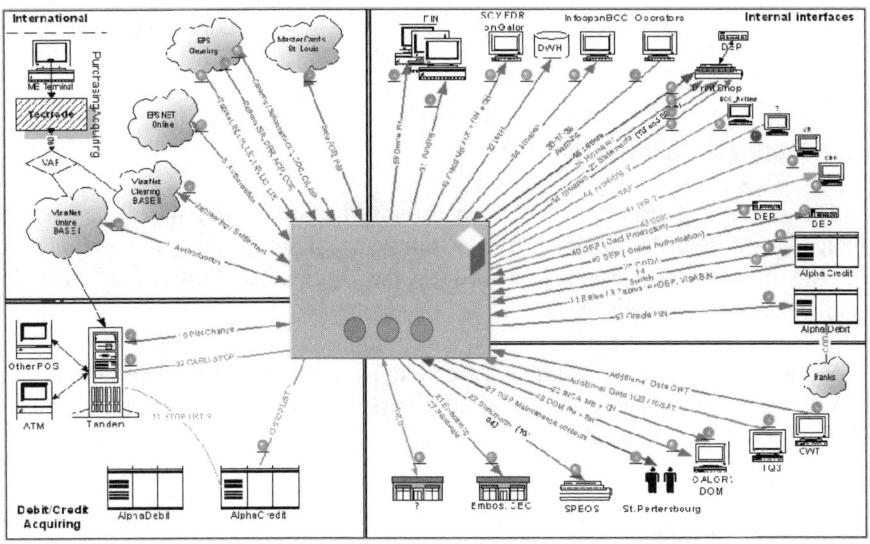

Figure 3.13. *Example of geographical visualization dashboard (© Axway, 2006)*

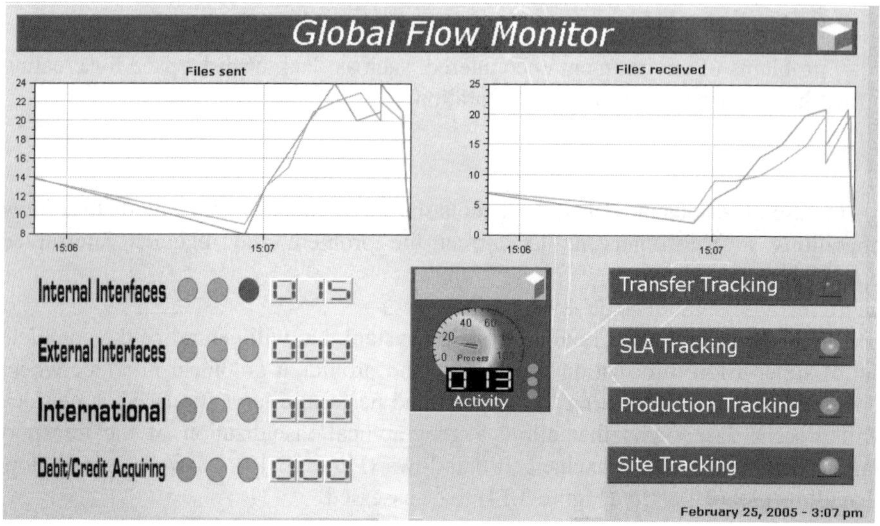

Figure 3.14. *Example of global activity indicators in the transport layer (© Axway, 2006)*

3.2. Adapting the information

The capture, transport and delivery of information to the recipients are not enough to address the complete set of problems of integration. It must also be possible to adapt the events produced by the original applications to what the recipient applications expect.

Moreover, it must be possible to determine these recipient applications and deliver what they expect at the right moment. This is the objective of the information adaptation level.

3.2.1. *Transformation*

An event must be transformed when it is expressed in a format or using a syntax that is not directly comprehensible by the recipient application(s). However, the necessity for transforming an event can also originate in the fact that it holds information used to generate other events of a different nature (for example, a purchase order could be used to generate stock movements).

An application integration infrastructure should therefore provide the tools necessary to describe the transformation rules for the events and execute them, whatever the nature of the transformation to be performed. The appearance of new formats linked to the Internet has further reinforced this necessity.

3.2.1.1. *Data formats*

Flat format – fixed length/position

This is the oldest but also the best performing format in the domain of computing management: each item of data is found at a predetermined position and always has the same length, which can be represented in the form:

[datum 1] [datum 2] [datum 3].......[datum n]

When the effective length of an item of data is shorter than the projected length, we complete the information with an agreed-upon value (blanks, zeroes, etc.). In the same way, when an item of data is absent, its position contains an agreed-upon value (blanks, zeroes, etc.) on the projected length. This simple format, close to the internal functioning of computers, makes it possible to locate a specific item of information immediately and therefore does not impact performance when it comes to manipulate the data.

Flat format – variable position-length

This is a variant of the previous format. Data is always scheduled in the same way but the position of a specific datum will depend on the effective length of the data that precedes it. In this case, the value of each item of data is preceded by a *counter* that indicates its length, in this pattern:

[ctr 1][datum 1] [ctr 2][datum 2] [ctr 3][datum 3]...... [ctr n][datum n]

When an item of data is absent, the length counter is at zero. To locate a specific item of information, the length of the data that precedes that item must be analyzed. This necessitates an analysis of the content of the message or record (parsing) that can impact performance when it comes to manipulate the data.

Flat format with delimiters

Here, we can distinguish the flat format with delimiters and sequenced data from the flat format with delimiters and non-sequenced data.

In a flat format with delimiters and sequenced data, data is always arranged in the same order and separated by an agreed-upon character (commas, for example) with the following pattern:

[datum 1],[datum 2],[datum 3], ... ,[datum n]

Here again it is necessary to analyze the message or record to determine the separators and locate an item of data depending on its relative position (1st, 2nd, etc.). Again, this analysis will have an impact on performance in the case where the data must be manipulated.

In a flat format with delimiters and non-sequenced data, given that this time the data could arrive in any order, thus in addition to the delimiter, "keywords" are required to identify the data. This type of format is used for example in command-line at computer consoles, where *[delimiter 1]* is often the equals sign "=" and *[delimiter 2]* is a comma or a blank. In this case, the structure would be, for example, of the type:

keyword 2=datum 2,keyword n=datum n, ...,keyword 1=datum 1

Here as well, the analysis required to locate data will have an impact on performance if the data must be manipulated.

Hierarchical (or tree-structure) format

Hierarchical or tree-structure format can be combined with the different formats described to this point. It is characterized by the fact that certain data that we will call "composites" are constituted by assembling other data – either "elementary" data or data that is itself composite. In addition, each item can be repeated several times to constitute the data for the next level up. This tree or hierarchical type format mixes the formats described above, as shown in this simple example:

keyword1=(datum 1, datum2,keyword11=(datum 11a, datum11b),keyword5=datum 5),keyword 7=datum 7, ...

It is obvious that for this type of format, locating the data continues to complicate the analysis, and therefore degrade performance yet again.

XML formats

In the family of hierarchical formats, XML (eXtensible Markup Language) is a standard from the W3C (*World Wide Web Consortium*), the consortium that groups public and private users with manufacturers and suppliers of the computing technologies on which the Internet is founded. For a complete vision of what XML is and its possible uses, consult for example the work of Jean-Christophe Bernadac and François Knab [BER 99]. Below, we provide some elementary notions required to understand certain points raised in the rest of this work.

XML is a language that makes it possible to describe the logical structure principally of textual documents, with the help of a system of tags that mark the elements composing the structure and the relationships between these elements. The goals of this language are to separate the form of documents from their content, to formalize their structure, to standardize the tags (syntax) and to constrain these documents using (semantic) models, to facilitate their computing treatment. Three XML document types exist:

– XML document instances, containing data (Figure 3.15);

```
<Order>
<CurrencyCode>FRF</CurrencyCode>
<PaymentMode>transfer</PaymentMode>
<OrderDate>20000310</OrderDate>
<CustomerReference>
     <Name>Mr BEAN</Name>
     <CustomerCode>007</CustomerCode
     <Company>Editions HERMES</Company>
          <Address>
               <Address1>Editions HERMES</Address1>
               <Address2>8, quai du Marché-Neuf</
Address2>
               <PostalCode>75004</PostalCode>
               <City>Paris</City>
               <Country>FRANCE</Country>
          </Address>
</CustomerReference>
     <OrderLine>
     <Quantity>25</Quantity>
     <ProductDescription>PC, Pentium III 500 MHz,
     8 processors, RAM 256 Mb</ProductDescription>
     </OrderLine>
</Order>
```

Figure 3.15. *Emission of an order for computers (XML format)*

– DTDs (Document Type Definition), document models used to describe the elements in and the default values for document attributes, with the help of a specific language (Figure 3.16);

```
<!ELEMENT doc (A, B, C?, (D|E)+, F*) >
<!ATTLIST doc Date CDATA "20000114"
                    Color (Red|Black) #IMPLIED >
```

- *A, B, C and the group D/E are ordered elements,*
- *C is optional, F has cardinality 0,N,*
- *D/E has cardinality 1,N,*
- *Conditioned presence: D or E,*
- *Date is a constant «20000114 »,*
- *Color is an optional list of values*

Figure 3.16. *Example DTD*

– XML Schemas, also document models, are used to define the properties of elements, the relationships between these elements, the types of data, and hierarchies of classes, but they do this using the XML language itself (Figure 3.17):

```
                    XML Schema
<elementType id= "Book" >
<element type= "#title" occurs= "OPTIONAL" />
<element type= "#author" occurs= "ONEORMORE" />
</elementType>
```

```
               XML Document generated
<Book>
<author>Henry Ford</author>
<author>Samuel Crowther</author>
<title>My Life and Work</title>
</Book>
```

Figure 3.17. *Example XML Schema*

The W3C completed XML by publishing a description language that can be used to define the way in which an XML document must be restored during display or printout. This language, XSL (eXtensible Stylesheet Language), is used to construct *style sheets* that are applied to the elements of an XML document where they are referenced.

XML is now used in numerous domains and gives rise to the definition of new standards that use its syntax:

– in the domain of graphical applications, the standards for representing vectors, VML (Vector Markup Language) proposed by Microsoft and PGML (Precision Graphics Markup Language) proposed by Adobe;

– in the domain of multimedia, SMIL (Synchronized Multimedia Integration Language) for representing multimedia elements on a Web page;

– in the domain of science, MathML (Mathematical formula Markup Language), CML (Chemical Markup Language) and AML (Astronomical Markup Language).

In the domain of management, numerous providers of computing solutions have adapted their new products or developments in existing products to the XML language. This fashion has led to the appearance, notably in the domains of industry and finance, of numerous initiatives that have united to make XML into a new document exchange standard (see section 4.3).

Unfortunately, when it is a question of manipulating or transforming the data of this type of documents, the analysis required to locate each item of information will have a very serious impact on performance. Moreover, the use of the system of tags considerably burdens the content of each document and can sometimes pose network load problems during the transmission of these document types. This explains why it is appropriate to use XML with discernment (see section 7.2).

3.2.1.2. *Syntactical transformation*

The goal of syntactical transformation is to modify the representation of an event in order to render it usable by the application(s) responsible for processing it. This type of transformation can concern the global format of the event, but also the representation of each item of information that goes to make up the event. It can therefore generate the modification of the order of information inside the event or the modification of the mode for representing an item of information (alphabetical, alphanumeric, extended numeric, binary, etc.).

Consider the example of an order carried out by a client on a commercial Internet site. The order involves information expressed in XML syntax. Before the order can be processed by an aging proprietary application written in COBOL, it must be transformed in order to make it usable by this application. This transformation will not therefore modify the meaning of the event but simply formulate it in a syntax acceptable by the application which will process it. In our example, the transformation would give the result illustrated in Figure 3.18.

XML Order

```
<Order>
<CurrencyCode>EUR</CurrencyCode>
<PaymentMode>transfer</PaymentMode>
<OrderDate>20000310</OrderDate>
<CustomerReference>
      <Name>Mr BEAN</Name>
      <CustomerCode>007</CustomerCode
      <Company>Editions HERMES</Company>
            <Address>
                  <Address1>Editions HERMES</Address1>
                  <Address2>8, quai du Marché-Neuf</Address2>
                  <PostalCode>75004</PostalCode>
                  <City>Paris</City>
                  <Country>FRANCE</Country>
            </Address>
</CustomerReference>
      <OrderLine>
      <Quantity>25</Quantity>
      <ProductDescription>PC, Pentium III 500 MHz,
      8 processors, RAM 256 Mb</ProductDescription>
      </OrderLine>
</Order>
```

Order for application written in COBOL

```
.........10.........20.........30.........40.........50.........60
EURtransfer 20000310Mr BEAN                      007HERMES
.........70.........80.........90.........100.........110.........120
Editions HERMES          8, quai du Marché-Neuf  75004Paris
 ........130........140........160........170........180........190
France          25PC, Pentium III 500 MHz,8 processors,
........200
RAM 256 Mb
```

Figure 3.18. *Syntactical transformation of an order*

3.2.1.3. *Semantic transformation*

The goal of semantic transformation is to modify the meaning of all or part of the information for an original event, or from that event, to deduce other events that will be introduced into the information system.

Let us return to the example of the order placed by a client from a commercial Internet site (see Figure 3.19). In this example, the purchase order completed by the client can be used to generate:

– a message to the client confirming the order;

– a delivery order for the delivery management application;

– a request to create an invoice for the billing application.

To carry out this type of transformation and creation of events requires more complex manipulations, for example:

– recover the messaging system address of the client to send him the confirmation message, and calculate the amount of the purchase;

– supply the ordered product reference for the delivery application;

– modify the customer number to conform to the repository for the billing application;

– supply the billing information for the invoice request.

These manipulations require access to external repositories to search for the messaging system client address, the reference and the pricing for the ordered products, as well as to convert the customer number. A certain number of calculations must also be performed. Figure 3.20 provides the generated events from the event on input.

The example that we have just examined contains in reality two problems to be processed:

– the first consists of generating the events necessary to complete the business process that handles the order; this problem is covered by the semantic and syntactical transformation that will generate the expected events when applied to the event on input;

– the second problem consists of determining the recipient applications for these events; this is the problem of routing.

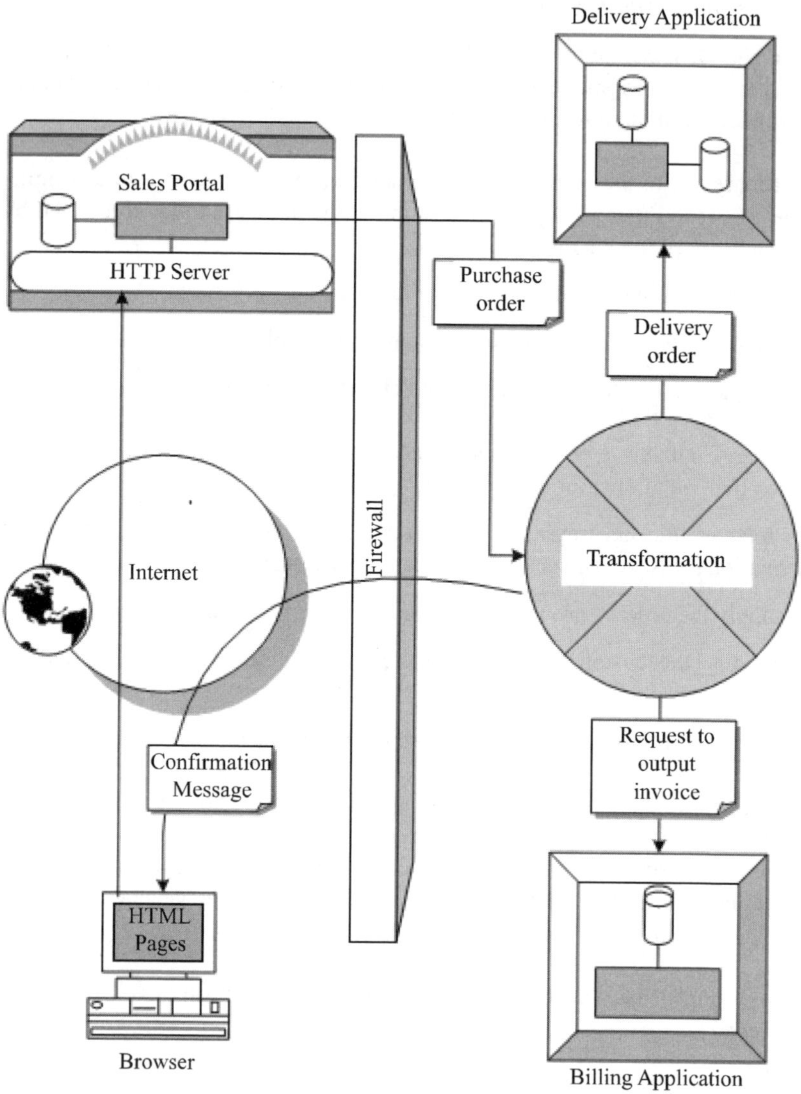

Figure 3.19. *Example dataflows generated by an order*

XML Order

```
<Order>
<CurrencyCode>EUR</CurrencyCode>
<PaymentMode>transfer</PaymentMode>
<OrderDate>20000310</OrderDate>
<CustomerReference>
<Name>Mr BEAN</Name>
<CustomerCode>007</CustomerCode
<Company>Editions HERMES</Company>
<Address> <Address1>Editions HERMES</Address1>
<Address2>8, quai du Marché-Neuf</Address2>
<PostalCode>75004</PostalCode><City>Paris</City>
<Country>FRANCE</Country></Address>
</CustomerReference><OrderLine><Quantity>25</Quantity>
<ProductDescription>PC, Pentium III 500 MHz,
8 processors, RAM 256 Mb</ProductDescription>
</OrderLine>
</Order>
```

Delivery request for COBOL application

```
........10........20........30........40........50........60
25   REF025643220000310 CLI007Mr BEAN              Editions
........70........80........90.......100.......110.......120
HERMES                   8, quai du Marché-Neuf
.......130.......140.......160.......170.......180.......190
75004Paris                         France
```

Billing request for COBOL application

```
CLI00720000310Mr BEAN                     007HERMES
........70........80........90.......100.......110.......120
Editions HERMES                8, quai du Marché-Neuf
.......130.......140.......160.......170.......180.......190
        75004Paris             France                 25REF0256432
.......200.......210.......220.......230.......240.......250
PC, Pentium III 500 MHz,8 processors, RAM 256 Mb
.......260.......270.......280.......290.......300.......310
```

Text format message

```
beans@editions-hermes.com;;Confirmation of order;Sir ,CRwe
have the pleasure of confirming your order dated CR10/03/
2000CRforCR25 x PC, Pentium III 500 MHz,8 processors, RAM 256
MbCR for a pre-tax amount of CR EUR  200.000CRSincerely,CRJ.
DupondCRCustomer Service
```

Figure 3.20. *Example semantic transformation*

3.2.2. *Routing*

Routing consists of determining the recipient of the events or data generated by an application. This determination can be carried out in different ways.

In the case of a spaghetti system, the application directly addresses the recipients of the information that it produces. It is the application that knows them and it is therefore the application that carries out the routing function (Figure 3.21).

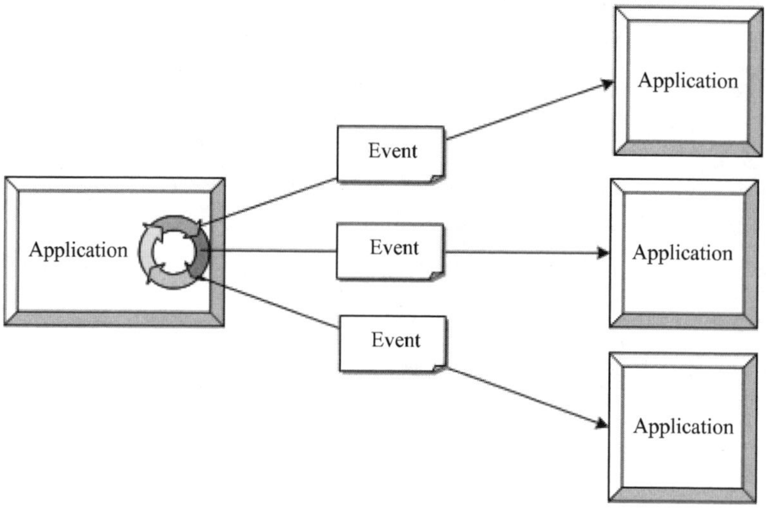

Figure 3.21. *Routing by application*

Given that one of the objectives of the integration solution is ensuring the independence of applications from each other, the routing function should necessarily be handled in a system outside the applications.

To do this, the first mechanism available for use is the publication/subscription mechanism that we have already featured in section 3.1.2.3. An application that creates an event "publishes" that event to make it available to the interested applications that will "subscribe" to receive this event (Figure 3.22).

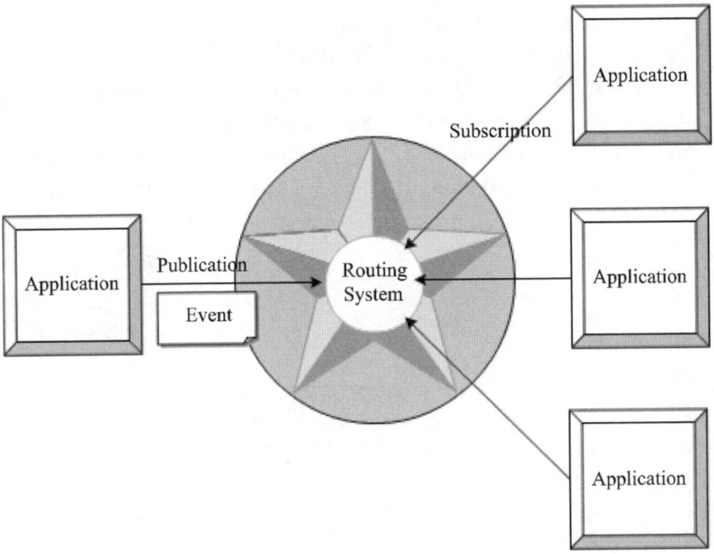

Figure 3.22. *Mechanism of publication/subscription*

To perform this, the recipient application indicates to the routing system the nature of the event concerned on its publication. This indication could be based on different levels, which, from the preceding example, could be:

– theme: customer relations;

– event: purchase order;

– client: “Editions Hermès”.

Interested applications sign up to the routing system by providing the same information. The routing system will then be able to determine the recipient applications for each event produced. If a new application is a candidate to receive this event, it only has to subscribe to it. There is no impact on the existing system.

This system seems ideal, but at the same time, it presents two drawbacks:

– the application must be designed from the start to use the publication/subscription mechanism;

– between the applications, a link is maintained that consists of an agreement concerning the denominations of publications (in our example: customer relations, purchase order).

In order to eliminate these roadblocks, the system must allow the implementation of publish and subscribe operations external to the applications. These operations can be performed perfectly well by a person or a group of persons who would be responsible for defining denominations and performing subscription operations for the application accounts. In this case, they would use a user interface for entering and storing this information in a database which the routing system could use (Figure 3.23).

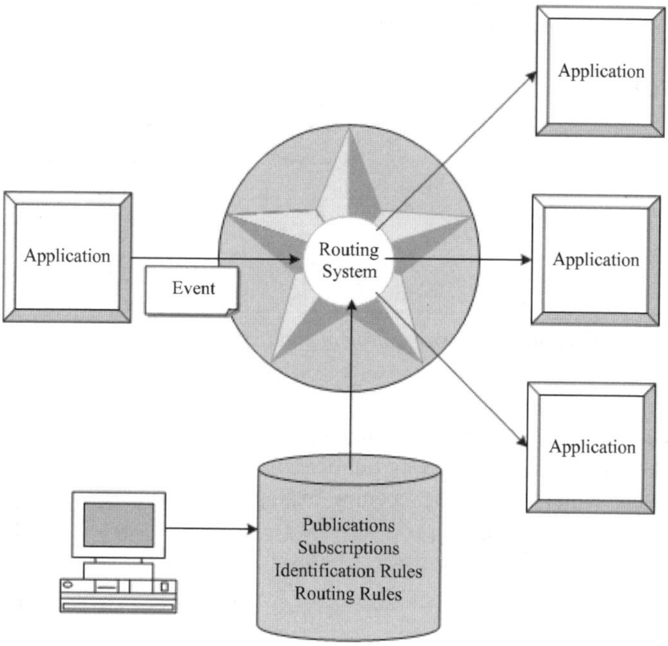

Figure 3.23. *Externalization of routing rules*

The problem of publication remains to be resolved. For applications that produce only a single type of event, this can be processed simply: in the database intended for the routing system, indicate that any event that originates in this application must be published with the predefined characteristics that appear in this database.

Unfortunately, a significant number of applications produce events of multiple natures. It is therefore indispensable to be able to define *identification rules* that will let the routing system use one of:

– declarative information originating in the application that publishes it;

– analysis of the content of the event to determine its nature.

In our example we could imagine a simple identification rule of the type: "if the event contains in position 2 the character string [Order] then the type of event is [purchase order] and the theme is [customer relations]".

In addition, routing will in certain cases depend on the specific content of the event. In our example, we could easily imagine that the event "request to output an invoice" should also be transmitted to a statistics application if the number of objects ordered is greater than 5. In this case, a *content-based* routing rule must be described so the system can analyze the content of the event in order to determine the recipient applications.

The implementation of these publication/subscription mechanisms will therefore necessitate respect for the sequencing of the following operations:

– identification of the event on input;

– transformation;

– identification of the generated events;

– application of subscriptions and of content-based routing rules.

We will see later that the notions of publication/subscription, identification rules, and routing rules can contribute to implementing SOA.

3.2.3. *Storage*

As we saw in section 2.4.2, different application types have different operational rhythms. When events transit between the applications to be integrated, it must be possible to adapt the exchange to the operating pace of each application. To do this, the integration infrastructure should provide mechanisms for temporary storage of these events in order to make them available to recipient applications *at the right moment*.

Depending on how the event is supported, this storage will be carried out in the appropriate environment:

– file management systems;

– databases;

– queues.

This necessity to store events temporarily could also follow from the conditions defined for their handover to the application. For example, an application for statistical consolidation could be set to execute its processing only if it has command of the complete set of messages originating in the applications that input it. As long as the last event has not arrived, other events must not be given to this application. The application adapter (see section 3.1.3.2) will therefore not be activated as long as the condition is not met.

3.2.4. *Defining the rules*

The adaptation of the events to the operation of the applications necessitates the definition of rules for transformation, routing and storage. These rules must be centralized in a global dictionary then distributed for operation by the integration infrastructure. This dictionary will include notably:

– the definition of the events circulating in the system;

– the definition of their structure;

– the identification rules for these events;

– the transformation rules to apply;

– information concerning publications and subscriptions;

– the itinerary taken by the event before handover to the recipient;

– the routing rules;

– the rules that allow temporary storage.

The integration infrastructure should make available an environment that offers – in particular – a user interface for defining the rules. The particularity of this interface is that it should be usable equally by business specialists in the enterprise and by IT staff.

Indeed, only the business specialist knows the information required to constitute each of the events or rules to apply in order to generate one event from another. Only the specialist knows how to define the rules for determining the applications to input with these events. The business specialist must therefore have access to a simple (and if possible graphical) interface for defining, via drag-and-drop mechanisms, the sequence of routing rules and/or transformation rules to be executed (refer to the example in Figure 3.24) as well as to a collection of functions for manipulating the data carried by the events in order to be able to manage complex rules (see Figure 3.25 and Figure 3.26).

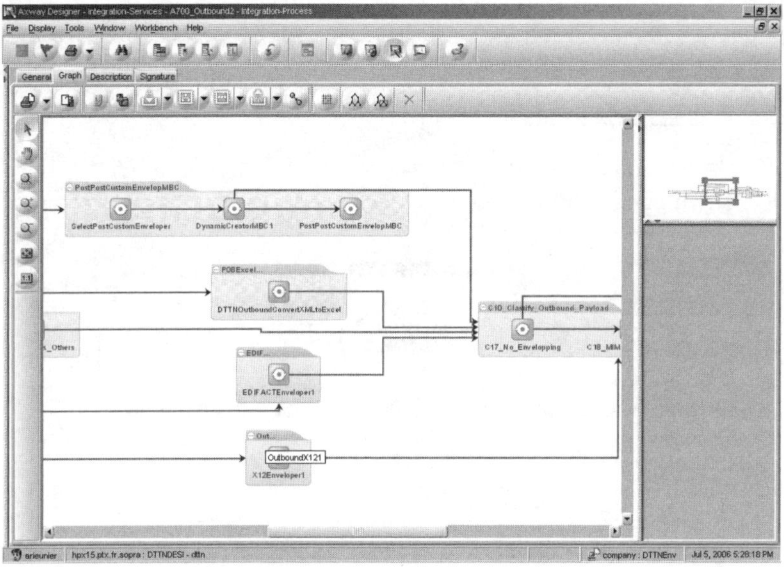

Figure 3.24. *Example sequencing rules definition (© Axway, 2006)*

In addition, to implement these rules, IT staff provide the set of technical elements required to translate the information defined by the business specialists. For example a business specialist describes the content of the purchase order, while IT staff construct its representation in XML (Figure 3.27).

The business specialist describes the process of passing one event to another (Figure 3.25), and IT staff describe the characteristics of the adapters and the middleware that will carry out this process (Figure 3.28).

To summarize, this interface should therefore be shareable between two populations, specialists in business and specialists in IT, and as a result, present the ergonomic characteristics and simplicity indispensable for use by non-IT staff. One of the solutions consists of dedicating distinct work environments that use technical and business transformation engines which share common objects such as descriptions of formats. It should moreover use an extremely powerful rules definition language in order to be able to deal with the complex cases of transformation and routing that we commonly find in information systems.

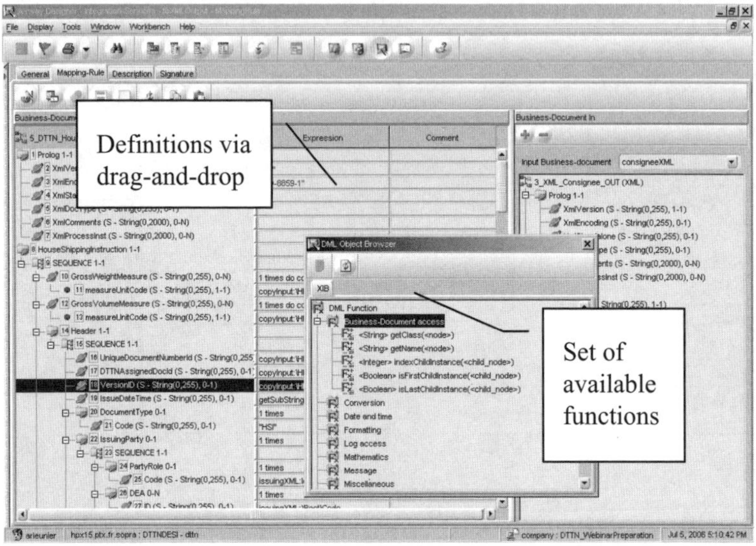

Figure 3.25. *Example of transformation rule definition (© Axway, 2006)*

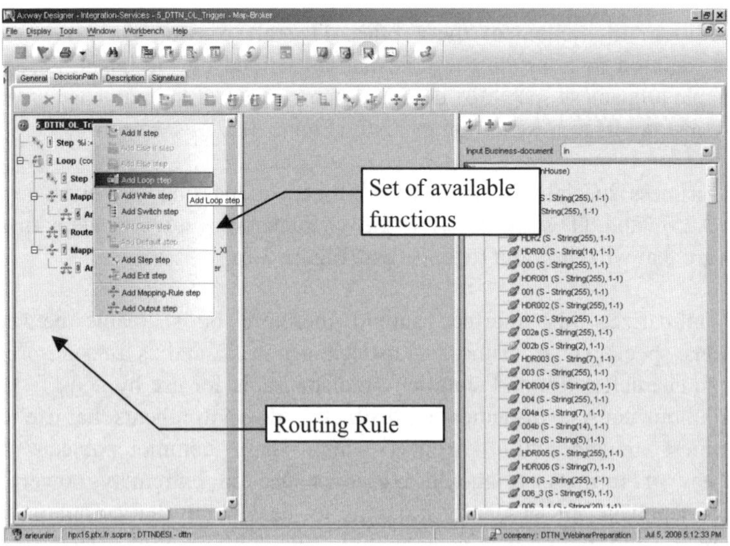

Figure 3.26. *Example of routing rule definition (© Axway, 2006)*

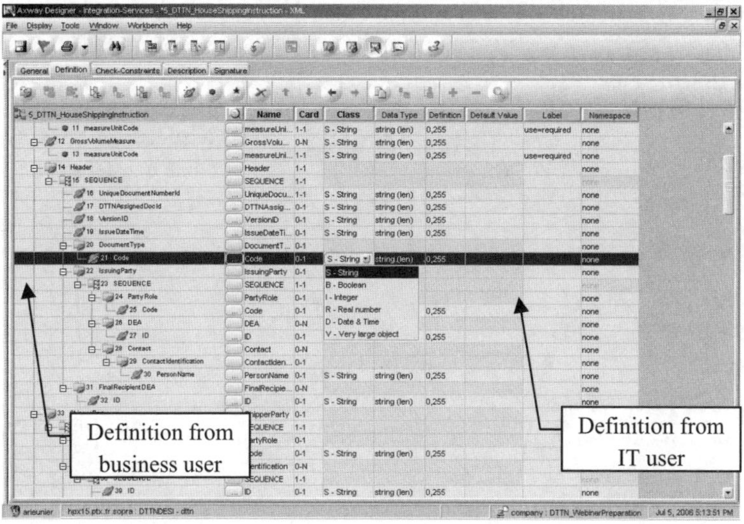

Figure 3.27. *Example of event structure definition (© Axway, 2006)*

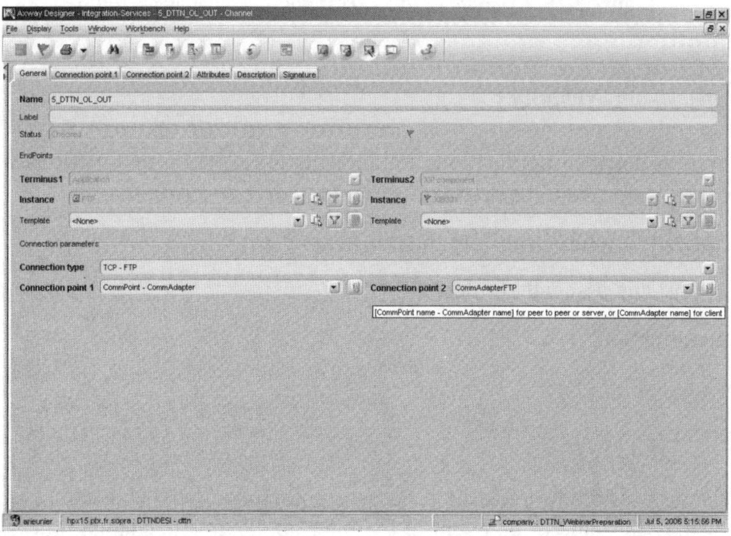

Figure 3.28. *Example of middleware usage definition (© Axway, 2006)*

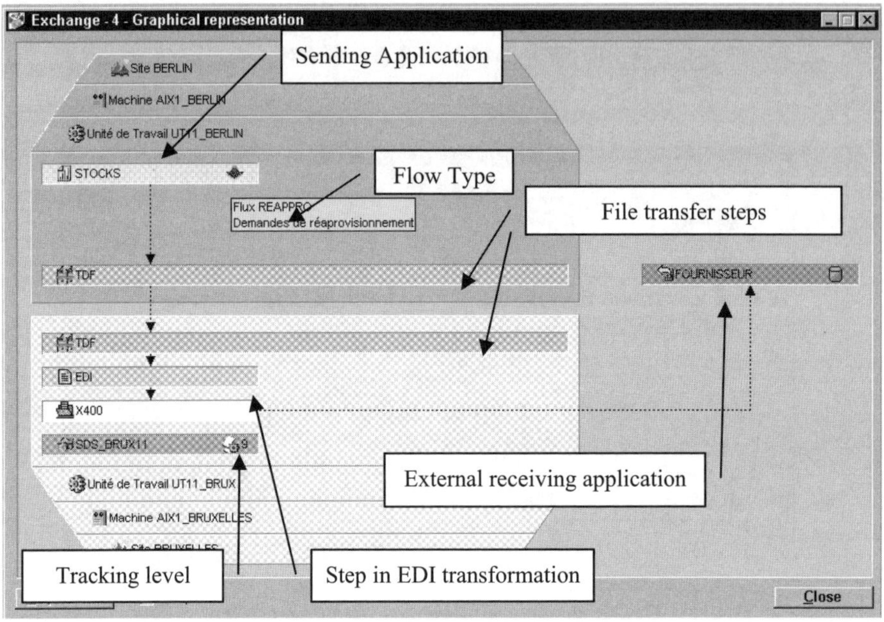

Figure 3.29. *Example of itinerary definition (© Axway, 2006)*

3.2.5. *Supervising exchanges*

Integration between applications implements a collection of functions which in certain cases can prove to be relatively complex:

– adapters to capture or restore the information;

– transport and associated rules;

– transformation;

– routing;

– storage.

It must be possible to track the process of integration from end to end, and to be able to display the state of an event in the inter-application exchange process at any moment.

We saw previously that transport tools as well as adapters should post information about the progress of routing operations. This is also true for transformation and routing components. Supervision thus provides an overview of exchanges and their status, with the possibility of zooming in on specific steps.

To do this, the global supervision system already discussed in section 3.1.4 must be usable to constitute dashboards that can display the indicators for assessing global activity (Figure 3.30), as well as the information and alerts concerning the transformation/routing processes (Figure 3.31).

Alerts take two forms:

– directly linked to the detection of errors during different processing steps (transformation, transport, etc.);

– deduced from checking rules, such as "excluding delay", "in the right order", etc., implemented as part of supervision of the exchanges.

In addition, in the case where an event is rejected by transformation and routing functions, a tool for intervening is indispensable. Thus, business specialists could manually correct the events in error and recycle them in the exchange circuit without having to re-execute the original application (Figure 3.32).

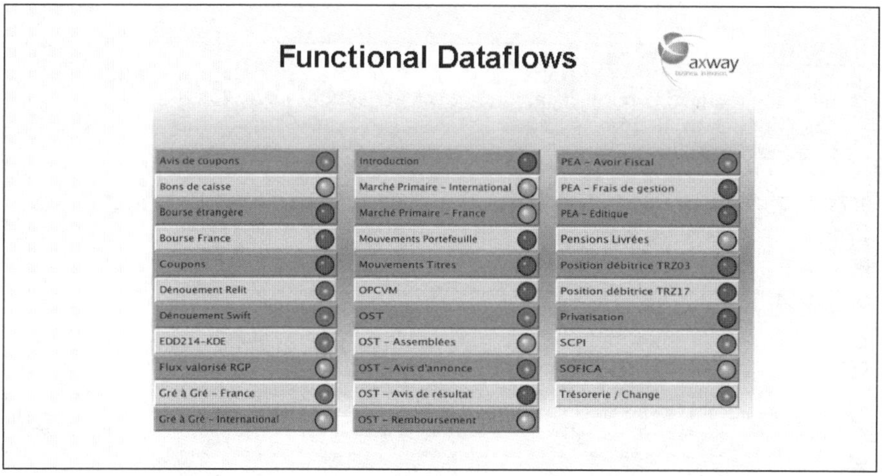

Figure 3.30. *Example of exchange supervision dashboard (© Axway, 2006)*

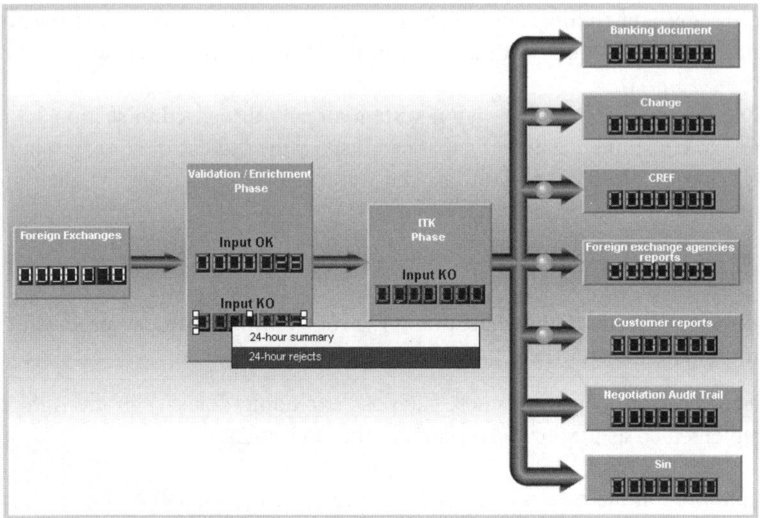

Figure 3.31. *Example of tracking dashboard for translation/transformation (© Axway, 2006)*

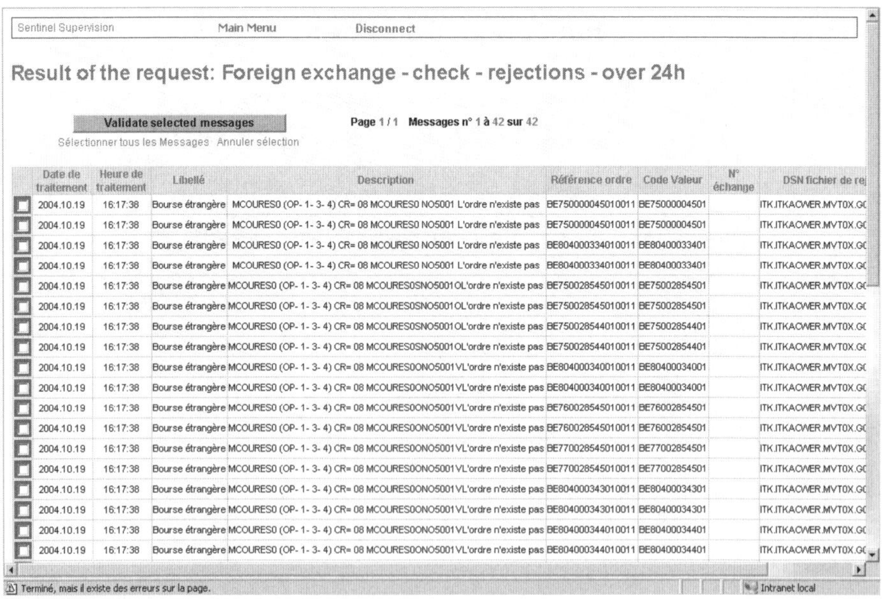

Date de traitement	Heure de traitement	Libellé	Description	Référence ordre	Code Valeur	N° échange	DSN fichier de re
2004.10.19	16:17:38	Bourse étrangère	MCOURES0 (OP- 1- 3- 4) CR= 08 MCOURES0 NO5001 L'ordre n'existe pas	BE75000004501 0011	BE75000004501		ITK.ITKACWER.MVT0X.G(
2004.10.19	16:17:38	Bourse étrangère	MCOURES0 (OP- 1- 3- 4) CR= 08 MCOURES0 NO5001 L'ordre n'existe pas	BE75000004501 0011	BE75000004501		ITK.ITKACWER.MVT0X.G(
2004.10.19	16:17:38	Bourse étrangère	MCOURES0 (OP- 1- 3- 4) CR= 08 MCOURES0 NO5001 L'ordre n'existe pas	BE80400033401 0011	BE80400033401		ITK.ITKACWER.MVT0X.G(
2004.10.19	16:17:38	Bourse étrangère	MCOURES0 (OP- 1- 3- 4) CR= 08 MCOURES0 NO5001 L'ordre n'existe pas	BE80400033401 0011	BE80400033401		ITK.ITKACWER.MVT0X.G(
2004.10.19	16:17:38	Bourse étrangère	MCOURES0 (OP- 1- 3- 4) CR= 08 MCOURES0SNO5001 OL'ordre n'existe pas	BE75002854501 0011	BE75002854501		ITK.ITKACWER.MVT0X.G(
2004.10.19	16:17:38	Bourse étrangère	MCOURES0 (OP- 1- 3- 4) CR= 08 MCOURES0SNO5001 OL'ordre n'existe pas	BE75002854501 0011	BE75002854501		ITK.ITKACWER.MVT0X.G(
2004.10.19	16:17:38	Bourse étrangère	MCOURES0 (OP- 1- 3- 4) CR= 08 MCOURES0SNO5001 OL'ordre n'existe pas	BE75002854401 0011	BE75002854401		ITK.ITKACWER.MVT0X.G(
2004.10.19	16:17:38	Bourse étrangère	MCOURES0 (OP- 1- 3- 4) CR= 08 MCOURES0SNO5001 OL'ordre n'existe pas	BE75002854401 0011	BE75002854401		ITK.ITKACWER.MVT0X.G(
2004.10.19	16:17:38	Bourse étrangère	MCOURES0 (OP- 1- 3- 4) CR= 08 MCOURES0ONO5001 VL'ordre n'existe pas	BE80400034001 0011	BE80400034001		ITK.ITKACWER.MVT0X.G(
2004.10.19	16:17:38	Bourse étrangère	MCOURES0 (OP- 1- 3- 4) CR= 08 MCOURES0ONO5001 VL'ordre n'existe pas	BE80400034001 0011	BE80400034001		ITK.ITKACWER.MVT0X.G(
2004.10.19	16:17:38	Bourse étrangère	MCOURES0 (OP- 1- 3- 4) CR= 08 MCOURES0ONO5001 VL'ordre n'existe pas	BE76002854501 0011	BE76002854501		ITK.ITKACWER.MVT0X.G(
2004.10.19	16:17:38	Bourse étrangère	MCOURES0 (OP- 1- 3- 4) CR= 08 MCOURES0ONO5001 VL'ordre n'existe pas	BE76002854501 0011	BE76002854501		ITK.ITKACWER.MVT0X.G(
2004.10.19	16:17:38	Bourse étrangère	MCOURES0 (OP- 1- 3- 4) CR= 08 MCOURES0ONO5001 VL'ordre n'existe pas	BE77002854501 0011	BE77002854501		ITK.ITKACWER.MVT0X.G(
2004.10.19	16:17:38	Bourse étrangère	MCOURES0 (OP- 1- 3- 4) CR= 08 MCOURES0ONO5001 VL'ordre n'existe pas	BE77002854501 0011	BE77002854501		ITK.ITKACWER.MVT0X.G(
2004.10.19	16:17:38	Bourse étrangère	MCOURES0 (OP- 1- 3- 4) CR= 08 MCOURES0ONO5001 VL'ordre n'existe pas	BE80400034301 0011	BE80400034301		ITK.ITKACWER.MVT0X.G(
2004.10.19	16:17:38	Bourse étrangère	MCOURES0 (OP- 1- 3- 4) CR= 08 MCOURES0ONO5001 VL'ordre n'existe pas	BE80400034301 0011	BE80400034301		ITK.ITKACWER.MVT0X.G(
2004.10.19	16:17:38	Bourse étrangère	MCOURES0 (OP- 1- 3- 4) CR= 08 MCOURES0ONO5001 VL'ordre n'existe pas	BE80400034401 0011	BE80400034401		ITK.ITKACWER.MVT0X.G(
2004.10.19	16:17:38	Bourse étrangère	MCOURES0 (OP- 1- 3- 4) CR= 08 MCOURES0ONO5001 VL'ordre n'existe pas	BE80400034401 0011	BE80400034401		ITK.ITKACWER.MVT0X.G(

Figure 3.32. *Example of acknowledgment/recycling screen (© Axway, 2006)*

3.3. Automating business processes

Therefore, the functions of transport and connectivity – to which we could add the function of information adaptation – make it possible to handle the problems of application integration linked to the propagation of data. At the same time, processing the cases that correspond to the classification type of multi-step process integration requires the complementary functions of business process automation.

This is the domain of integration of business processes, or BPM (Business Process Management).

The WfMC (Workflow Management Coalition) defines a business process [WFM 99] as *a collection of one or more linked procedures or activities that together accomplish a business objective, in the context of an organizational structure that define roles and relationships*.

For example, in a financial institution, granting a loan is a business process which can be automated by chaining multiple applications, but that in certain cases could require approval from the service manager.

A business process can be supported entirely by a single organizational structure, or extended over several of these structures, as for example in a client-supplier relation. It possesses predefined conditions for triggering its initialization on each new instance (on each arrival of an event), and outputs defined for its completion.

3.3.1. *Modeling business processes*

The modeling of business processes is not a new approach. First, it has served as a documentary objective in clarifying, and often improving, the business process itself. Document- and graphics-oriented tools will appear, initially intended for use by business specialists in the enterprise. Once a modeling tool has been used to optimize the process around the business, then a more operational slant is useful in the case of application integration.

Above all, the modeling of a business process must represent the process so that it can be implemented automatically. It defines a collection of activities, the relationships between them, the criteria that define the beginning and the end of the process, and all information concerning each activity, such as participants (persons), applications, data, etc.

The activities can be manual or automatic (i.e., performed by computing applications). Figure 3.33 provides a simplified representation of the structure of a business process.

In 2004, BPMI.org (Business Process Management Initiative) published version 1 of the specifications for the BPMN (Business Process Management Notation), a graphical notation for describing business processes in the form of diagrams (BPD – Business Process Diagram) [BPM 04]. In June 2005, BPMI.org and OMG™ (Object Management Group™) merged their activities around BPM in the group BMI DTF (Business Modeling and Integration Domain Task Force) within the OMG. The adoption of BPMN as an OMG standard is being finalized at the time of writing.

The BPMN notation is projected for extension, if necessary, to allow the addition of non-standard elements or of artifacts for satisfying particular needs, for example, to respond to requirements linked to a particular vertical sector. BPMN does not prejudge the language that will be used for the execution of the business processes, but offers an example of correspondence with the Business Process Execution Language (BPEL – see section 3.3.2).

This notation is composed of four categories of basic elements:

– connections (connecting objects);

– actions (flow objects);

– groups of elements (swimlanes);

– artifacts.

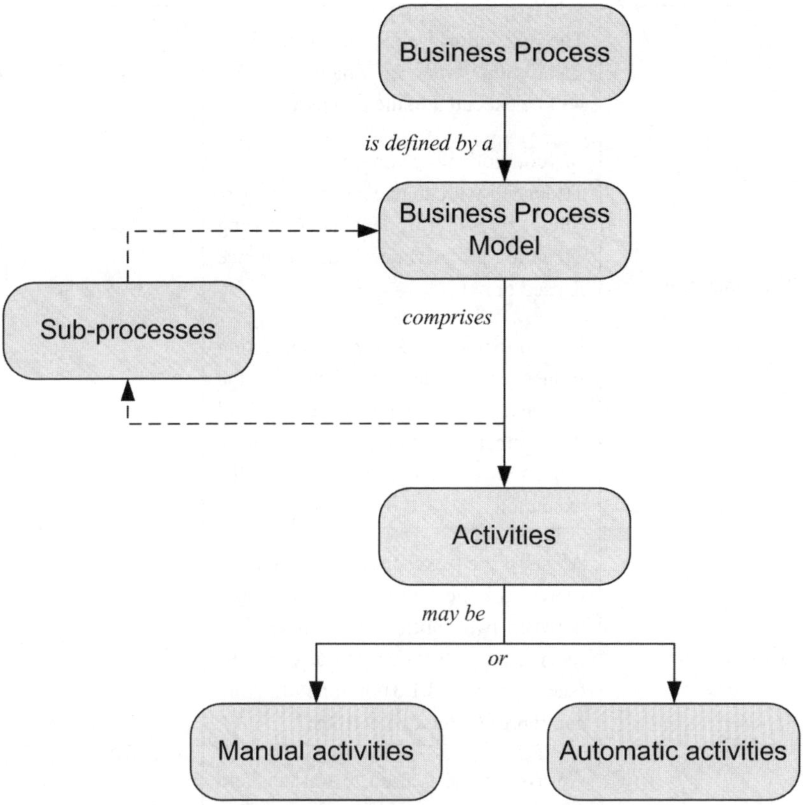

Figure 3.33. *Definition of a business process*

3.3.1.1. *Connections*

These are the graphical representations used to connect elements to each other. There are three types of connection:

– execution sequence (sequence flow);

– exchange of messages (message flow);

– associations.

Table 3.1 below provides a brief description of these elements.

Sequence flow	The execution sequence is used to specify the order in which activities will be executed in the process.	
	A conditional expression can be associated with an execution sequence. This expression is evaluated during execution to determine if the sequence is used or not.	
	It is possible to define an execution sequence by default. This is the sequence that will be executed if all the other conditional execution sequences are not checked during the execution.	
Message flow	A message exchange is used to represent the flow of messages between two entities ready to send or receive them. Two groups of elements (see section 3.3.1.3) in one diagram can represent the two entities.	
Association	An association is used to link an item of information with actions. This information can comprise text or graphical objects that do not represent actions.	

Table 3.1. *BPMN: graphical representation of connections*

3.3.1.2. *Actions*

Actions are the principal graphical elements for describing the functioning of a business process. There are three of these objects:

– events;

– activities;

– gateways.

Table 3.2 below provides a brief description of these elements.

Events	An "event" is something that occurs during the execution of a business process. It impacts the progression of process execution, and can arise at the beginning of the process (single line) to trigger it, during the process (double line) to trigger an activity, or at the end of the process (bolded line) to terminate it.	
	Message: a message arrives from a participant.	
	Timer: date, expiry of time period, etc.	
	Exception: an error occurs during the execution of an action or a process; processing is typically associated with this error.	
	Cancel: cancels the transaction in progress.	
	Compensation: used to return to the original situation when a transaction is canceled (following an error for example).	
	Rule: triggers an event if the conditions for the rule are verified.	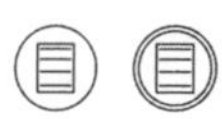
	Link: for connecting sub-processes.	
	Multiple: several types of events can occur.	
	Terminate: terminates immediately all activities in the process.	

Activities	These are the different operations that the process must execute. An activity can be simple or composite. Three types of activities can be represented in a business process diagram: tasks, sub-processes and processes. *Task*: represents an operation to be executed by the process. *Sub-process*: a composite activity that contains a sequence of other activities. The representation of the sub-processes can be performed in mode: - masked activities or - expanded activities.	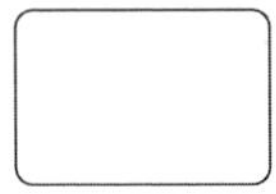 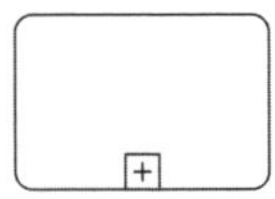 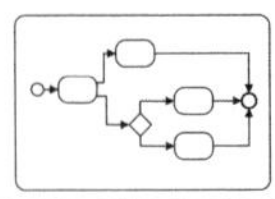
	The activities (tasks, sub-processes) can have associated attributes that specify how they function: - loop - execution in parallel - compensation.	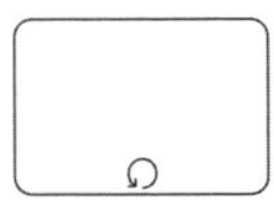 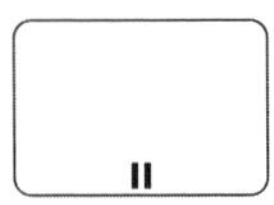 

Gateways	Gateways define the way that execution sequences in a process can converge, diverge or execute in parallel.	
	Exclusive decision/merge (XOR): a single sequence can be executed. The switch can be performed on:	
	- data	
	- events.	
	Inclusive decision/merge (OR): multiple sequences can be executed.	
	Parallel fork/join: several sequences are executed in parallel, or indication of a joining point between multiple sequences.	

Table 3.2. *BPMN: graphical representation of actions*

The modeling of a process with BPMN notation makes it possible to define the execution conditions for different activities in conformity with the examples supplied in Table 3.3 below.

<table>
<tr><td>- Exclusive gateways on data

- without marker</td><td>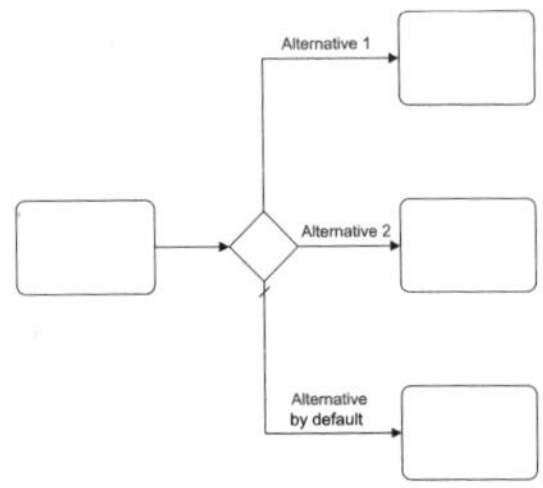
</td></tr>
<tr><td>- with marker

- Exclusive gateways on events</td><td>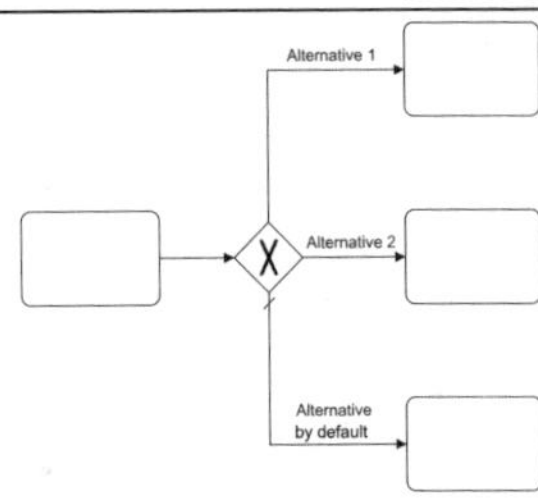

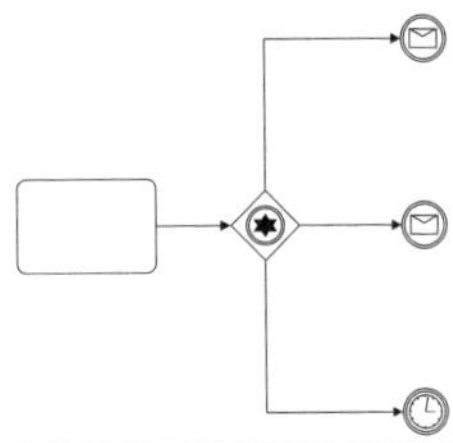</td></tr>
<tr><td>- Inclusive gateways

- using conditional sequences

- using gateways</td><td>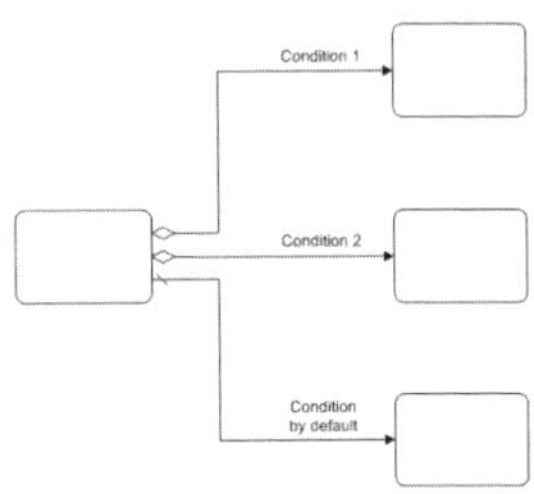

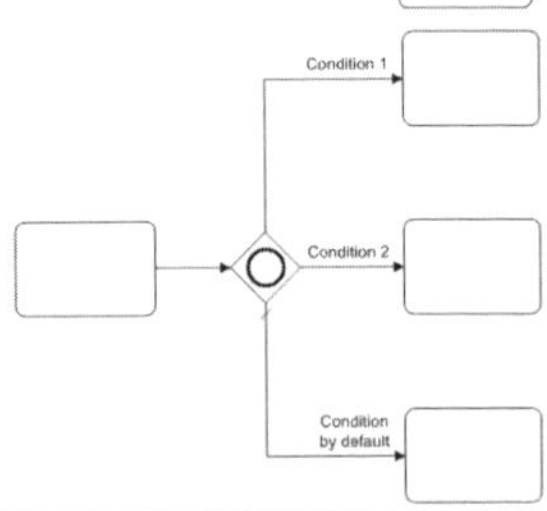
</td></tr>
</table>

- Joins	
- exclusive	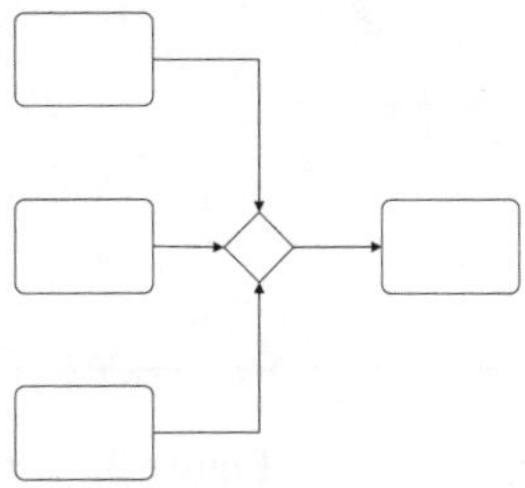
- inclusive	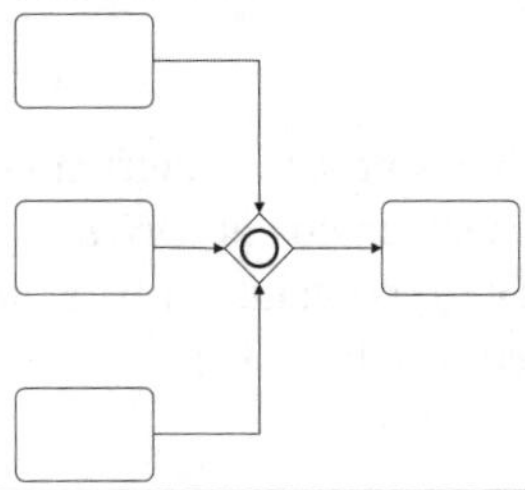
- Iterations	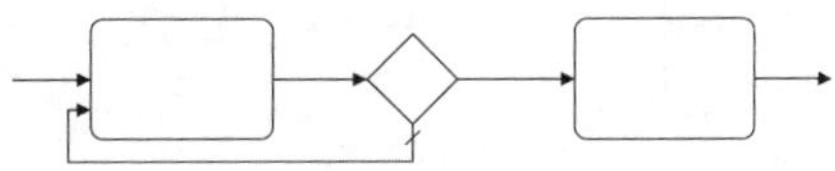

Table 3.3. *BPMN: examples of sequences of activities*

3.3.1.3. *Groups of elements*

Groups of elements can be used to assemble the actions performed by each participant of a process.

A *Pool* (Figure 3.34) represents a participant in a process, which can be an organizational entity in an enterprise (customer services, accounting, etc.) or more generally a role (purchaser, vendor, etc.).

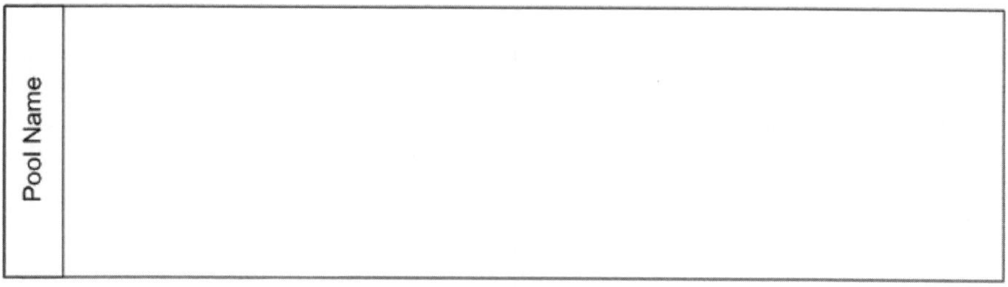

Figure 3.34. *BPMN: Representation of a Pool*

A business process diagram contains at least one *Pool*. In most cases, since the process represented is *private* (internal to a given organization such as an enterprise), it contains only a single *Pool*. In that case, its limitations are not represented (Figure 3.35).

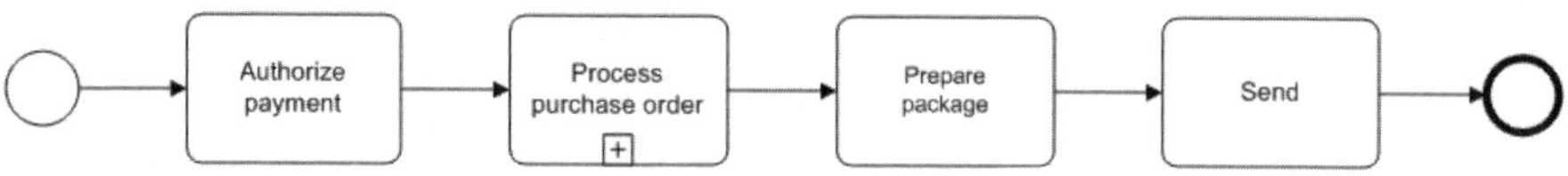

Figure 3.35. *Example representation of private process*

A *Lane* is a subset inside a *Pool* that makes it possible to organize and categorize activities (Figure 3.36). The meaning of the *Lanes* is left to the discretion of the process model designer, but most of the time they are used to represent internal roles (accounting, purchaser, etc.), systems (applications of the enterprise) or organizational entities internal to the enterprise (customer services, accounting, etc.). For example a warehouse management process could comprise a *Pool*, represented by a "Welcome" *Lane* and a "Check" *Lane*.

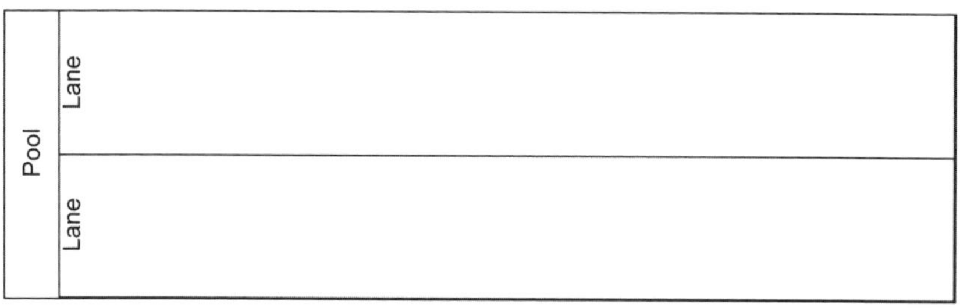

Figure 3.36. *BPMN: Representation of Lanes*

As part of the integration of inter-enterprise exchanges (see section 4.3), the internal business processes that are proper to each enterprise must be distinguished from the "collaborative" business processes most often defined by value-added network providers. These make it possible to automate the whole of the exchange process.

Consider the example, in a client/supplier relationship, of the process for handling an order (Figure 3.37). The global process of treatment between the client and the supplier takes the form of a chain of internal and public processes. Each partner should therefore be capable of defining this chain for the portion that concerns its information system (its internal process + the public process).

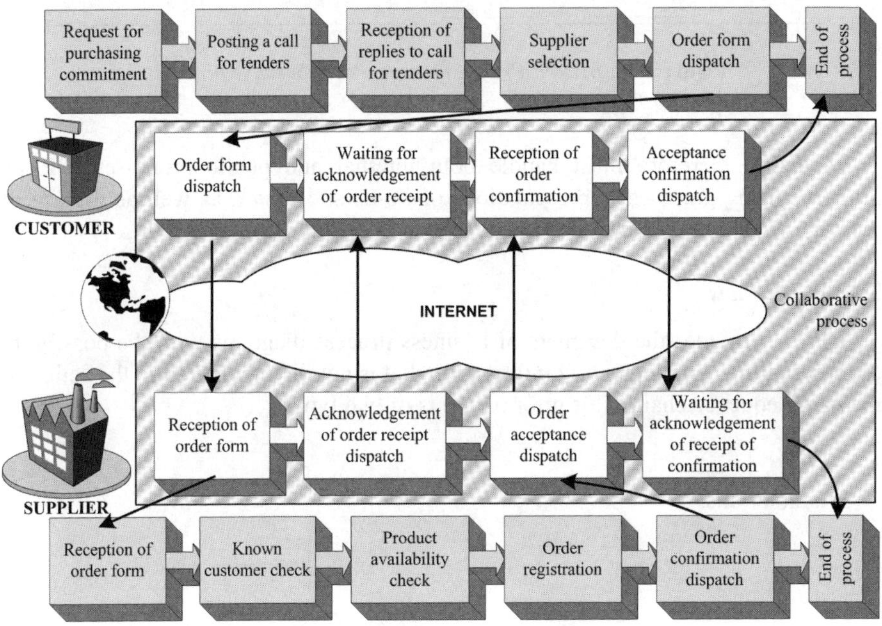

Figure 3.37. *Internal process – collaborative process*

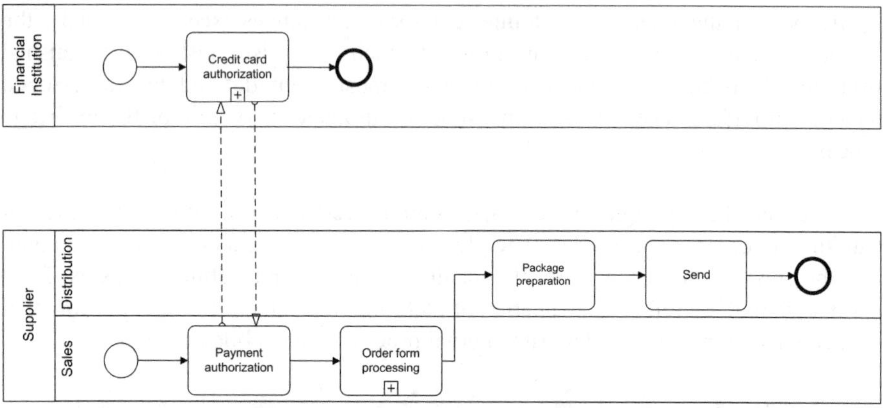

Figure 3.38. *BPMN: Private process – collaborative process*

Modeling therefore must handle both internal and public processes. BPMN proposes using graphical representations of *Pools* and *Lanes*, as well as the use of message exchange connections to represent such diagrams (Figure 3.38).

3.3.1.4. *Artifacts*

BPMN provides the designers of business process diagrams with the possibility of representing complementary information that is not directly linked to the action or message sequence chain. This information is of two types:

– data;

– annotations.

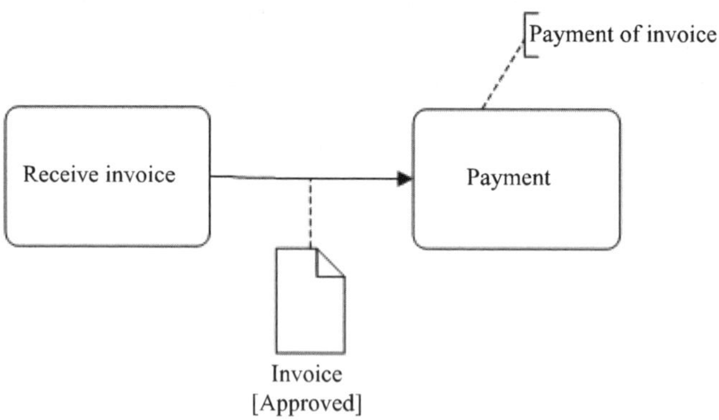

Figure 3.39. *BPMN – artifacts*

3.3.1.5. *Graphical interface*

It should be possible to carry out modeling using a graphical user interface, and one that presents the same characteristics as the interface used to define the rules for adapting information (see section 3.2.4). Furthermore, the interface should be usable by both business specialists in the enterprise and by IT staff.

Business specialists graphically draw a process by manipulating activities, data, conditions and constraints. The drawing establishes the connections between the various elements, generating the logic chain that enables process execution. It also defines the performance indicators for measuring the efficiency of the process as well as the indicators for providing a summary view of the business activity via dashboards that are also defined at this point.

IT staff, for their part, provide the complete set of technical elements required to execute these sequences.

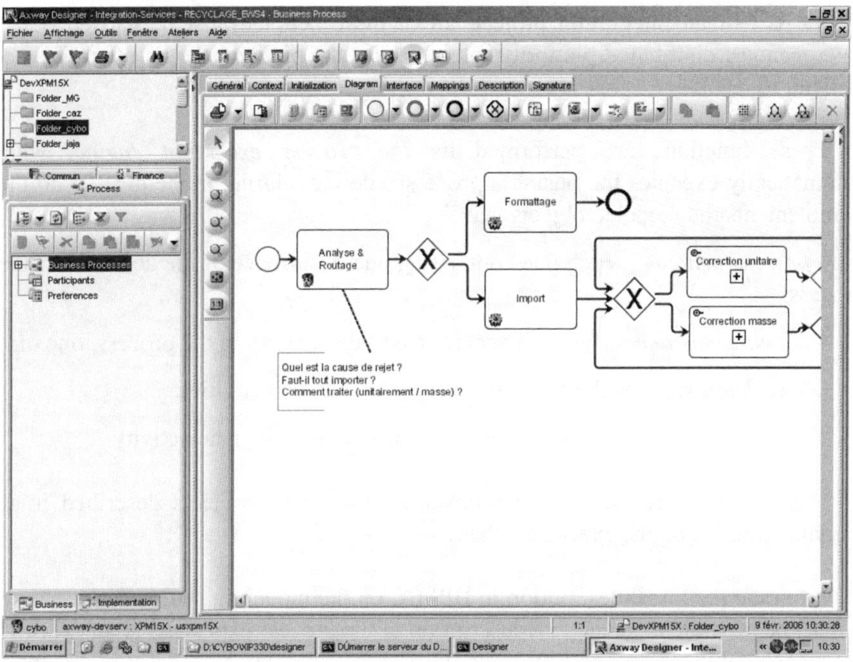

Figure 3.40. *Graphical modeling interface (© Axway, 2006)*

3.3.2. *Executing business processes*

3.3.2.1. *The orchestration of activities*

Once modeling has been completed, the described sequences must be executed:

– launching each activity in the defined order;

– recovering the results of each step;

– applying the rules for chaining depending on the results observed;

– ensuring that the successive activities are input with the data or the events that they require;

– posting information to the supervision system;

– managing each step of the process, omitting none, over the whole of its life span.

As part of an integration project, all of these actions must be carried out on heterogenous, distributed platforms, which poses the problem that is often the most difficult to resolve.

These functions are performed by *the process execution engine*, which automatically executes the business processes defined during modeling. To do this, it implements the modeled objects via:

– *process instances*, each one comprising one occurrence of the defined business process;

– *activities instances*, for each occurrence of the activity in the process, one of:

- *work units*, for each of the occurrences of manual activities,

- *application instance*, for each occurrence of an automatic activity.

Figure 3.41 illustrates the relationships between the objects described in the modeling phase and the execution phase.

From the graphical description in BPMN, on the modeling station for processes, it must be possible to generate a description of the process expressed in an execution language usable by the execution engines, and to deploy this description on the platforms which host those engines.

The process execution language that, on current trends, looks increasingly established today is the BPEL standard from OASIS.

At the origins of this standard are IBM and Microsoft, each of whom had already defined their own execution language, respectively WSFL and XLANG. IBM and Microsoft have decided to combine these two languages to define BPEL4WS (Business Process Execution Language for Web Services). In April 2003, BEA Systems, IBM, Microsoft, SAP and Siebel Systems submitted BPEL4WS V1.1 to OASIS to have it adopted as standard. BPEL4WS (since abbreviated to BPEL) describes the process in an XML format by utilizing a certain number of other standards as XPath and WSDL (refer to section 4.5.3.1).

However, in the current state of the BPEL standard, this description, in the form of structured blocks imposed by the use of XML, does not *cover all the representations of processes authorized by the graphically oriented BPMN.* From this fact, for the moment, an inconsistency exists between what we are capable of modeling with BPMN and what can be executed by a BPEL engine.

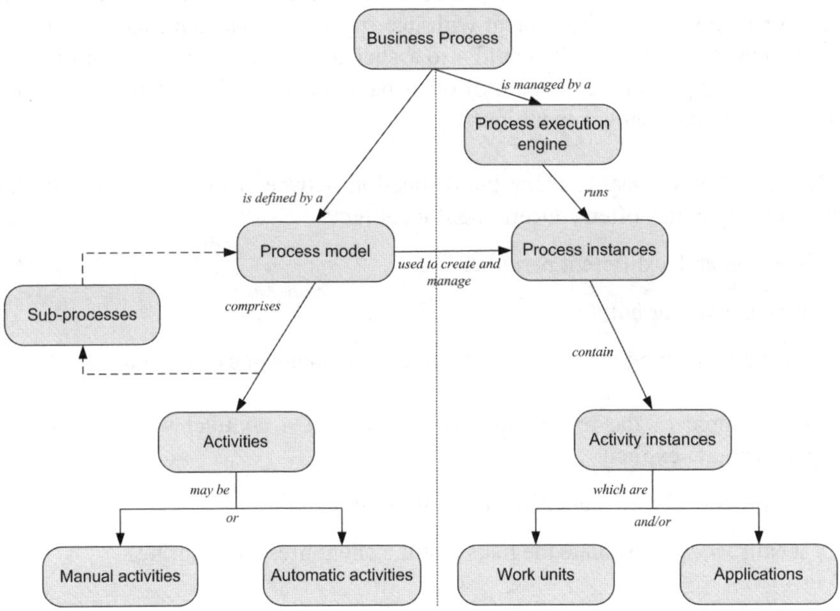

Figure 3.41. *Relationship between business process modeling and execution*

3.3.2.2. *The execution of business rules*

In addition to the execution engine of the processes, an execution engine for the business rules (Business Rules Engine, or BRE) is also required to describe and execute the rules that will guide the process through the various possible paths in the model. This is a fundamental element in the automation of processes, since it allows the coding rules for the applications to be externalized, and therefore, from this fact, avoids modifying the applications in case of a change to the business rule, a determinative factor for IT agility. In addition, another advantage is to be able confer on business management the responsibility for developing and refining rules and thus lightening the workload for the development teams.

The definition of these rules could be (and sometimes is) performed directly during the modeling by using a programming language such as Java in the description of the process. However, for graphical or natural-language definition of these rules, it is preferable to use an external rules engine. This avoids modifying the modeling of the process in case the rule needs to be modified. All that is needed is to modify and redeploy the rule, with no impact on the logic of the process.

The use of such an engine makes possible the management of extremely elaborate rules: for example, in the case of a resupply process during an out-of-stock, we do not have to be content with just specifying "backup" suppliers in case the principal supplier fails. We could also associate periods when different rules will be applied, along with a collection of other parameters that help optimize the costs of resupply during such an operation.

It is not always easy to make the distinction between *rules* and *processes*. The distinguishing points often concern their updating:

– with generally different periodicities;

– dynamically or not;

– by distinguishing the profiles authorized to manage one or the other.

The example of the process for subscription of a contract with an insurance company is quite explicit:

– the process allows management of the contract request;

– it calls *rules* to evaluate the risks that the client presents (scoring).

3.3.3. *Supervising business processes*

The supervision of business processes consists of ensuring the correct sequence of the various applications or tasks that comprise the process. Moreover, with process execution coming between the levels of adapting and transporting information, it is up to supervision to provide a global view of all these operations.

Using dashboards, the global process supervision system provides users with information about what the process is doing, and its current advancement at the step-level. It must also detect processes that do not respect the constraints of execution timeframes defined during modeling (Figure 3.42). It posts alerts to business specialists and operators so that they can intervene in case of incidents.

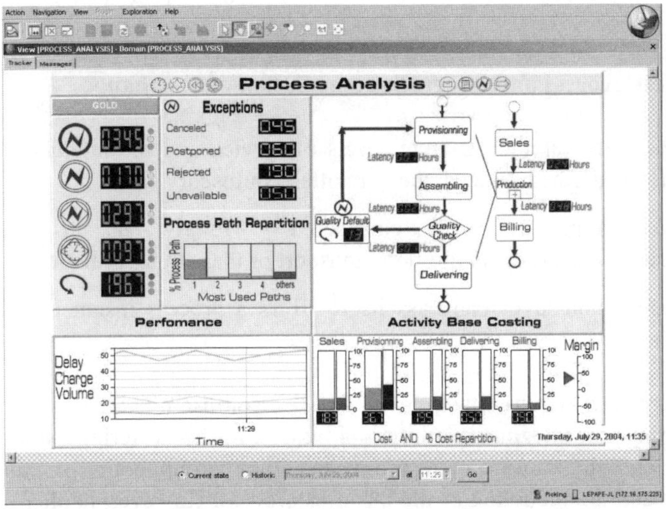

Figure 3.42. *Supervision of the processes (© Axway, 2006)*

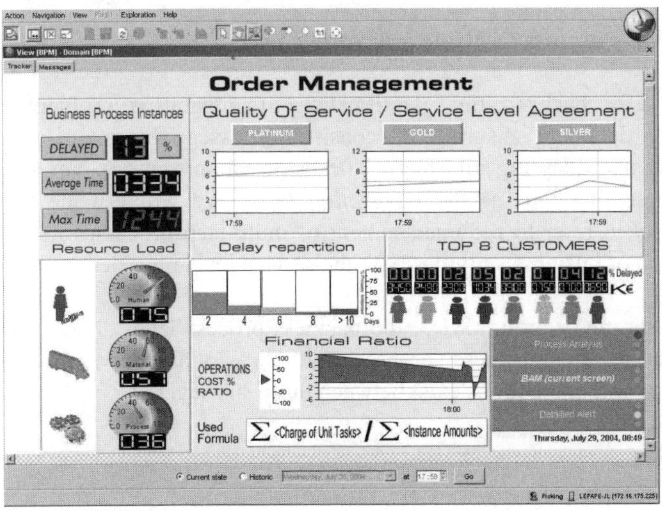

Figure 3.43. *Example of BAM dashboard (© Axway, 2006)*

As we have previously mentioned (see section 2.7), BPM is closely associated with Business Activity Monitoring. BAM gives users real-time indicators for evaluating the efficiency of enterprise processes, and takes account of the context to alert users in case of abnormal activity. The BAM system is continuously input, in particular by the process execution engine, and provides users with information on what is happening globally in enterprise activity (Figure 3.43).

3.4. Business process and integration: mediation and exchange

Both the roles for the different levels of service and the interactions for each service must be defined. Indeed, they are often confused:

– a business process can be considered – wrongly – as an orchestrator of integration activities, such as file flow transport or mass transformation;

– an integration layer can pass itself off as a process instance orchestrator – which it is not.

Clarification is required then, given that this confusion is sometimes fostered by certain application integration solution providers. In their offerings, under the same formalism and the same data entry screen, they group both the content of an integration and the modeling of the business process. However, neither the rhythms of modification, nor the user profiles, nor the technical and business preoccupations are the same.

3.4.1. *Business process level and integration level*

If we refer back to our classification of integration problem types, then propagating data and ensuring its consistency essentially require functions for transporting and adapting information (transformation/routing). For simplicity, we refer to these functions as the *integration level*. We will use the term *business process level* to refer to the management of multi-step processes necessitating the orchestration of business activities with the service level provided by BPM.

As we saw in section 3.3.1.3, the business process level divides into two sub-levels: the private business process and the collaborative process. Various relationships and interactions exist between these sub-levels.

3.4.2. *Mediation process sub-level*

In conformity with our definition, the integration level comprises different infrastructure services that are part of the transport and connectivity layer in our model (as is the management of file transfers (MFT) or the queue managers), as well as services in the information adaptation layer. Each group of services is executed by what we will call a *mediation process* in the integration level. Figure 3.44 provides an example of the use of a mediation process.

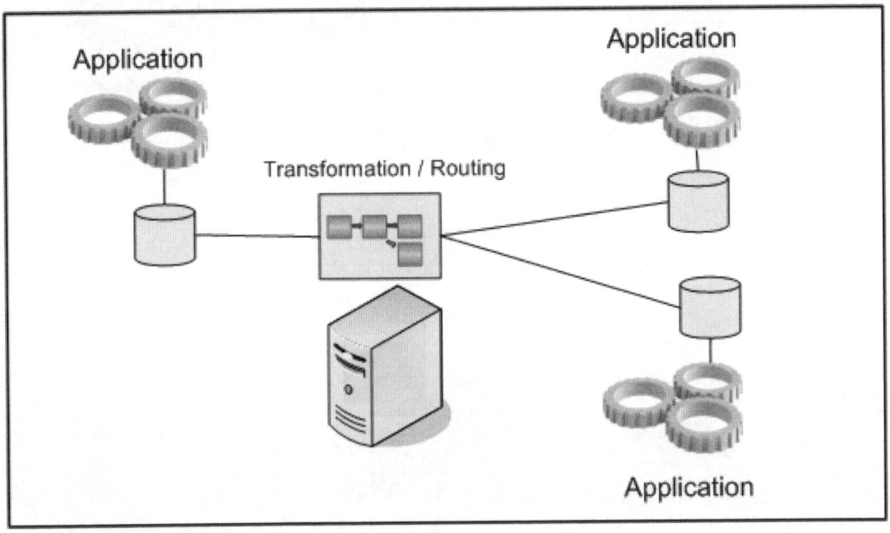

Figure 3.44. *Example of mediation process*

3.4.3. *Exchange process sub-level*

Each group of services can be used separately, but most of the time in a distributed environment (see section 3.5.2.2), multiple services distributed over different platforms have to be chained in sequence. End-to-end control over the execution of these services is carried out by what we will refer to as an *exchange process sub-level*. Figure 3.45 illustrates the use of this sub-level.

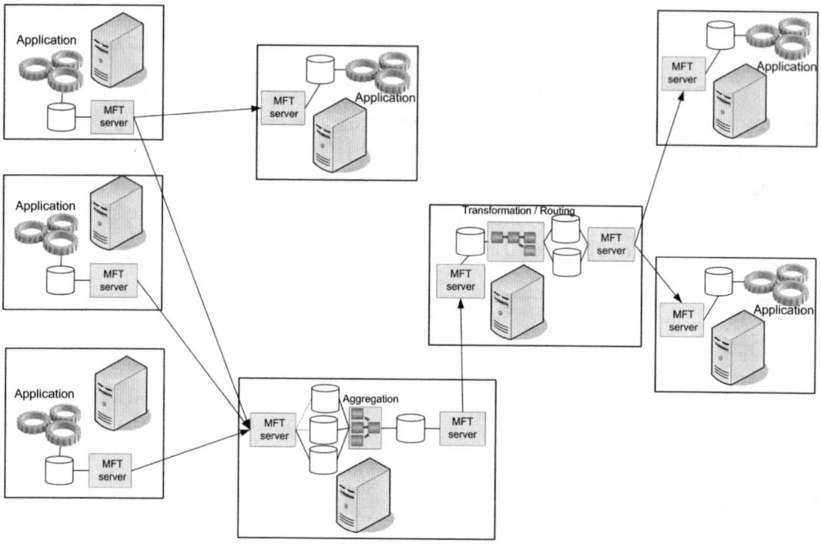

Figure 3.45. *Example of exchange process*

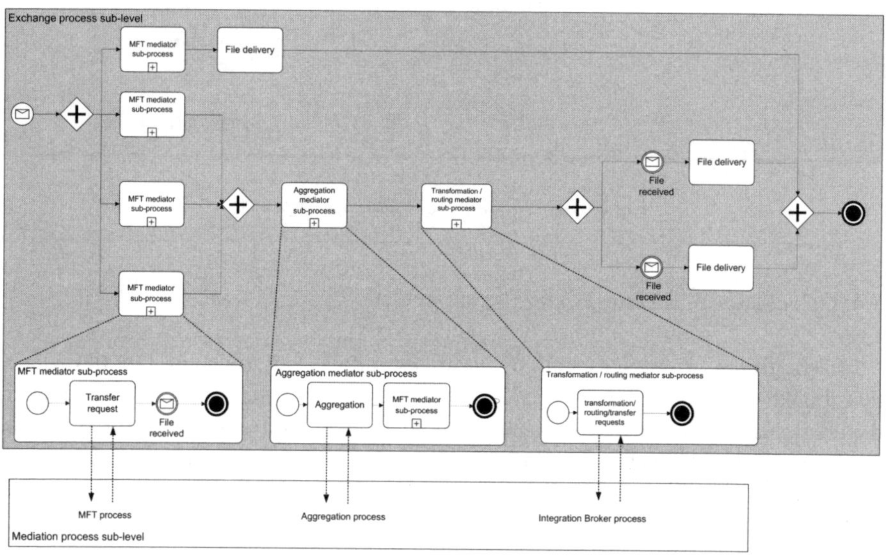

Figure 3.46. *Relationships between the mediation process and the exchange process*

3.4.4. *Interaction between the sub-levels*

The interactions/relations between the mediation processes and exchange process can take the form illustrated in Figure 3.46. As a case in point and since we have already described it, this illustration uses BPMN notation to represent the exchange process illustrated in Figure 3.45.

3.4.5. *Interaction between integration and business process (BPM)*

By themselves, the services in BPM do not cover data propagation, which can be necessary to make the data available to an activity in the business process. There will therefore be a certain number of relations and interactions between the process level and the integration level:

– the same data propagation can input activities that belong to different business processes;

– one business process could require several data propagation processes to input the different activities that compose it. That business process should therefore orchestrate the different activities required to carry out those data propagations;

– in addition, the process level and the integration level do not necessarily change at the same pace.

These relations are represented by Figure 3.47.

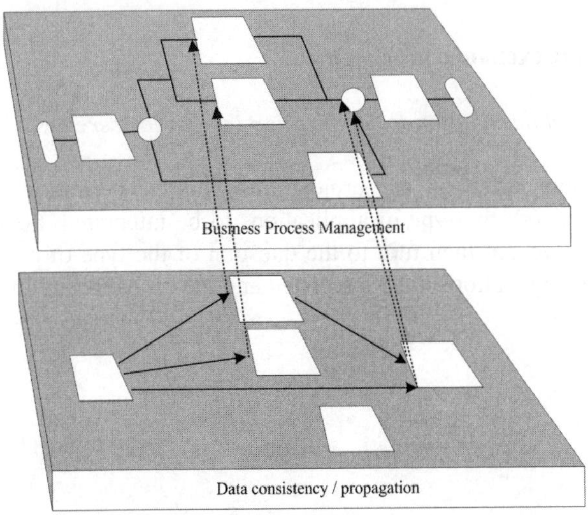

Figure 3.47. *Inter-level relationships*

Finally, the drawing in Figure 3.48 presents the complete set of relations and interactions possible between the different levels and sub-levels.

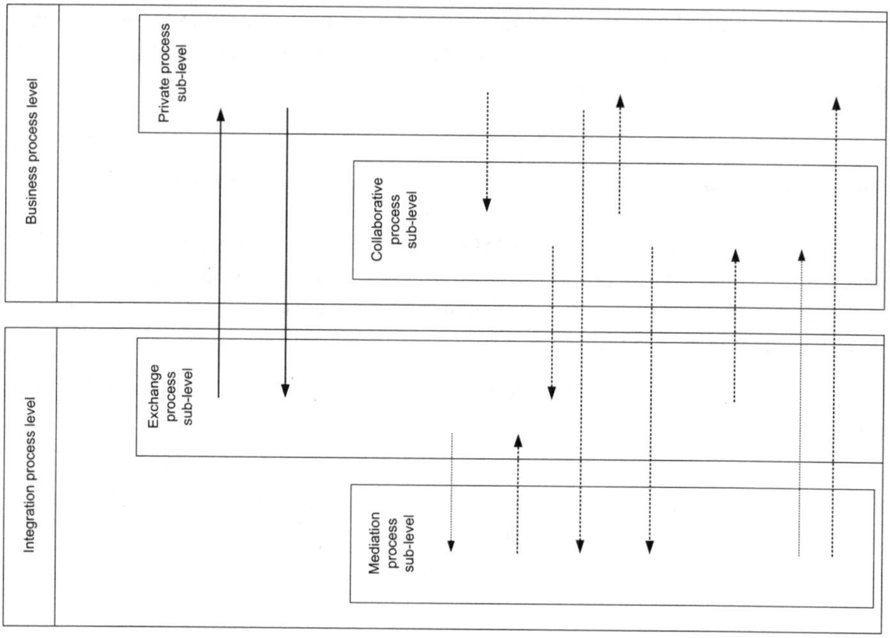

Figure 3.48. *Relations and interactions between levels and sub-levels*

3.5. Choosing the exchange architecture

"Types of physical distribution for application integration services"

Once the boundaries of the project have been determined – the targeted integration domain(s), the type of applications to be integrated, the cartography of the exchanges – we can then turn to the question of the type of communication to use between the applications to be integrated and the exchange architecture to be put in place.

3.5.1. *Synchronous/asynchronous communication*

The result of integration between applications must not recreate a spaghetti system inside the integration solution. Thus, to keep the information system flexible and reactive, loose coupling between these applications should be favored. Furthermore, close study of the different integration types (see section 2.4.1) confirms this for us: integration by data propagation or integration of multi-step processes only implement asynchronous and uni-directional interactions. In this case, we prefer to use means of asynchronous communication, such as MOMs or file transfer managers.

Only the integration of composite applications necessitates synchronous and bi-directional interactions for which we should use technologies such as DBMS bridges, ORBs (Object Request Brokers), RMI (Remote Method Invocation) calls or RPC (Remote Procedure Call), or currently as well, calls to Web services as part of an SOA approach.

3.5.2. *Architecture: centralized or distributed?*

Once the type of communication has been determined, the question of the desired exchange architecture must be asked. The choice of this architecture could, in addition, directly influence the choice of the tool(s) that go to make it up.

3.5.2.1. *Centralized architecture*

Centralized architecture concentrates in one focal point the complete set of services ensured by the infrastructure. The applications to be integrated to connect to this focal point using the appropriate adapters (see section 3.1.3.3). In a multi-machine environment, this architecture, designated “hub and spoke” in the terminology of EAI tools (Figure 3.49), makes it possible to not have to deploy all of the components in the infrastructure on the complete set of platforms. On the downside, if the platform that supports the hub becomes unavailable or overloaded, it can potentially generate a single point of failure (SPOF) and contention in the information system.

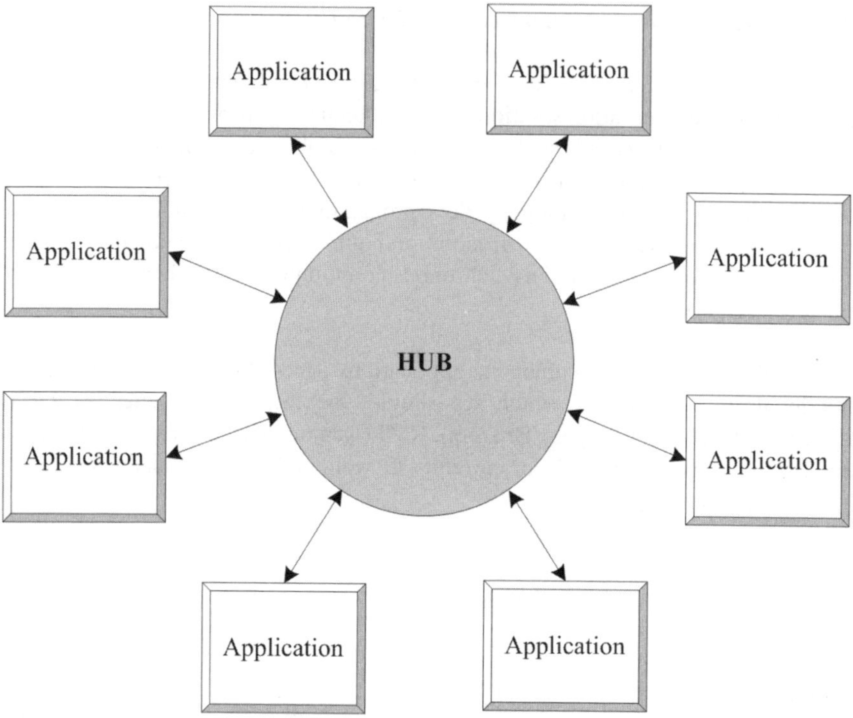

Figure 3.49. *Hub-and-spoke architecture*

3.5.2.2. *Distributed architecture*

A distributed architecture shares out the infrastructure over the set of machines that support the applications to be integrated, with each application connecting locally to that infrastructure through adapters. This architecture does not introduce any single point of failure or contention. However, on the downside, it requires tools adapted to the heterogenity of the platforms where its components must be deployed, as well as tools for supervising and maintaining those components on the various platforms.

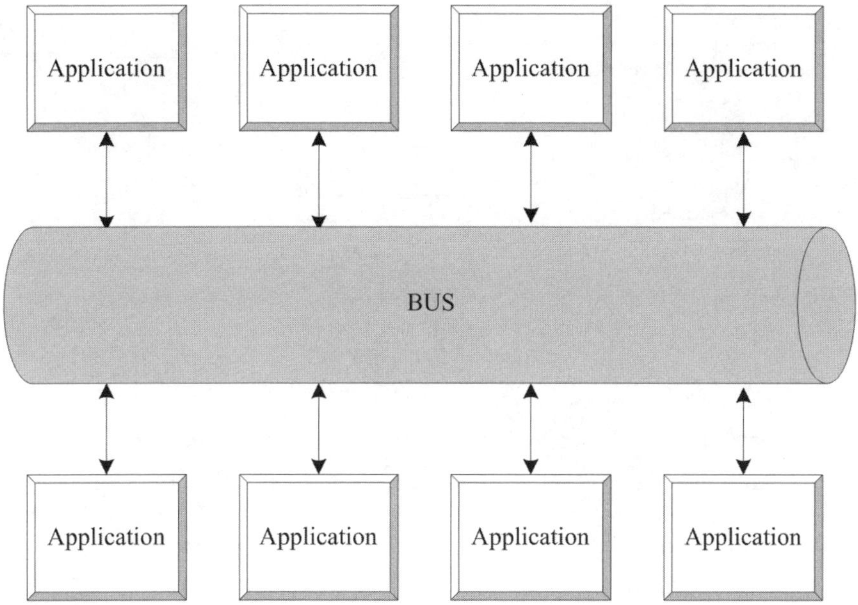

Figure 3.50. *Bus architecture*

Since distribution can work at the level of the integration services themselves, we thus find ourselves in the presence of a bus-type architecture (Figure 3.50). The integration services are therefore themselves distributed in what ensures a "meshing" of the exchange infrastructure, rendering the solution more robust (no "SPOF" (single point of failure) service on the critical path).

This can also be carried out by deploying multiple integration platforms in the system, creating a *snowflake* architecture (Figure 3.51). This type of architecture is particularly relevant in the case of large-scale deployment of infrastructure inside large enterprises. Each domain of responsibility is in control of its exchanges, and communicates in a standard way with other large entities of the enterprise. This is an operational illustration of handling the range of problems in A2B, or Business Collaboration, as expressed in section 2.7.

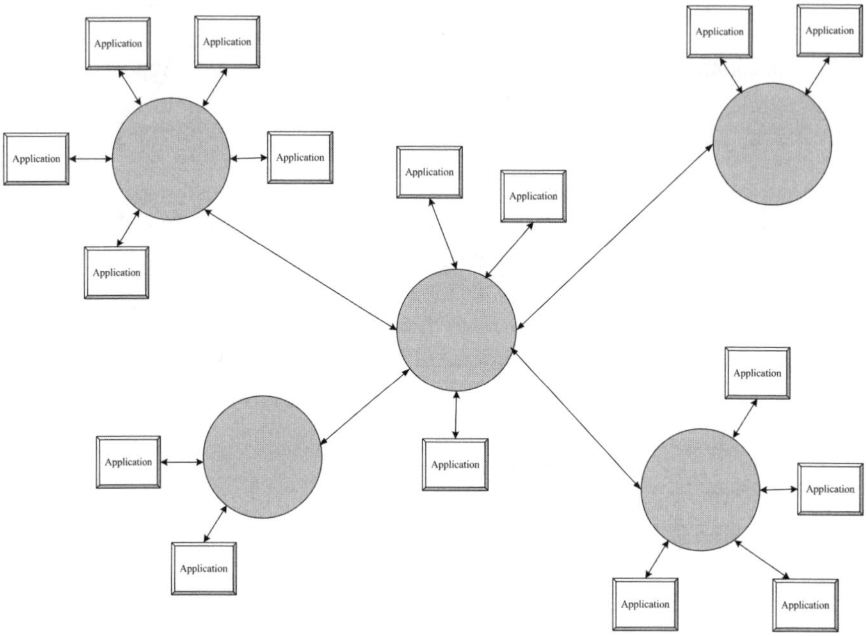

Figure 3.51. *Snowflake architecture*

Once the type of architecture has been determined, the next step considers the choice of the tool(s) that will make up the infrastructure. This choice will be guided by the complete set of results of the analysis carried out under the different focal points that we examine, and must make it possible to respond to detected needs and constraints.

Chapter 4

Types of Integration Projects

4.1. Integrating a single application

4.1.1. *Exchange cartography*

The appearance of the EAI phenomenon in 1996-1997 correlated with the emergence of software packages for Integrated Management.

Indeed, ERP (SAP R/3, Oracle Applications, PeopleSoft, etc.) initially put forward the replacement of the entire information system with a collection of modules developed using the same technologies and sharing the same repository. ERP seemed therefore to constitute a response to the range of problems in application integration, since it provided a system that was already entirely integrated.

At the same time, in the real world, they did not cover all of the business needs of an enterprise and have often proved difficult to implement, precisely because their modules were not designed to communicate with other applications, though they exchange perfectly with each other.

ERP systems have in reality only reinforced and amplified the problem of integrating applications of the enterprise. In addition, the ERP phenomenon occurred along with the implementation of software packages for Customer Relationship Management (CRM) or Supply Chain Management (SCM).

The introduction of ERP or of CRM or SCM software packages into an information system requires EAI-type integration projects to be implemented, and as a result, has constituted an essential factor in the development of the EAI “wave”.

These one-off, *ad hoc* integration projects make up one of the most widespread cases of use for an integration solution of the EAI type: it is often the need to put a new business service in place or to renovate one IT application that leads to integration. There is no global objective of achieving a general infrastructure for exchange management. Rather, each project deals with its own integration problem. At first, this involves purely tactical projects.

We will therefore strive to shed light on how to complete the interface between a new application and the rest of the information system. This type of project typically deals with problems of data propagation and repository data consistency (refer to section 2.4.1.1) between the applications of the enterprise IT – thus, A2A.

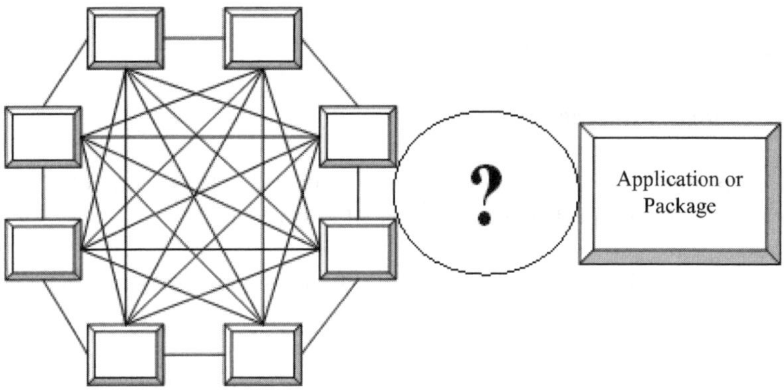

Figure 4.1. *Integrating a new application in the information system*

To correctly carry through such a project, the following steps must be performed:

– first identify all the existing applications with which the new application will have to communicate;

– subsequently, determine the nature and volume of information to be exchanged between these applications;

– then evaluate the way in which each of these applications can communicate with the outside (using a file or database, sending a message, etc.);

– finally, determine the rhythm of the exchanges (in real-time, in sessions, in batch or delayed mode).

The result of this analysis is the production of a cartography of the exchanges and of their constraints that will help determine what needs to be covered by the integration tools to be put in place.

4.1.2. *The integration platform*

The addition of the new application in the information system goes along with the implementation of an integration software platform that provides the complete set of services required to carry out mapped exchanges in an organized fashion. These services constitute a subset of the services detailed in Chapter 3, and include in particular:

– services in the transport and connectivity layer:

  - acquisition and delivery (adapters),

  - multi-channel communication bus;

– services in the information adaptation layer:

  - checking,

  - transformation,

  - routing;

– administration services (modeling);

– supervision services;

– etc.

As this involves addressing the integration of a limited number of applications, the software integration platform will be implemented in the majority of cases using a hub-and-spoke architecture, to avoid having to deploy this infrastructure on the complete set of hardware platforms.

The cartography completed previously (see section 4.1.1) will be used to set the parameters needed to exchange through the integration platform. The example below illustrates how a typical exchange progresses via an integration platform.

Consider an application in an operational "means of payment" system, which generates a collection of events around "debit dates for amortizable loans" in a file. Two applications, "client accounting" and "general accounting", are responsible for a certain number of accounting postings from these events, some of them only being taken into account two days after the corresponding debit event is created. These two applications can only receive information through files.

In order to ensure data propagation between these applications, they must be put into relationship with each other. This propagation will be carried out via the integration platform by chaining the following steps (Figure 4.2):

1. a file is created, containing the events in "debit dates for amortizable loans" by the means-of-payment application;

2. this file is taken in charge by the acquisition service (adapters) of the integration platform;

3. as required, the file is transported to the platform which hosts the integration services;

4. once the list of the recipients has been determined, the transformation process is executed (checks, enrichment, transformation), generating the associated accounting entries;

5. following the application of various checks, certain operations are placed in exception. They are signaled to the supervision system for possible correction by a user and/or the operations in exception are returned to the sending application;

6. certain (*N*) operations are held over for processing on Day+2. They are signaled to the supervision system. These events could be liberated either automatically by services in the integration platform, or manually by a user;

7. the integration platform creates the files intended for the Client Accounting and General Accounting applications;

8. as required, the file is transported to the platforms which host the accounting applications;

9. the respective files are made available to the applications for Client Accounting and General Accounting.

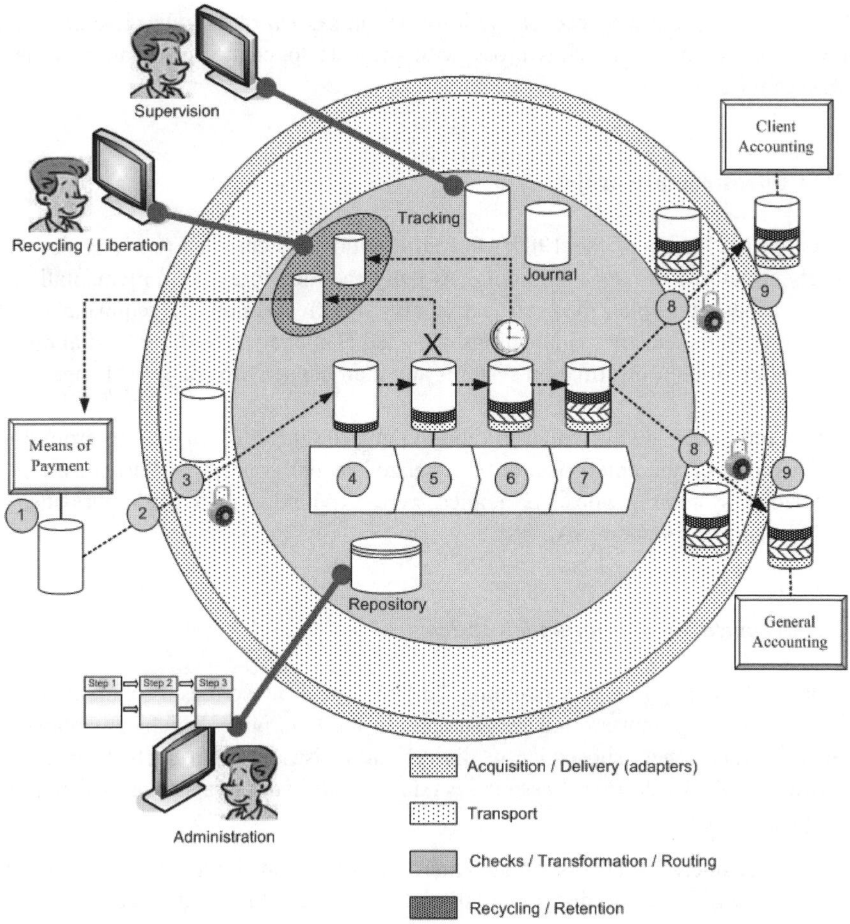

Figure 4.2. *Example exchange progressing through an integration platform*

This *ad hoc* approach, which integrates a single application or software package, presents major inconveniences, such as not pooling the cost of the integrations required for each individual project, and often, multiplying the number of tools required by these integrations.

This explains why projects that implement a single new application often drag on the coattails of projects that genuinely implement a global exchange infrastructure, where the implemented solutions and thus their costs are pooled. This subsequently results in the launch of a more ambitious project to restructure the entire information system. This is a classic "bottom-up" approach in pragmatic programs.

Clearly, strategic projects for the information system of an enterprise are found where "top-down" approaches cross with projects to create information systems infrastructure.

4.2. IT infrastructure projects

At the beginning of the 1980s, the information systems in French banks were entirely structured around accounting. At that time therefore, the implementation of a new accounting plan had an extremely significant impact, requiring costly adaptations to the existing applications. This led IT managers to think hard about the organization of their information systems and their capacity to adapt to changes.

This rethinking was oriented to reorganizing the information system around the core business of the enterprise. It materialized in the concept of "urbanization of information systems", whose principles were expounded in a work published in 1998 by Jacques Sassoon [SAS 98].

4.2.1. *Urbanization of information systems*

Using the analogy of city planning, "urbanization" prescribes a segmentation of the information system around departments in the enterprise. This segmentation is used to define zones, subsequently divided into districts, with each district itself divided into blocks. Jacques Sassoon lays down seven rules to apply in this approach to segmentation:

– the business processes of an enterprise are divided into zones, which are subsequently divided into districts, with each district itself being divided into blocks;

– each block is autonomous, and treats an event from end to end without calling any other block;

– blocks are asynchronous, i.e., each of them treats events with no concern for the processing carried out by other blocks;

– a block disposes of only a single point on input and a single point of output from the events;

– each block owns its data and is the only entity authorized to update that data;

– each block posts standardized reports on its processing;

– all communication between blocks transits necessarily by a flow management system.

This seventh rule concerns us directly here: it gives rise to the necessity for an exchange infrastructure in the information system, the *flow manager*. Further, Jacques Sassoon provides a description of its more important functions: administering exchanges, routing and transforming data, scheduling and aggregation. Certainly, we find these functions once again in EAI tools.

An example of a generic urbanization plan is put forward in Figure 4.3: the segmentation distinguishes:

– the distribution zone, where the exchanges with the outside world to acquire or restore the information are carried out;

– the production zone, that carries out the processes that make up the core business of the enterprise;

– the synthesis zone, that makes it possible to carry out the operations required for the functioning of the enterprise (for example: payment, accounting, etc.);

– the control zone, that groups the processes that provide the elements for reacting to the global functioning of the system;

– a repository zone that contains the complete set of enterprise reference data used by the different blocks;

– the flow manager, that plays the role of "expansion joint" between the different blocks;

– in each zone there are districts, and in each district, blocks – according to a representation that makes it possible to give form to some of the principles mentioned above.

Unfortunately, IT reorganization projects built using the concept of urbanization have only occasionally reached completion, since they were often much too ambitious and forgot one of the fundamental principles of the approach: *the progressive development of the system.*

This involves stretching the existing system little by little, progressively reaching a system closer to the target system that was defined. In fact, the first objective of urbanization is to maintain competitiveness by rendering business processes, and in particular, the processes in the value chain, more efficient. Urbanization is not therefore a goal in itself. It is instead a way to increase efficiency, and its implementation is of no interest for applications that do not contribute to the agility and global efficiency of the system.

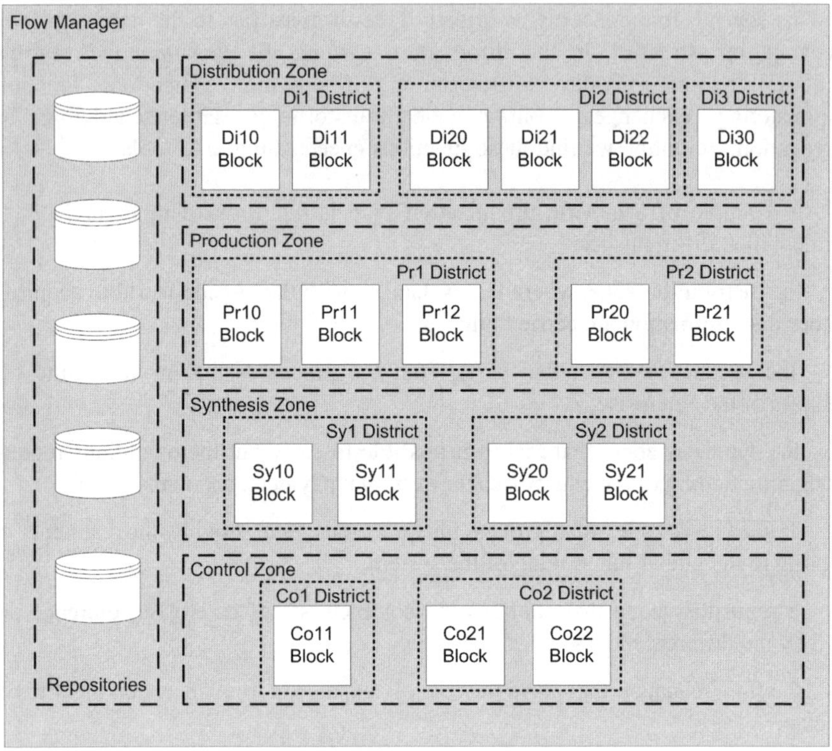

Figure 4.3. *Generic urbanization plan*

If many urbanization projects have not reached their ultimate goal, they have on the other hand greatly contributed in French enterprises, particularly banks, to the implementation of integration tools such as the software package RDJ (now Synchrony AccountingIntegrator) from Axway. For more on getting the most out of integration and urbanization, see Chapter 8.

4.2.2. *IT exchange infrastructure*

Projects that implement an IT infrastructure proceed therefore on a different path from the *ad hoc* projects that integrate individual applications: they first define the target information system they are aiming at, and they subsequently consider the various steps required to achieve this target system. To return to the culinary metaphor, this is a question of determining how to change a plate of spaghetti to something much more organized – say, a plate of lasagne (Figure 4.4)!

We can consider that the concept of IT urbanization constitutes the oldest approach to integration of enterprise applications and that EAI finds its source in urbanism. Roy Schulte in his report *Architecture and Planning for Modern Application Styles* [SCH 97] directly refers to this as the principles of "City Planning".

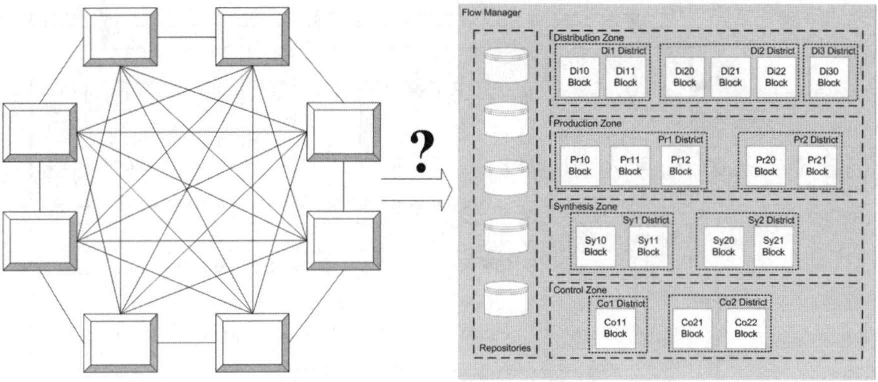

Figure 4.4. *IT infrastructure project*

As for the integration of a new application in an existing system (see section 4.1.1), the general cartography of the exchanges must be established, then a solution must be selected and implemented, using one or more tools to compose the infrastructure of the system (the flow manager).

The set of exchanges is carried out between the application blocks and the flow manager. There are no longer any point-to-point links between blocks which no longer "know" each other (Figure 4.5).

At the same time, the centralized hub-and-spoke architecture selected for the integration platform (to integrate a new application in an existing system, as described in section 4.1.2) could not be selected for the enterprise IT flow manager. For the flow manager to be accessible and usable by all the applications, it should be deployed using a distributed bus or snowflake architecture (see section 3.5.2.2), and could potentially contain the complete set of services described in Chapter 3.

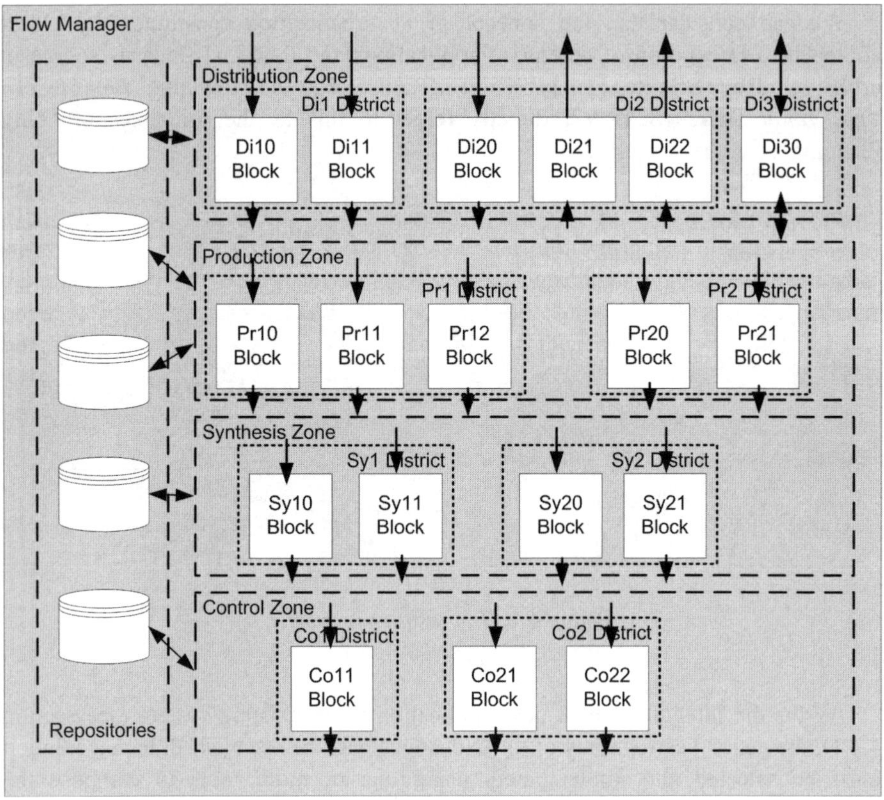

Figure 4.5. *Exchange infrastructure*

In this case, of course, the previously completed cartography is also used to set the parameters required for exchanges via the infrastructure. The example detailed below (Figure 4.6), which is derived from the example provided in section 4.1.2, illustrates the steps in a typical exchange using the flow manager (to get the most out of the example, we chose to illustrate this exchange through file mode.)

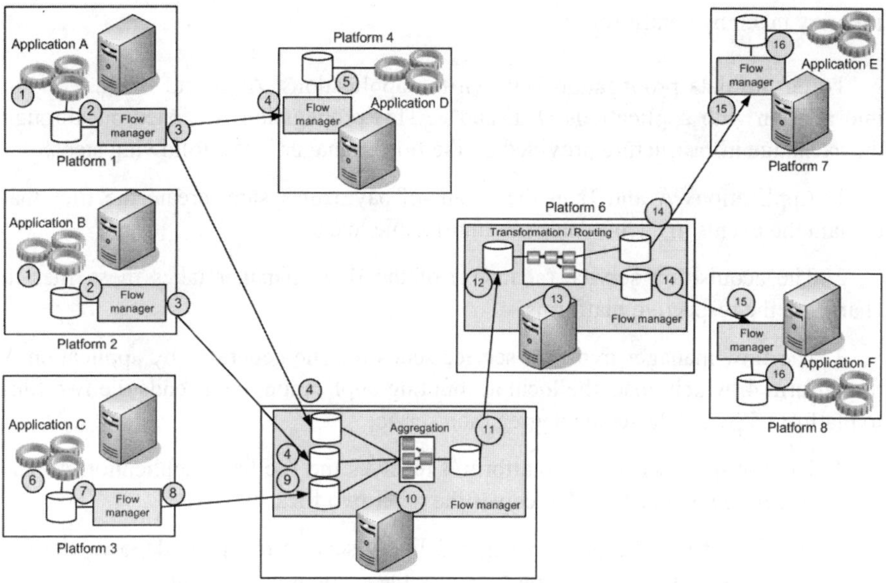

Figure 4.6. *Example exchange chaining using a flow manager*

Statement of the problem

The system of applications is distributed over several hardware platforms, each of which hosts, moreover, some portion of the services from the flow manager. The applications A, B and C of an operational "means of payment" system are distributed respectively on the hardware platforms 1, 2 and 3. Each application generates a file containing a collection of events around "debit dates for amortizable loans". Applications A and B generate this file at an instant *t*; application C generates the file at *t+1*. A copy of the file generated by application A must be supplied to a local accounting application D, which executes on hardware platform 4. When the files are generated, the information that they contained must be aggregated, transformed to generate a certain number of accounting postings that should be routed to application E, Client Accounting, executing on hardware platform 7, and application F, General Accounting, executing on hardware platform 8. The aggregation service is hosted on hardware platform 5, while transformation services execute on hardware platform 6.

Itinerary taken by dataflows

To ensure data propagation between the applications, A, B and C must be put into relation with applications D, E and F. This propagation is carried out through the exchange infrastructure provided by the flow manager in the following steps:

1. Applications A and B in the means-of-payment system create the files that contain the events in "debit dates for amortizable loans".

2. The acquisition service (adapters) of the flow manager takes these files in charge on the respective platforms.

3. The flow manager transport service sends the file generated by application A to platform 4, which hosts the local accounting application, then sends the two files to platform 5, which hosts the aggregation service.

4. The transport service on platform 4 receives the file from application A. The transport service on platform 5 receives the other two files.

5. On platform 5, the flow manager delivery service (adapter) deposits the file from application A in the reception space for the accounting application D.

6. Application C in the means-of-payment system creates a file that contains the events in "debit dates for amortizable loans".

7. The acquisition service (adapter) of the flow manager takes charge of this file on platform 3.

8. The flow manager transport service sends the file generated by application C to platform 5, which hosts the aggregation service.

9. The transport service on platform 5 receives the file from application C.

10. On platform 5, the flow manager aggregation service aggregates elements from the three files, and creates a file from the results.

11. The flow manager's transport service sends the file that results from this aggregation to platform 6, which hosts the transformation service.

12. The transport service on platform 6 receives the aggregated file.

13. Once the list of recipients has been determined, the transformation process is executed (checks, enrichment, interpretation), generating the associated accounting entries in the files intended for applications E and F.

14. The flow manager's transport service sends the files that contain those accounting entries to platforms 7 and 8.

15. The flow manager transport service receives the files on platforms 7 and 8 respectively.

16. On platform 7, the flow manager delivery service (adapter) deposits the file in the reception space of application E, Client Accounting. On platform 8, it deposits the file in the reception space of application F, General Accounting.

The flow manager thus constitutes the “backbone” of enterprise IT. It is thus nothing less than the implementation of the exchange process sub-level described in section 3.4.3. At the same time, beyond the exchanges between the applications in its information system, the enterprise will also have to get control over the numerous exchanges that it must carry out with its partners, clients, suppliers or administrations. This is the domain of inter-enterprise exchanges, Business to Business (B to B, or B2B).

4.3. Integrating inter-enterprise exchanges

Inter-enterprise exchanges are today the domain where the problem of application integration is most crucial. This is a question of bringing the applications of the enterprise IT into communication with the applications of an external information system as part of commercial transactions.

Let us consider the case of a client/supplier relationship between two enterprises A and B. The exchanges to be established in this case can, for example, take the form illustrated in Figure 4.7.

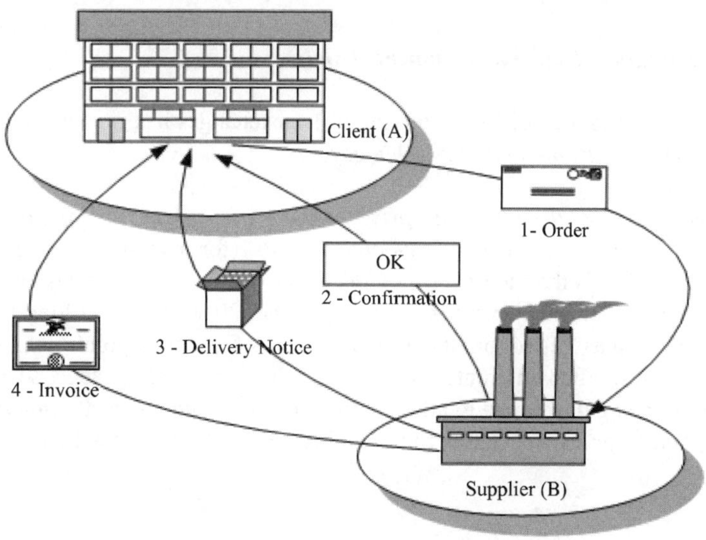

Figure 4.7. *Example inter-enterprise exchange*

– The SCM application of enterprise A (the client) sends a purchase order to enterprise B (the supplier).

– The order management application in enterprise B receives this order and sends a confirmation of the order to the SCM application for enterprise A. To the other applications in its own information system, the order management application in B will send the information for processing the order, notably to the applications for billing and delivery management.

– The delivery management application for B will send a delivery notice that will be received by the SCM application for A.

– The billing application in enterprise B will send an invoice that will be received by the accounting application for A.

The major problems which must be faced in these exchanges follow principally from the fact that most of the time, none of the participating enterprises is using:

– the same communication network;

– the same exchange format;

– the same exchange process.

In short, heterogenity must once again be dealt with, but this time in multiple information systems.

4.3.1. *Exchanging electronic documents (EDI)*

One response to the need for inter-enterprise exchanges has existed for a number of years: EDI (*Electronic Data Interchange*).

EDI is defined as *the inter-enterprise exchange, from computer to computer, of commercial transactions using standard formats* (for example purchase order, invoice, etc.). This is the oldest form of electronic commerce, but it has also made it possible to carry out B2B exchanges for more than 20 years. For a long time, EDI implementation has relied on the establishment of point-to-point links between enterprises, most often on rented lines. Little by little, value-added sector-based networks are being developed to allow participants to avoid the costly multiplication of these point-to-point links (sometimes ending up in a "spaghetti network").

The principal standards implemented for EDI exchanges are the following:

– EDIFACT: this is the norm from UN/CEFACT (United Nations) that defines the messages exchanged in the domains of international commerce, purchasing, transport, logistics, insurance, healthcare, etc.;

– ANSI ASC X12 (American National Standards Institute Accredited Standards Committee): this is the national standard in the USA for the same types of exchanges.

Among value-added networks, we could cite the following from the banking sector:

– SWIFT (Society for Worldwide Interbank Financial Telecommunications): this network for interbanking exchanges was created in 1973 by 239 banks in 15 principal countries, including the USA. SWIFT also provides the norm for the messages exchanged on its network.

– SIT (*System Interbanking de Télécompensation* (the French remote inter-banking settlement system)): GSIT, a group created in 1983 by the French banking community, set up the network for remote interbank clearing in France. This network conveys messages defined by the GSIT that contain banking operations documents that respect the norms set by the CFONB (*Comité Français d'Organisation et de Normalisation Bancaires* (French Committee for Banking Organization and Normalization)).

– In Italy, SIANET, which defined its own exchange standard with banks, holds the monopoly.

However, EDI presents a certain number of drawbacks, in particular:

– weak flexibility that leads to the emergence of proprietary "standards";

– a batch-processing orientation that introduces waiting periods into processing;

– the lack of integration in processes, which causes a tunneling effect in processing;

– a high cost, because EDI often operates on Value-Added Networks (VAN), which are frequently expensive – in turn, this holds up EDI adoption by the complete set of commercial partners, particularly small and medium enterprises.

4.3.2. *XML standards*

At the end of the 20th century, the Internet explosion greatly modified the way inter-enterprise exchanges are addressed:

– it imposed the Internet as the preferred (and often, the only) network for these exchanges;

– it helped bring about the emergence of XML, a new standard for the description of information (see section 3.2.1.1);

– it led to the appearance of a large number of new actors disputing the definition of norms for exchanged documents and the provision of value-added sector-based or even inter sector networks.

In the domain of inter-enterprise exchanges, numerous initiatives have driven XML to become a new standard for document exchange.

Among these initiatives we would cite principally:

– UBL (Universal Business Language): the result of work carried out internationally in a technical committee of OASIS (Organization for the Advancement of Structured Information Standards) defining the library of standard electronic commercial documents (purchase orders, invoices, etc.) and using XML. UBL also provides an implementation for small and medium enterprises participating in the international trading chain.

– ebXML (Electronic Business eXtensible Markup Language): launched in September 1999 by UN/CEFACT and OASIS, ebXML is an initiative aimed at creating a global XML/EDI standard utilizing an exchange infrastructure. The work performed by several technical committees in OASIS has resulted in a collection of specifications regarding:

- exchanging data in a common format (Core Components Technical Specification – CCTS v2.0.1);

- recording and providing services and objects for electronic commerce (ebXML Registry Services – ebRS v3.0 – and Registry Information Model – ebRIM v3.0);

- the technical configuration of contracts of exchange between commercial partners (Collaboration Protocol Profile and Agreements – CPP/CPA v2.0);

- providing a dependable and secured transport layer (ebXML Messaging Service – ebMS v3.0);

- process management (ebXML Business Process Specification Schema – ebBP v2.0.3).

– RosettaNet: this initiative dates from mid-1999 and brings together the largest manufacturers in the sector of electronics and computing, along with their suppliers, including Intel, Cisco, IBM, HP (Compaq), Toshiba, Microsoft, Oracle, SAP, etc. (www.rosettanet.org). Its objective was to define, develop and implement standardized exchanges of data as part of the business processes in the supply chain in the world of computing. Today, RosettaNet provides a collection of specifications that describe the way to implement collaborative business processes between the partners in the supply chain who use communicating applications. These specifications cover the definition of the processes and the technical elements for interoperability and communication:

- RosettaNet Partner Interface Processes® (PIPs®) define business processes between the partners;

- RosettaNet dictionaries provide a collection of common properties for the PIPs. The RosettaNet business dictionary defines the properties used in basic commercial activities. The RosettaNet technical dictionary provides the properties to define products;

- RosettaNet Implementation Framework (RNIF) describes the packaging, routing, and transport of all PIP messages and the signals associated with the destination of departmental applications.

– BizTalk: launched in March 1999 by Microsoft, BizTalk is positioned less as a standard than as a community of suppliers and users whose objective is to supply an environment that favors inter-enterprise exchanges (www.biztalk.org). BizTalk offers a collection of directives for publishing XML schemas (purchase orders are a standard example) as well as an exchange infrastructure (or framework), and a dictionary where XML schemas can be stored.

– cXML (Commerce XML): this is a collection of commercial document types expressed as XML DTDs. These documents were developed by Ariba for inter-enterprise commercial exchanges over Internet (www.ariba.com). cXML was launched at the beginning of 1999 and uses mechanisms of "equal to equal" message exchanges.

– Bolero.net (www.bolero.net): created by Bolero Operations Ltd., a corporation resulting from a partnership agreement between SWIFT and the Through Transport Club (TT Club: international association for mutual insurance of transporters founded in 1970), Bolero.net offers an exchange infrastructure for documents and inter-sector data for international commerce.

– OAGIS (Open Applications Group Integration Specification): the Open Application Group (www.openapplications.org), a consortium created at the end of 1994, strives to promote the implementation of solutions for electronic commerce and application integration utilizing XML, especially as part of the management of the supply chain involving the different participants in international commerce (banks, transporters, importers, exporters, insurance corporations, etc.).

Application integration as part of inter-enterprise exchanges will therefore necessitate a certain number of choices, each of which leads to consequences in the functionalities served by the implemented infrastructure:

– What type of network must be used: point-to-point links, EDI value-added networks (VANs), or VANs using the Internet?

– What document types must be exchanged with the partners, using which norm or standard?

– How far should we go in integrating the processes of the enterprise with the processes of the partners?

– How should the pace of the applications be adapted in relation to exchanges with the outside, in other words, how should the business processes be realigned around the needs of exchange?

4.3.3. *Inter-enterprise "spaghetti" system*

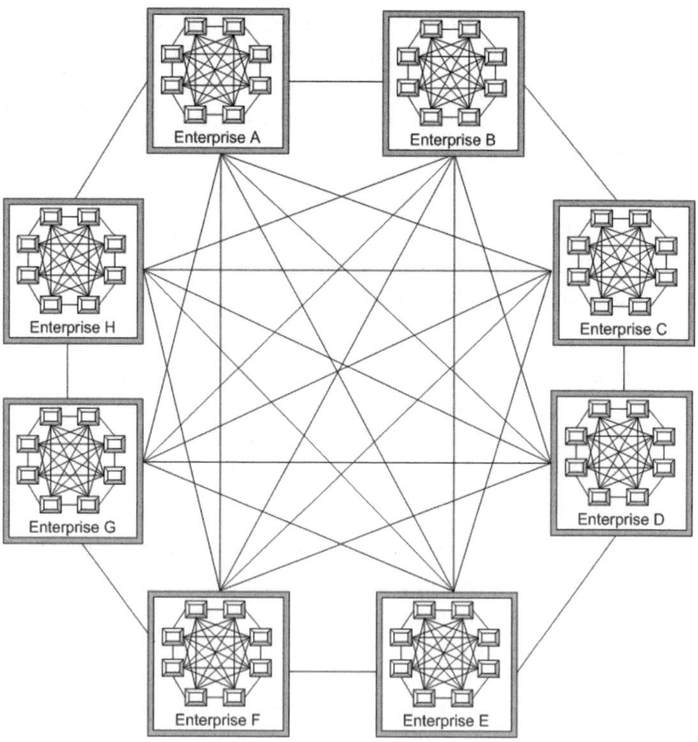

Figure 4.8. *Inter-enterprise spaghetti system*

The implementation of EDI-type links in enterprises developed over time and around identified needs, and was most often carried out by different teams who adapted the means to the partners with whom connections were required. In the same way that the anarchic creation of interfaces between applications resulted in "spaghetti" information systems, the anarchic implementation of links between partners results in the *inter-enterprise spaghetti* system illustrated in Figure 4.8.

In fact, it is a "mega" spaghetti system, given that links or interfaces are established directly between the applications of each partner. The question that arises here involves knowing who will complete the interface for exchanging with the partner i.e., which enterprise is going to have to adapt its system?

The response will result most of the time from the balance of power existing between the partners, or from their capacity to carry out this adaptation. For example, when connecting a smaller enterprise with limited computing competencies, a large enterprise should carry out the required adaptation rather than risk losing this potential client. In the end, the result is an allocation of the interfaces in the information systems of the different communicating enterprises (Figure 4.9).

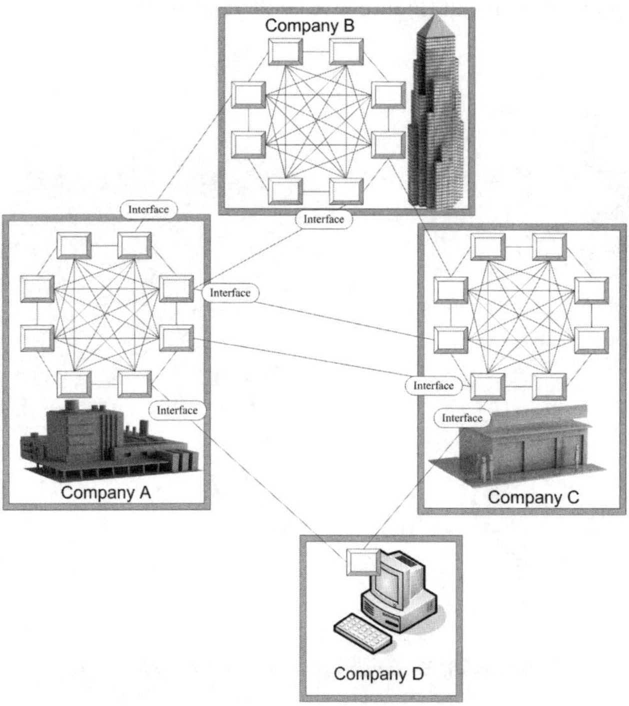

Figure 4.9. *Allocation of the interfaces*

4.3.4. *Inter-enterprise exchange platforms*

From the point of view of individual participating enterprises, the problems linked to exchanges with partners may vary, but they all relate to heterogenity.

A large enterprise whose information system uses a distributed architecture, must overcome the challenges linked to the need for connecting partners of quite different types:

– small enterprises, who do not often have deep information technology competence, particularly where it concerns networks;

– medium enterprises, also with limited competencies, but who can still exchange information electronically on simple, low-cost infrastructures;

– large enterprises or groups, with significant computing services with strong competencies in the domain of the electronic exchanges, but from this fact, also have a tendency to want to dictate the technologies that they will use.

In most cases, because these connections are carried out without using an organized approach, the result (Figure 4.10) will generate numerous problems:

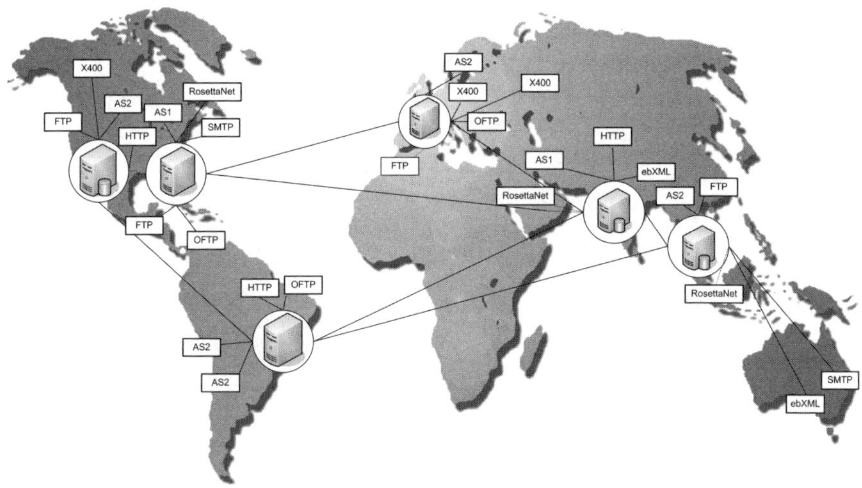

Figure 4.10. *Exchanges in a distributed architecture*

– difficulties in offering the variety of communication protocols to connect each partner: all too often, the appropriate protocol is not available on the necessary platform;

– difficulties in offering the variety of document formats required for exchanges: this requires access to different transformation tools on the different platforms involved in the exchanges;

– requirement for different support teams that can deal with operational problems in exchanges with partners in different locations;

– difficulties in connecting small enterprise partners with no particular IT competence;

– etc.

These problems have an impact at different levels in the enterprise:

– high hardware costs, because different platforms are implicated in the exchanges and must be equipped accordingly (CPU processing power, memory, network connections, etc.);

– high software costs, because the different platforms must be equipped with the software needed to support the exchange protocols and process documents that are sent and received;

– high personnel costs, due to various factors:

- significant time required to connect small enterprise partners with reduced computing skills,

- complexity of daily system operations,

- complexity of system maintenance;

– impossibility of managing SLAs due to the lack of visibility on the exchanges that transit the system.

In order to augment reactivity while optimizing the use of their resources, large enterprises have undertaken to rationalize exchanges with their partners by creating platforms for integrating B2B exchanges ("B2Bi Gateways"). These Gateways centralize the complete set of services involved in network connections, exchange protocols, equipment for processing electronic documents and supervising the exchanges.

Figure 4.11 illustrates the implementation of such a platform (for enterprise A) on an existing "spaghetti"-type information system.

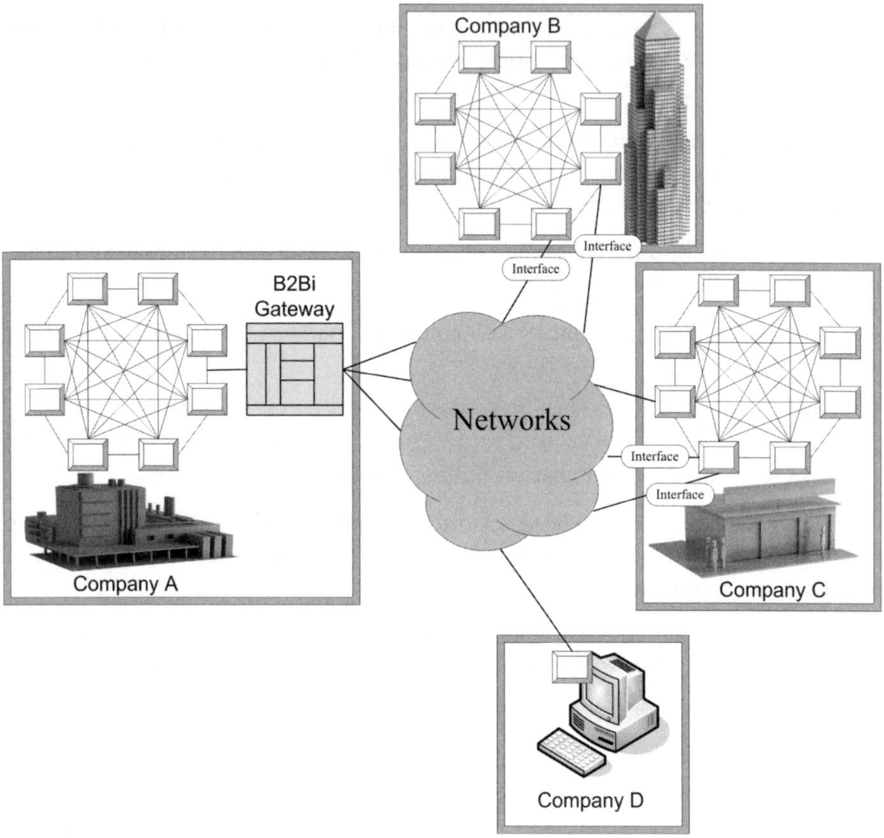

Figure 4.11. *Integration of inter-enterprise exchanges*

If we apply the analysis from IT urbanization, this is in fact a question of adding the services required to exchange with partners (Figure 4.12) to the flow manager, often extending its hold beyond business IT.

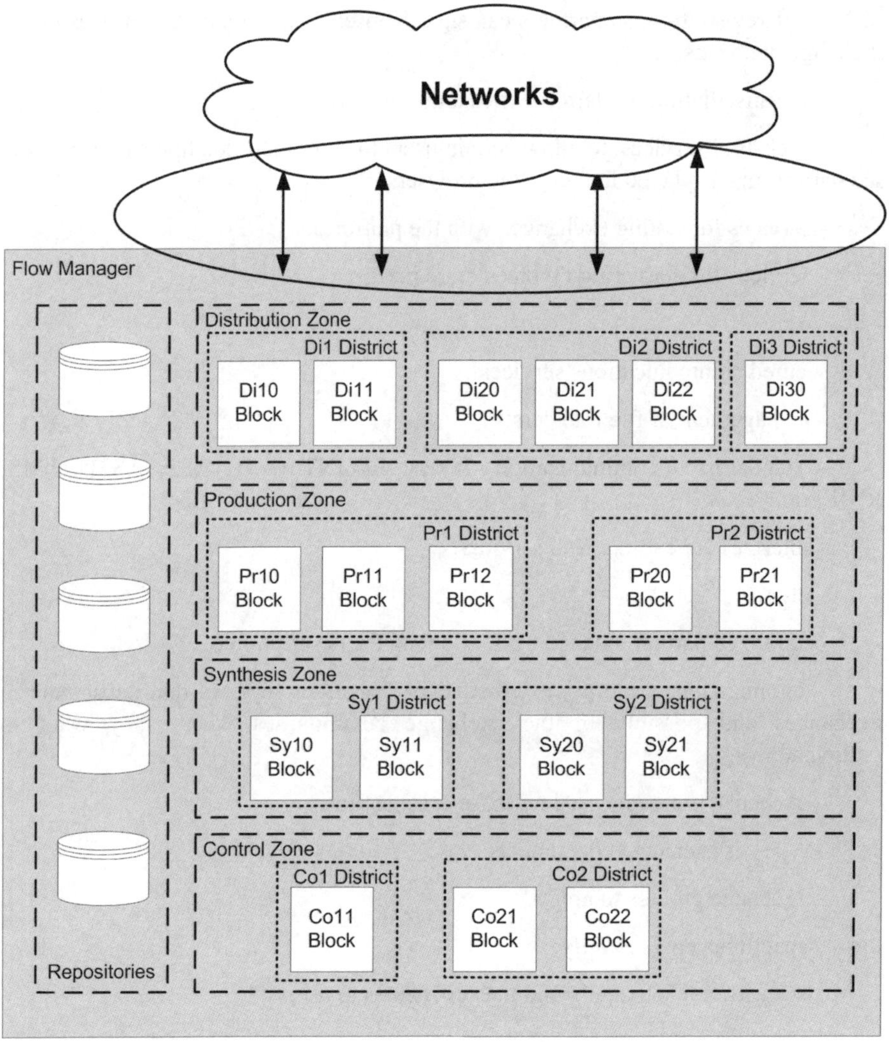

Figure 4.12. *Exchanges between the flow manager and enterprise partners*

The services in the exchange platforms cover the following aspects (Figure 4.13):

– an access portal for partners, providing the interface with a certain number of available services:

- self-registration, so partners can sign themselves up to use the services in the exchange platforms;

- self-installation of platform exchange software;

- Web-EDI services, to allow certain users to enter their documents directly via standard forms displayed in their Web browsers;

- services for testing exchanges with the platform;

- services for delivering invoices on request;

- etc.;

– secured communications services:

- management of file transfers;

- standardized communications layers: EDIINT (AS1, AS2, AS3), ebMS, RNIF, etc.;

- interface for calling Web services;

- etc.;

– centralized partner management, allowing the description of:

- organizations (enterprises), their departments or services that participate in exchanges and possibly of the exchange communities where they want to participate;

- exchange protocols used by those organizations;

- types of exchanged documents;

- exchange process to apply;

- specific events to notify;

- security levels to apply and the certificates to use;

- etc.;

– transformation services: EDIFACT, X12, XML, HL7, SWIFT, etc.;

– adapters: to provide connection to the applications in the business IT (legacy applications or software packages – ERP, CRM, etc.);

– security services: for operations of authentication, encryption and electronic signature;

– collaborative process management services: for orchestrating interactions between partners by utilizing the selected standards (eBPSS from ebXML, RosettaNet PIPs, etc.);

– services for tracking dataflows and for business supervision that supply the elements required for managing Service Level Agreements between partners, as well as the business dashboards indispensable to measuring the efficiency of the platform. These services also provide the complete set of technical or business alerts for correcting and often anticipating possible problems during exchanges.

Finally, the platform offers a services registry for exposing available services to partners, as well as how to call them. The invocation of these services is performed by an internal service bus.

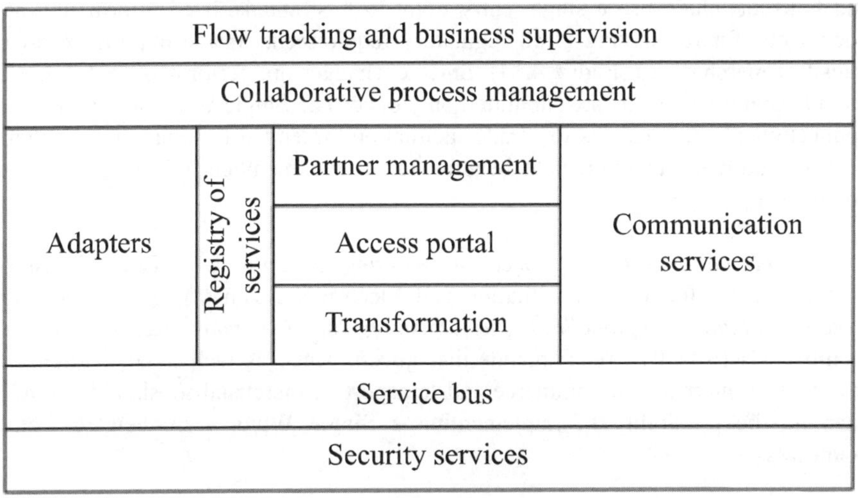

Figure 4.13. *The services of the B2B exchange platforms*

4.3.5. *"Single Window" initiatives*

In most countries, enterprises that carry out operations in international commerce must provide a significant volume of information and numerous documents to governmental authorities in order to comply with regulatory requirements in importation, exportation or transit of merchandise. In the majority of cases, this information and these documents must be supplied to different services, through different processes, and using forms specific to each one of them. These constraints, associated with the costs intrinsic to these regulatory requirements, constitute a burden not only for enterprises but for governments, and can also constitute a major obstacle to the development of international commerce.

The implementation of a "Single Window" solution represents one means of handling this problem: a Single Window improves the availability and the manipulation of information. It also simplifies and accelerates the flow of information between commercial enterprises and governments. In addition, it brings greater harmonization and a better sharing of pertinent data between governmental services, and from this fact, generates significant benefits for all the stakeholders in international commerce. Ultimately, through its best use of resources, it improves the pertinence and efficiency of official controls and reduces their cost, initially for enterprises but for governments as well.

The Single Window is a solution that lets different participants in the commerce and transport chain use a single entry point to host standardized information and documents, for responding to all regulatory requirements in the import, export or transit of merchandise (Figure 4.14). Since exchanges are performed electronically, the information elements are submitted only once. The Single Window is a practical application of the concepts of "trade facilitation" intended to reduce related trade barriers and provide immediate benefits to all the members of the commercial community.

The *International Trade Procedures Working Group* of UN/CEFACT (United Nations Center for Trade Facilitation and Electronic Business), in the document *Recommendation and guidelines on establishing a single window* (Recommendation Number 33) [R33 05], recommends that governments, as well as all participants involved in international commerce and transport of merchandise, should carefully examine the possibility of implementing a Single Window in their respective countries.

According to this recommendation, a Single Window must provide for:

– hosting of standardized information and documents through a single input point to respond to all the regulatory requirements with regards to importation, exportation or transit of merchandise;

– sharing of information concerning international commercial transactions, by signing up to a legal framework that provides confidentiality and security in the exchange of information;

– adding services for providing governmental information concerning commercial exchanges and for receiving the payment of taxes and other costs;

– providing a single input point to give access to or distribute pertinent information to participating governmental authorities or to authorized governmental services;

– coordinating checks and inspections carried out by various governmental services.

A Single Window allows participants in the international trading chain to obtain substantial benefits:

– for governments:

- improvement in the collection of taxes;

- improvements in regulatory compliance from commercial enterprises;

- more efficient and pertinent deployment of resources;

– for commercial enterprises:

- reduction in costs through a reduction in delays;

- greater rapidity in customs clearance and notices;

- explanations and predictable applications of regulations;

- more efficient and pertinent deployment of resources.

For example, according to studies from UN/CEFACT, when the Republic of Mauritius put a Single Window in place, the average time for customs clearance for undisputed declarations of merchandise went from four hours to 15 minutes. In the same way, the mechanism of the Single Window in Senegal was able to reduce to one day the administrative processes that previously took two or three days.

The costs of implementing a Single Window vary depending on the approach: for example, in the case of a Window financed by governmental funds, these costs are most often integrated in the commercial development policy budget for the country.

Different implementation models exist for a Single Window, depending on the requirements and local or regional conditions:

– financing can come from the government (as in Finland, Sweden or the USA), the private sector (as in Guatemala or Germany), or via mixed private/public initiatives (as in China, Republic of Mauritius, Senegal, Malaysia or Singapore);

– the use of the Single Window can be mandatory (as in Finland, the Republic of Mauritius, Senegal or Guatemala), or based on voluntary participation (as in China, Germany, Malaysia, Sweden or the USA);

– services are variable, and can be free (as in Finland, Sweden or the USA), or use various billing schemes (as in Guatemala, Germany, China, Malaysia, Republic of Mauritius, Senegal, and Singapore).

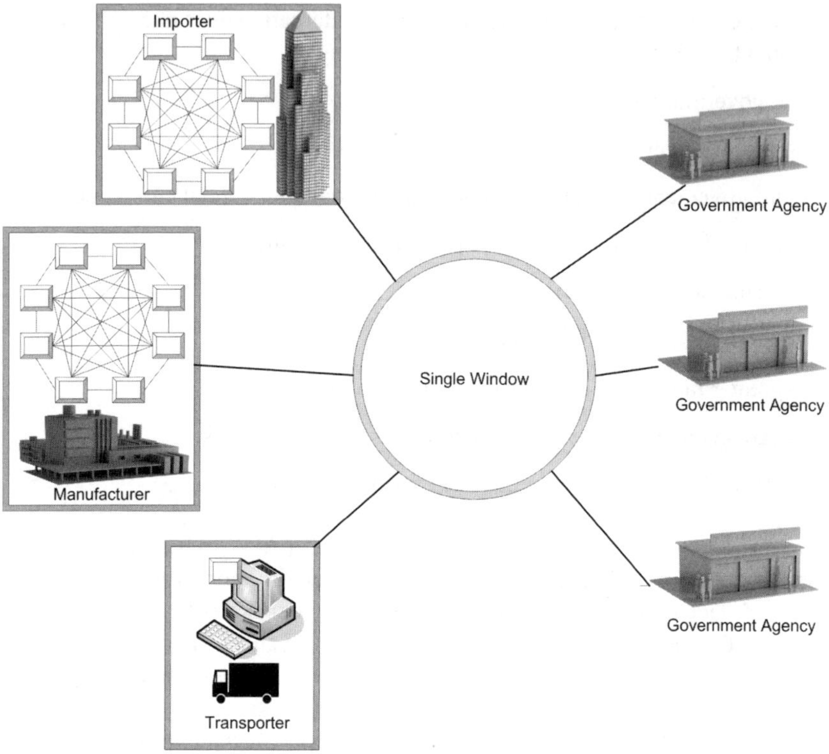

Figure 4.14. *Single Window*

Despite these differences, all countries that have put a Single Window in place present this experience favorably, with revenues and benefits largely carrying the costs of creation and operation. Moreover, a common set of key success factors can be drawn from different experiences, among which are:

– strong leadership, whether from the public sector (as in Malaysia, Senegal, the USA or Singapore), or the private (as in Guatemala);

– cooperation and strong commitment from all participants, public and private;

– a friendly system, that does not introduce greater complexity into commercial procedures;

– investments in modern technologies;

– a progressive and flexible approach;

– a technical solution that is neutral, transparent and robust.

The solutions implemented as part of Single Window initiatives utilize the technologies for exchange platforms presented in the previous section (4.3.4), this time, however, not to process exchanges between partners and enterprise IT, but to intermediate between partners, each of whom can, moreover, use their own exchange platform to connect to the Single Window.

The addition of inter-enterprise exchange platforms to the flow manager as part of IT urbanization makes it possible to assume responsibility for exchanges in the information system, in an approach that we could qualify as *A2B* (application to business) integration.

However, in order to accomplish A2B integration, it is important to keep in mind the ultimate goal of IT urbanization, which is in point of fact to reorganize IT for a better and faster response to the business requirements of the enterprise: it is a matter of building an information system adapted to the business processes and to their developments (Figure 4.15).

4.4. Managing business processes

As we already explained at the beginning of this work to introduce the notion of spaghetti system (see section 2.3), the construction of the information system in enterprises followed what is now a well known process: year after year, applications were created, deployed and updated to automate the tasks of certain departments in the enterprise: human resources, accounting, sales, marketing. This approach, which aims to improve the level of operational efficiency of each of those departments, resulted in a system of applications which "line-traced" over the functions in the enterprise.

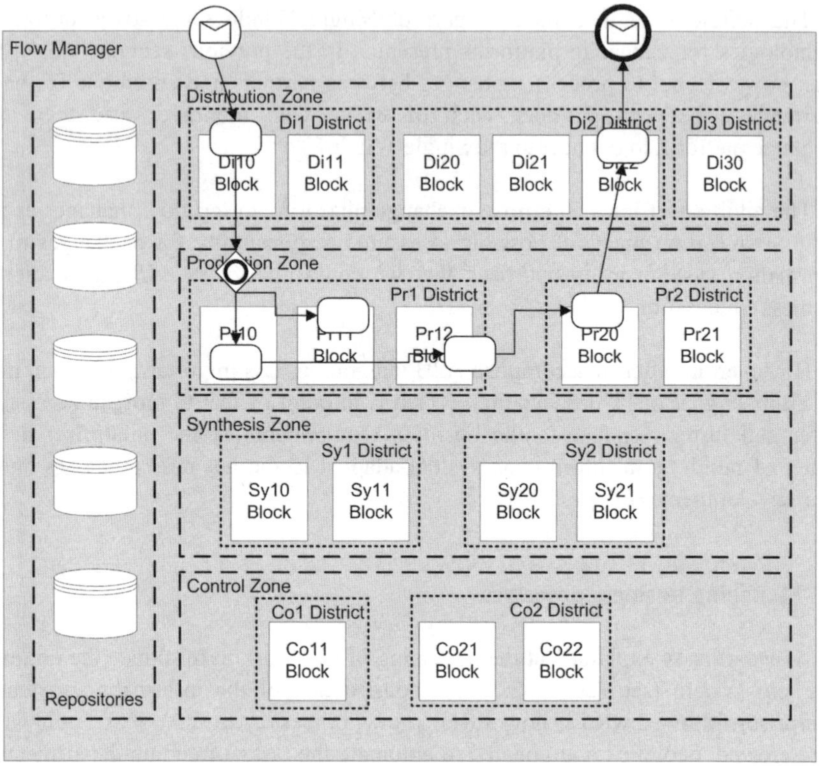

Figure 4.15. *Urbanization and processes*

4.4.1. *Points of departure*

Since integration solutions now make it possible for different applications to carry out exchanges, their implementation ensures better consistency of services of the enterprise, not only inside its boundaries, but also outside. This is because, as we saw above, the applications of the enterprise are linked to those of partners and suppliers, improving the reactivity and the competitiveness of all the participants (see section 2.7).

Most approaches to application integration still address the movement of data between applications, and are therefore still far from completed. In fact, the objectives of integration are primarily business objectives, not just technical milestones, including objectives such as increased competitiveness, improved quality of service, and more efficient management of information exchanges via electronic data exchanges between the various participants. The next step in the integration path is therefore naturally the management of certain business processes (Business Process Management – BPM).

By "business process", we understand the processes in the value chain of the enterprise, i.e., those processes which help create competitive advantage for the enterprise. These are horizontal processes (see section 2.4.1.2), necessitating interaction between applications and/or human users in different entities, whatever the heterogenous information systems to which they belong.

Let us consider an enterprise that is trying to reduce the delivery delay for its products and services, something that is a determining factor for competitive advantage. This objective can be applied to enterprises in different sectors of activity, such as an insurance company (investigating claims), a telecoms operator (providing high-speed Internet access), or government agency (sending administrative forms or documents). Whatever the sector, reducing the delays of delivery by hours – even days – necessitates:

– working with multiple organizations, not only within the enterprise, but also upstream with suppliers, downstream with clients, or in cooperation with public administration;

– involving different actors of different types appropriately at different steps of the process – sales directors, legal services, purchasing services, logisticians, customs services, etc.;

– interacting with multiple information systems: managing orders through the SAP ERP, processing purchases and logistics with the PeopleSoft package, managing customer relations with the Siebel CRM tool, etc.

In other words, making business process management possible in turn leads to answers to a series of questions, such as:

– Who knows the business process from end to end?

– Who is responsible for aligning the process with the needs of the business?

– Who is responsible for the performance of process execution?

– Who controls process modification?

– Does the information system support the execution of the process as the business requires it?

– How is it possible to organize the horizontal business processes in an enterprise, without putting into question the existing organizations and the information system currently in place?

– How can business process execution be automated?

One result of implementing a business process management solution is that it will require the launch of a project inside the enterprise. What is the right time to launch a BPM project, and how should the candidate processes be determined?

4.4.2. *BPM project opportunity: choosing the processes*

As with any integration project, the opportunity for launching a BPM project will follow from modifications to the general context of the entire enterprise or to its information system (see the work of Bernard Debauche and Patrick Megard [DEB 04]). It can involve the appearance of new requirements linked to the business of the enterprise:

– improvements in quality of service;

– reduction in costs;

– new regulatory obligations – for example the accounting requirement to apply the rules in IFRS (International Financial Reporting Standards), or to comply with directives such as the Sarbanes-Oxley Act, which aim to reduce fraud and conflicts of interest;

– an increase in volumes to be processed;

– the appearance of new imperatives in time-to-market;

– etc.

However, modifications can also be linked to business IT:

– the loss of competencies (for example the mass retirement of COBOL programmers);

– software obsolescence;

– the need to reduce costs in corrective or development maintenance for applications;

– the need to change operating systems;

– etc.

Whether linked to the business or the information system, these contextual modifications will sometimes necessitate operations that modernize all or part of the information system. It is then that questions can be asked about the opportunity of launching a BPM project.

However, if we are modernizing the information system, does it only affect processes involving supervision or support? If the answer is yes, then now is not the moment to launch a BPM project.

If the modernizing phase touches the business processes (operational, functional), these processes satisfy most of the following characteristics:

– Do these processes have a central position in the value chain? Are they complex? Are they often required to adapt to developments in the market, or in production, for example (frequency of change)?

– Do these processes deal with significant volumes, or in other words, what is the number of new instances of these processes in a given month, day, or even hour (with 10,000 instances per month as a threshold for "significant" volume)?

– Are these business processes closely supervised by management or upper management?

– Do these processes require a high degree of computerization and/or automation, i.e., are they closely linked to the information system?

If the impacted business processes satisfy none of these characteristics, they are not appropriate for launching a BPM project. On the other hand, the more the impacted business processes do satisfy these characteristics, the higher the return on investment from implementing them in the information system with a BPM solution.

Whether the project concerns implementation of a new application in the information system, or IT system "urbanization" projects, or the integration of inter-enterprise exchanges, all of them end up in some way modernizing at least part of the information system and therefore make a BPM project auspicious, if the impacted processes respond to the criteria above.

4.4.3. *The "top-down" approach*

Once the BPM project has been launched, and the business processes have been selected for processing, it will be necessary to implement a way of working that will process the complete set of steps, from the initial design of the model for each process right up to the deployment of a version that can be executed in the selected environment.

Two approaches are possible:

– the *top-down* approach starts from the business and modeling know-how in the business requirement team, and computerizes that model for the project execution teams;

– the *bottom-up* approach starts from what the information system can do, as designed and modeled by the project execution teams, then subsequently makes those process models visible to the business requirement team.

The most appropriate approach most of the time is one that researcher Bernard Debauche describes as a "yo-yo": successive iterations first from the business requirement team, then from the project execution team, and from both in concert, converge towards the business process models that best satisfy the requirements and the constraints in the business on the one hand, and IT on the other.

In this approach, it can be useful for the business requirement team to start by modeling their business processes, initially not interacting with the project execution teams.

When the business requirement team has sufficiently converged on a model for the business process, this model is picked up by the project execution teams, who analyze it to determine how it can be implemented in the information system. This analysis can lead in turn to exchanges between project execution teams and the business requirement team, adjusting the process if necessary around the capacities of the information system (availability of functional services, openness of the applications, limitations and constraints of the existing architecture, etc.). Here we can see the "yo-yo" effect.

This back-and-forth "process" between project execution teams and the business requirement team is facilitated by the adoption of a notation such as BPMN, which is comprehensible by both types of actors.

Once the process model is set, the work of the project execution teams consists of:

– setting the technical parameters for the process model;

– carrying out the required IT development;

– refining, validating and testing the resulting models;

– deploying the models on the production servers and making them available to the process actors.

4.4.4. *Expected results*

If enterprises implement solutions to manage business processes, it is because they expect genuine advantages. Among them, we could cite:

– increased agility in the information system, by making it possible for the processes managed by IT to rapidly adapt to changes in the organization, to the arrival of new products or services on the market, to the use of new suppliers, etc.;

– a rationalization of these business processes, by providing the capacity to model and execute them in the information system in the most automatic way possible;

– an improvement in operational efficiency: by increasing automation and limiting human involvement to exception management, process execution is accelerated. In turn, this enhances the global capacity of the enterprise (for example, processing a larger number of orders in the same period of time). In addition, this increase in efficiency produces knock-on effects, including reduced error rates, better exception management, and improvements to the quality of service;

– an increase in traceability and transparency in process execution: by implementing performance indicators, the enterprise can determine the state of its processes at all times, and facilitate communication between services to handle exceptions or possible slowdowns in execution. For example, a client can be warned of a delay in the delivery of a product, with the explanation that the delay arises from an out-of-stock at the supplier or a transport problem. By implementing dashboards, the enterprise can also verify compliance with regulatory obligations in real time, such as with directives like Sarbanes-Oxley (Figure 4.16);

– added value for and capitalization on the information system: by adding a level of abstraction that works through standardized interfaces, these solutions add value to the existing applications. The capacity to orchestrate calls to services increases system flexibility and allows new services to be created by encapsulating existing applications instead of developing or acquiring new applications, making “old” applications into assets.

This last point leads us then to suggest that BPM is closely linked to what is today known as *SOA* (Service-Oriented Architecture), discussed in the next section.

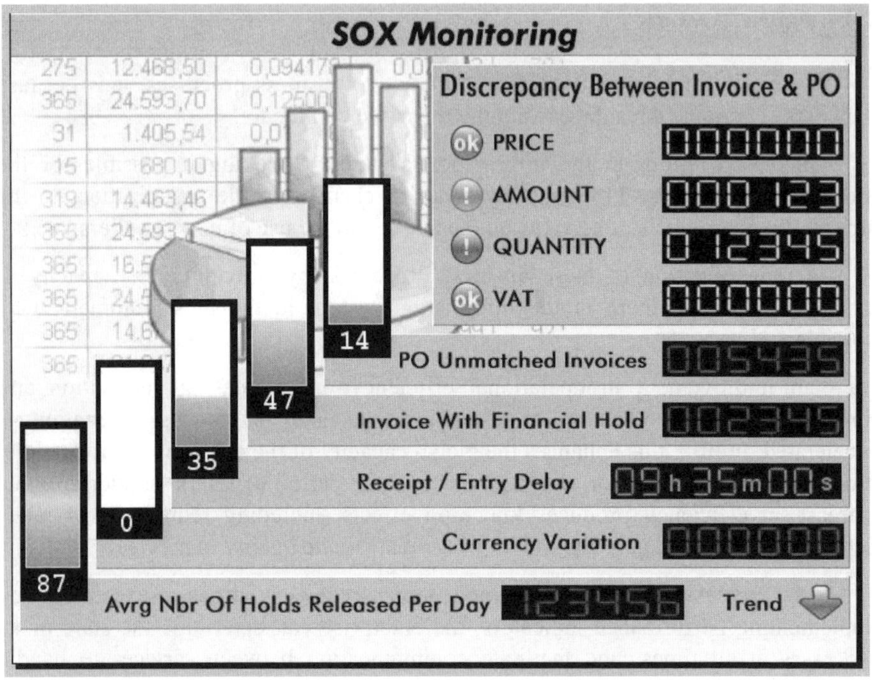

Figure 4.16. *Example dashboard tracking compliance with Sarbanes-Oxley (© Axway, 2006)*

4.5. Implementing a service architecture

If we refer to our classification of integration into three types (projects to implement a new IT application, projects to urbanize the system and projects to integrate inter-enterprise exchanges), we can see that all three types must handle integration problems by propagating data between applications (see section 2.4.1.1). Furthermore, all three types could lead to the launch of a business process management project (BPM project) that begins in multi-step process integration (see section 2.4.1.2). The impulse that drives implementations of service architectures is often found in the problem of composite application integration (see section 2.4.1.3), or in many cases, follows from and supports a BPM approach. This means that this approach is not therefore associated with a particular type of integration.

SOA is an approach intended to confer greater agility and reactivity on distributed, heterogenous information systems by providing a new way to integrate and manipulate the various bricks and application components of a computing system, and to manage the links that they support.

What do we mean by service?

A service presupposes the existence of the following actors and elements:

– a producer: this is the actor who provides the service;

– some consumers: these are the clients or service requesters;

– the service contract: it defines the terms of the service rendered, the format of exchange between consumer and producer, and the quality of service rendered. It is a genuine interface and interchange contract which remains stable over time.

In an information system, three large categories of services exist:

– *Business services,* which provide business functions, such as for example "submit order" or "status of client activity", and are designed to provide units of business work inside business processes.

– *Application services,* which also provide business functions, but are designed around the implementation of a particular application.

– *Infrastructure services,* which provide technical functions, such as: access to the data, access to the communication channels, print services, etc.

The concept of service did not appear out of nowhere; it draws its roots from technologies of "objects" and "components" well known in the computing industry.

The concept of "object" aims at the design and the programming of software. The notion of "Class" is a concept from programming and is referred to as a "module" in programming languages like C++ or Java. The class encapsulates the programming logic and the data of the module in such a way that programmers can use the module (and therefore the class) without having to understand how the module is structured or coded internally. An object is a particular instance of a class. This concept has yielded the method of "object-oriented programming", where we find the notions of interface and of encapsulation in particular.

The concept of "component" is addressed to information system architects. A component is an artifact at a finer granularity level than an object. A component is often, but not always, developed with an object-oriented language and itself contains objects. A component executes a certain function and possesses a well defined interface. A component can interact with other components. However, an understanding of the technology used is necessary to manipulate or deploy components. CORBA, DCOM, J2EE are examples of distributed component architecture.

The concept of "service" is intended for users. A user can be a person or a system, internal or external. A user should not need to know the underlying technology or the implementation of a service. The user only needs to know the interface for the service, i.e., the way to use the service. A service can be an aggregation of components.

The degree of coupling decreases as we pass from objects to services:

– in general, objects are contained in the same memory space allocated to the application, and while the application is executing, they are closely linked;

– components can reside on physically different machines; their coupling is therefore less tight. On the other hand, interactions between components depend on (homogenous) technology, such as CORBA, DCOM, RMI, etc. Furthermore, they are often complex;

– services can be implemented through components that use heterogenous technologies, but their interfaces are standardized and technologically independent. Further, the communication protocol is standardized and simple.

The SOA approach is therefore not new. The design of client/server software in which one application comprises software services and software consumer has effectively existed for quite some time: RPC (Remote Procedure Call), defined in 1976, was already a "service" approach. Distributed architectures and invocation of remote methods such as DCE or CORBA also covered the notion of "service". Moreover, those last two technologies largely inspired SOA itself.

However, these models have suffered from the lack of exchange standards between the calling process and called process. They have not achieved universal acceptance, nor reached the objective of interoperability that was set for them. On the contrary, the SOA approach was developed along with the emergence of technologies linked to Web services, which have permitted improvements to the concept of service:

– more delineated encapsulation (separation between interface and implementation) of components through the generalization of object-oriented concepts that simplify the segmentation of one monolithic application in an assembly of components or services;

– the standardization of protocols and exchange formats favors the interoperability of components and services from different platforms and suppliers;

– the functional level approach by which a service can correspond to a business service.

4.5.1. *Characteristics of an SOA*

Even if no unanimously accepted definition exists for service-oriented architecture, it is still possible to determine the characteristics that every observer accepts.

4.5.1.1. *The service interface: the heart of the SOA concept*

A service is an operational encapsulated software component presented as a pair of separately defined elements: the interface for the service and the implementation of the service (Figure 4.17).

The interface is the fundamental component of a service. A service is always intended for access via programming from another component (a service consumer). The service interface defines the "contract" of access through service programming: it establishes the identity of the service and the rules for calling the service. The service interface must have enough information to identify the service and use it without taking its internal design or its implementation content into consideration.

The implementation of the service fulfills the operational function of the service. During the design of the interface, it can be considered as a "black box". In the context of integration with an existing information system, the implementation of a service consists most of the time of writing a new module that encapsulates access to an older module, or a combination of several calls to new and pre-existing software modules, which correspond in our classification to the integration of composite applications. Generally, in the design of an SOA, implementation is secondary.

Fundamentally, an SOA relies on a dataflow of service interfaces and the set of relationships between them. The design of such an architecture implies defining service interfaces as well as their interactions: interactions between services and with service consumers.

The elements of the interface for a service are:

– the name of the service;

– the data on input and on output for the service;

– exceptions that could be raised by the service;

– metadata for identifying the objective and function of the service.

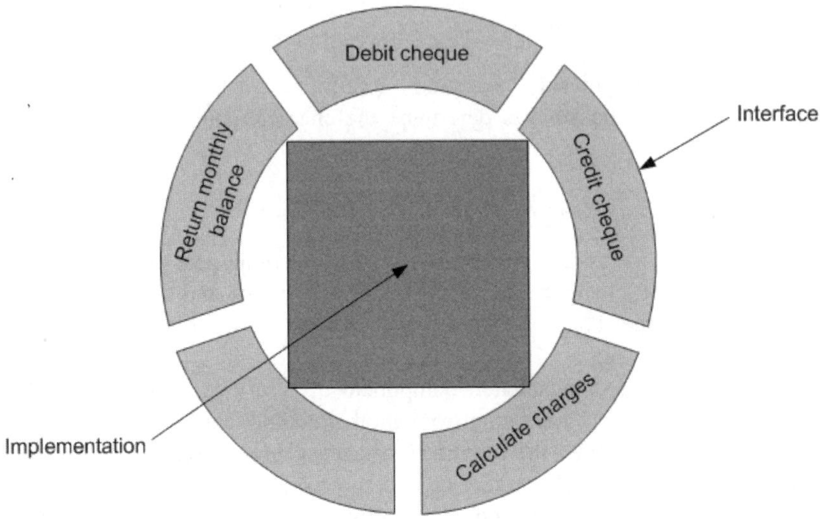

Figure 4.17. *Interface and implementation of a service*

4.5.1.2. *Technological neutrality*

The separation of the interface from implementation makes technological neutrality possible: the technology used to implement the services is not significant, since the service is accessed through an interface made available on a standardized protocol. The promise of interoperability that follows from this is one of the principal factors in the popularity of the SOA approach.

4.5.1.3. *Dynamic service discovery*

In a service-oriented architecture, service producers must publish their services, and service consumers must be able to search for published services (Figure 4.18). The operation is similar to a "Yellow Pages" type of registry. The data published provides the descriptions of the interfaces mentioned above. A repository of services that contains the set of service definitions (whatever the origins of the service) must be put in place in order to fulfill the function of services registry in an information system.

Just like a person searching for a service supplier in a "Yellow Pages" registry, the service consumer in a service-oriented architecture "discovers" the reference for the searched service during execution.

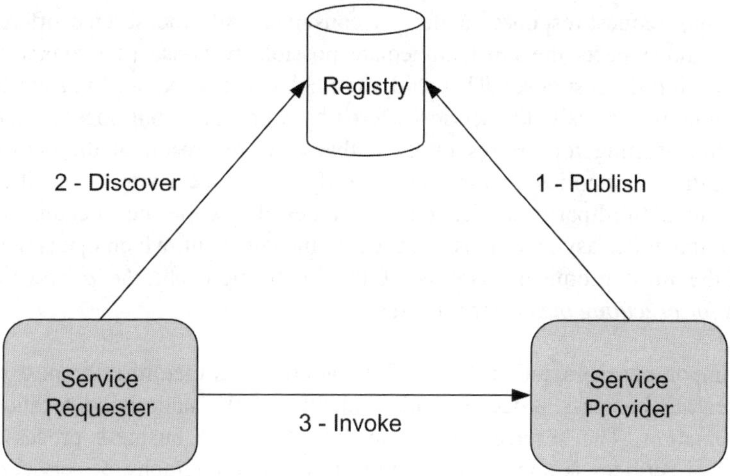

Figure 4.18. *The dynamic discovery of services*

4.5.1.4. *Reuse*

The reuse of existing components is a fundamental characteristic of services architectures. It is through reuse that agility and reactivity are conferred on the information system, by accelerated development of new applications that will use these components. To achieve this, callable components must be carefully selected and defined as services that can be used by a large number of clients. Technological neutrality and the exposition of services in a registry will facilitate this reuse, similar to loose coupling, discussed next.

4.5.1.5. *Loose coupling*

One of the principal characteristics of the SOA approach lies in how a service is organized with its consumers. Specifically, services are designed without regard for any particular service consumer. Inside the service, no assumption is made concerning the objective or nature – technical or functional – of the service consumer. In this way, a service is totally decoupled from the service consumer. On the other hand, the consumer is dependent on the service, since it refers to the service interface. As a result, the SOA approach allows the implementation of an architecture with loose coupling. It is thus differentiated from a monolithic architecture, in which all the software components are designed to function in the initially projected context (known as strong coupling logic).

SOA is principally used in the development of applications that function in synchronous request/response mode – a consumer calls the service offered by a producer and expects the most immediate possible response (it remains in place while awaiting the response). That said, the SOA can also be used in asynchronous mode – a consumer calls the service offered by a producer, but does not remain in place while waiting for the response. In this case, the result of the demand will subsequently be supplied to the consumer if the service contract specifies it, or supplied to a third-party service that continues the work thus begun. An SOA therefore integrates asynchronous event-based management, which opens the way to one of the most promising aspects of the SOA approach: *the orchestration of services for executing business processes*.

An important characteristic of the SOA approach is therefore the possibility of implementing business processes independently of the underlying technology of implementation. The services are chained to form the business processes (this chaining of services is sometimes referred to as "choreography of services"). The choreography is subsequently executed for each instance of the process by the BPM engine, which plays the role of service orchestrator. A business process can itself be exposed as a service, and can be deployed and distributed at several separately accessible physical points (Figure 4.19).

The orchestration of services is paramount to large-scale SOA deployment. However, *other functions are necessary* to, for example, play the role of intermediation between services and consumers of services by introducing the asynchronous communication mentioned above. These functions provide a level of abstraction such as *determining the "right" service*, a role of mediation between the consumer and the producer, possibilities for activating the transformation function on the information sent and received when the consumer and the producer have not previously agreed on the service contract (this is particularly the case for existing applications). In short, the implementation of SOA necessitates the deployment of a service infrastructure, often referred to as *SOA Backbone*.

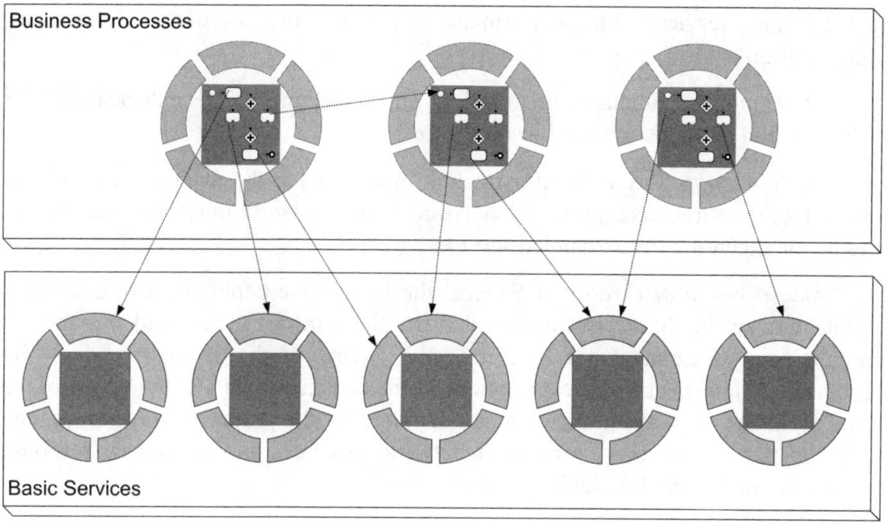

Figure 4.19. *Business processes and service calls*

4.5.2. *Elements of an SOA infrastructure*

Advocating the "de-correlation" of the call from the application to the SOA service directly: "a services infrastructure must be used".

Even if, today, no specific definition exists for what a services infrastructure must contain, it is still possible to list its principal functions:

– *Multi-channel communication*: to ensure dependable, high-performance communication with existing applications, such as with the new Web applications, the infrastructure must not be limited only to SOAP implementations, but offer different communication channels (such as message exchanges by queue managers).

– *Mediation/transformation*: these functionalities are necessary to make the deployment flexible in a distributed context, in particular with an existing application base. Mediation/transformation makes it possible to adjust the constraints between consumers and producers in, for example, data formats or type of communication used. It should be noted that these functions, which are at the core of EAI tools, are also the basis of service infrastructures.

– *Services registry*: a registry of services is an indispensable function for offering the functionalities of dynamic services discovery, and for responding to the need to manage the services lifecycle (management of the versions of services, configuration etc.).

– *Modeling*: the functions of modeling and development are indispensable for designing and implementing service interfaces.

– *Orchestration*: the SOA infrastructure must provide the means of assembling services to construct complex and horizontal processes. It must also supply the engine for executing the assembled services.

– *Measurement of Quality of Service*: the large-scale deployment of a services architecture in the enterprise implies that the SOA infrastructure will provide the complete set of elements for measuring the quality of the services rendered by producers with respect to the expectations of the consumers. In addition, most of the time, SLAs are included in the elements supplied by the producers of services, and make up part of the service contract between producer and consumer (response times, rates of availability, fault-tolerance, etc.).

– *Security*: the service infrastructure must manage the service access policy, both for internal calls to the information system and for external calls from partners.

– *Global management*: the infrastructure must provide functions for managing deployment as well as versions of services, plus mediation processes, exchange processes, and business processes. It must also offer the complete set of services registry mechanisms for managing the lifecycle for these services: in development, in production, etc. Finally, it must supply all the functionalities for managing access authorization to the various functions that it provides.

– *Supervision*: the infrastructure must provide functions for constructing performance indicators and tracking dashboards on the use of services and on the associated business activity.

We could note that the functionalities described above are part of the service-level integration required for implementing an integration infrastructure, such as is described in Chapter 3. They are not all necessarily present in the different tools. These functionalities are often limited to supplying the basic functions required for implementing Web services, to the detriment of the functions that can integrate existing applications in the SOA approach.

4.5.3. *Applicable norms and standards*

The norms and standards for implementing SOA made their appearance with the emergence of Web services and directly cover the phases required for invoking a service (Figure 4.20):

– the description of the service;

– the publication and search for the service;

– the invocation of the service.

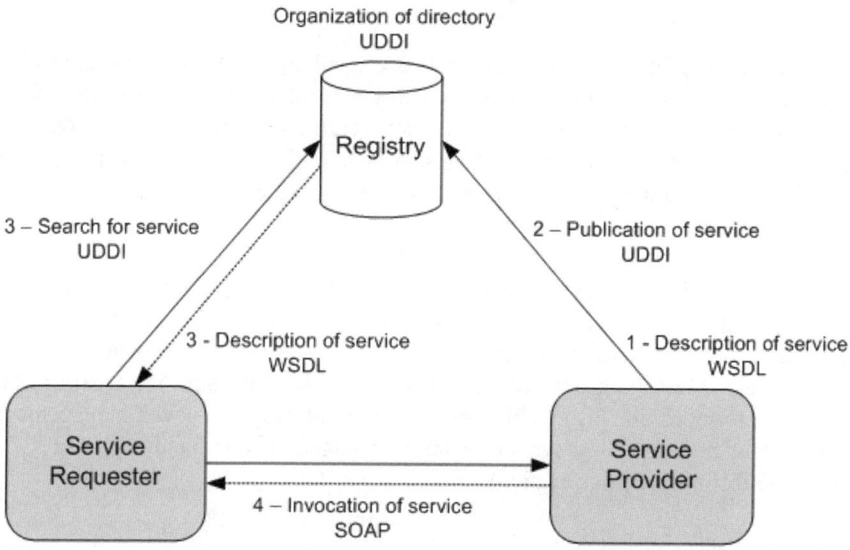

Figure 4.20. *Norms and standards in services architecture*

4.5.3.1. *The description of the service*

WSDL (Web Services Description Language) is the standard for describing the service interface. It uses a standardized XML format to describe the technical modes of access to a service, the name of the functions that it exposes, the data that it needs for execution and the data that it sends back in return.

WSDL version 1.1 was proposed by IBM and Ariba in 2001, and was largely implemented by software providers. Version 2.0, constructed under the aegis of the W3C consortium, was being validated at the time of writing.

4.5.3.2. *The publication and the search for services: the services registry*

UDDI (Universal Description Discovery and Integration) is a specification from OASIS that describes the structure of a services registry and defines the APIs used to publish and dynamically discover services. Version 3 of UDDI was approved by OASIS in February 2005.

4.5.3.3. *The invocation of the service*

SOAP (Simple Object Access Protocol) is a standardized XML request/response language for invoking services. It is used to encapsulate the data that allows the service to be executed, as well as the data returned by the service. SOAP is recommended by the W3C, which has also specified the WSCL (Web Services Conversation Language), used to describe the sequence of messages in a conversation between two services.

At the same time, a services architecture is not limited to Web services. Other means of communication can be used: this is notably the case in the exchange of messages through a queue manager. In this case, it is possible, for example, to use the JMS (Java Messaging Service) specification, defined by Sun, for access to the messaging services in Java. This specification allows high-level management: subscriptions, message files, synchronization management, etc., and is part of J2EE (Java 2 Platform, Enterprise Edition).

Chapter 5

Application Integration Tools

Few tools today exhibit the complete set of functions that we have detailed in the three integration types to cover and serve an integration problem. It will often be necessary to associate several of these tools to provide the global solution required for a project. The next few sections provide an initial approach to the tools used to implement integration solutions.

5.1. *Brokers*

Under this term, we group the complete set of tools identified under descriptions such as "Message Broker", "Integration Broker" and "Integration Server". *It is these tools that provide the functions basic to any integration solution.* As their name indicates, they are presented to other applications as a third party playing the role of communication intermediary.

However, brokers are not only communication tools or bridges between applications, even if several of them integrate or often utilize an inter-application messaging system. One example is IBM's WebSphere MQ (formerly MQSeries), the principal example of a "Message Broker". For their part, "Integration Brokers" provide the option of different communication modes (notably *file*). By definition, a broker should supply the principal functions of the second level:

– syntactical and semantic transformation of data and events;

– routing via publication/subscription mechanism or via implementation of content-based routing.

Moreover, to adapt to the operating pace of applications, most brokers offer functions that temporarily store events, and provide a certain number of adapters to allow the applications to connect directly.

To carry out these functions, brokers rely on:

– dictionaries that contain the description of the structures for events on input and on output, as well as the rules for transformation and routing;

– administration and supervision functions that make it possible to configure the rules and survey their execution;

Applications can connect to the broker either non-intrusively via adapters, or intrusively via a "Super API" which masks all the technical levels.

These brokers can be presented as a software package that integrates the complete set of functions, or as a group of modules each of which covers a function or group of functions, which can be implemented separately or simultaneously in order to construct a solution that is adapted to the scope and requirements in a project.

Brokers are most often used to carry out integrations for propagating data or for integrating multi-step processes.

5.2. *Application servers*

Application servers provide an environment for implementing transactional applications, most of the time utilizing Internet technologies. These are not, strictly speaking, tools that supply the basic functions of an integration solution, even if they are often positioned in this niche. They are, however, essential for projects to create Web applications that must integrate into an existing system (integrating composite applications).

They offer a collection of services particularly for managing communication with the user, providing the functions required to develop Web applications:

– HTTP server;

– SMTP server;

– session manager to ensure their persistence;

– ORB;

– EJB (Enterprise Java Beans);

– etc.

Moreover, they include adapters or bridges to databases so that applications functioning in their environment can communicate with the traditional applications of the information system.

Finally, in addition to their own adapters, most application servers can embed a broker to ensure the best integration with existing applications. We then obtain the architecture presented in Figure 5.1.

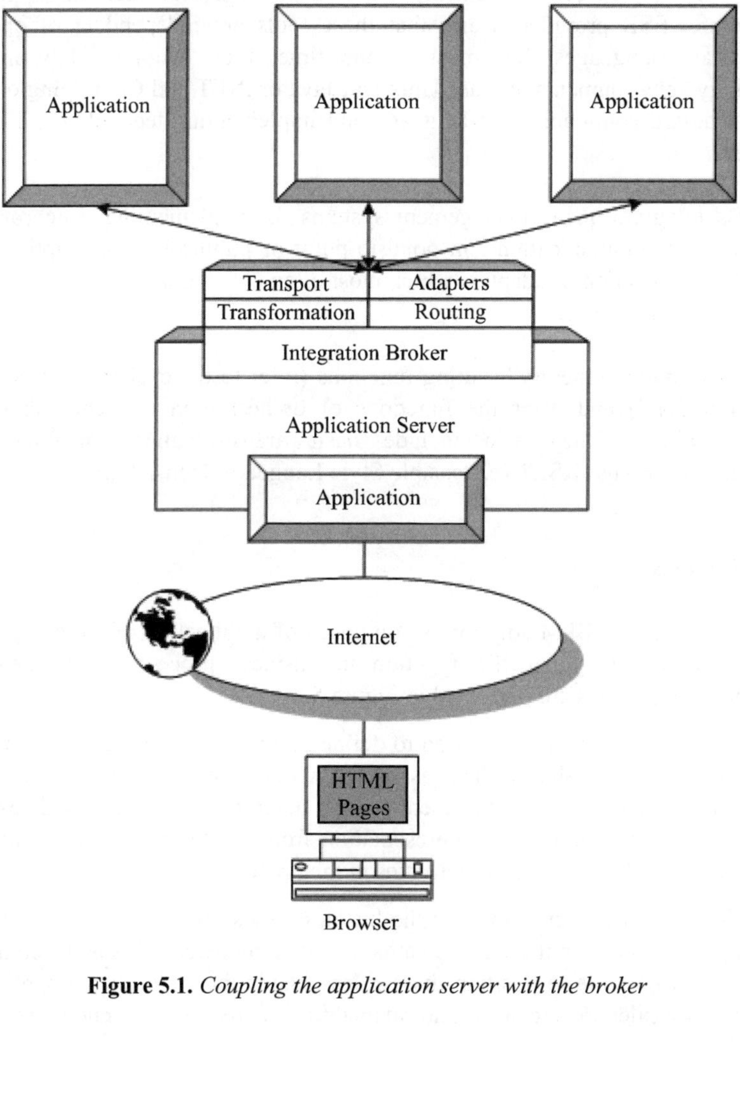

Figure 5.1. *Coupling the application server with the broker*

5.3. *Enterprise Service Bus (ESB)*

There exists no definition of an Enterprise Service Bus, or ESB that is widely accepted. It is, however, possible to list the characteristics on which everyone agrees.

An ESB implements the principles of service-oriented architectures, and as such, supplies the infrastructure elements required to construct such an application architecture. ESB providers claim that these tools are independent of operating systems and languages, but most of the time, they operate solely in "new technology" environments that use Unix and Java or .NET and C#, relying on XML as the standard communication language and implementing technologies linked to Web services.

ESBs integrate queue management systems for implementing synchronous or asynchronous communications, in point-to-point or publication/subscription mode, as well as a collection of adapters which most often use standards such as JCA (Java Connector Architecture).

ESBs provide "itinerary" routing functions (refer to the exchange process level in section 3.4.3) and offer the functions of orchestration and choreography of services. Finally, they also include basic transformation functions, often implemented through XSLT (eXtensible Style Language Translation).

5.4. *BPM tools*

In most cases, a BPM solution is composed of a collection of "bricks", each of which fulfills a very specific function in business process management. The following components are presented in Figure 5.2:

– The modeling component, used to define graphically the processes that should be executed by the solution. This is the component that implements the BPMN notation (see section 3.3.1) to represent process diagrams that are comprehensible by business users, decoupling this representation from the technical aspects linked to the applications that execute the activities in the process.

– The component for managing the business rules, used to define the rules for directing the process on the various paths that were modeled. This is the component that makes it possible to position these rules outside the code for the applications, and thus to render maintenance and adaptability of the system much simpler and faster.

– The execution engine of the processes, which instantiates a process each time necessary, i.e., on reception of trigger events (for example, reception of a purchase order). It then executes the different activities in the process, according to the defined business rules. It can also call activities from the integration level to perform processes, either of exchange or of mediation (see section 3.4).

– The supervision component, which collects the set of the events for monitoring process execution, alerting when necessary, and measuring the global activity of the enterprise with the help of dashboards that present the indicators defined during the modeling phase.

– Connectors, which allow the execution engine to interact with the applications responsible for executing the activities in the process.

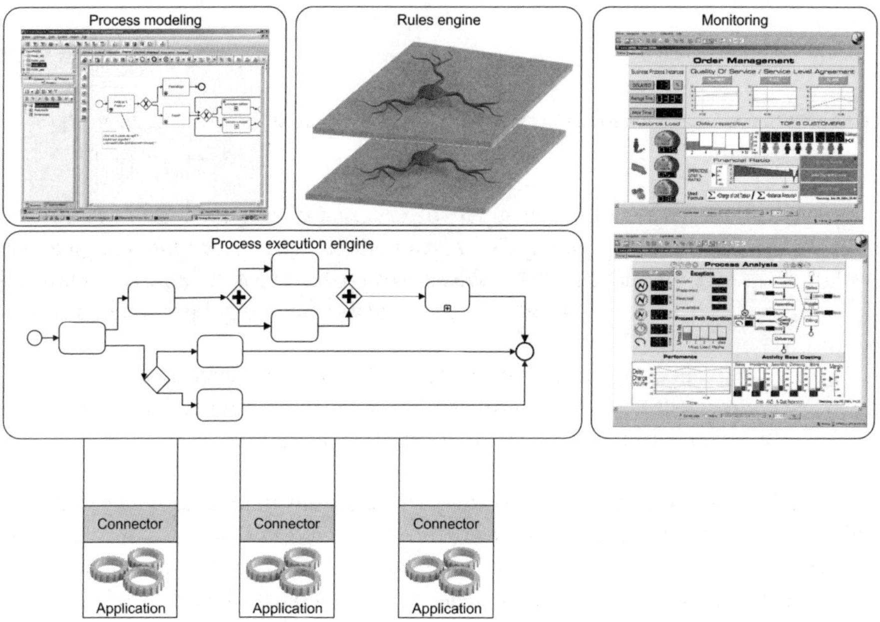

Figure 5.2. *The components of a BPM solution*

As we saw in our definitions, the implementation of application integration solutions does not rest solely on the tools; it also requires an appropriate methodology and the complementary services indispensable to the success of the project. It is precisely these aspects that very often determine success or failure in the implementation of an application integration solution – themes that we will develop in the next few chapters.

Chapter 6

Understanding Integration Failures

6.1. High failure rates

After reviewing the issues of application integration, the functions and levels of services, as well as the different technologies, what remains is not just putting them all into practice, but above all, concretely and durably succeeding application integration projects inside enterprises.

This last point sheds light on the implementation, the key points to be processed and the errors not to commit to rendering flexible – durably – its information system through the technologies of application integration.

Why raise this subject? Because a significant number of acquisitions of integration solutions, notably at the start of the 21st century in the exuberance of the Internet bubble, have ultimately led to implementations that are very restrained in scope, where the cost of getting results is out of all proportion to the problems at stake, leading to suspicion of, or even abandoning the projects in question.

After gathering a number of items of information emanating from large enterprises, from software providers and analyst firms in the USA and in Europe which specialize in integration, the plain facts are:

– one in four integration solutions purchased is not implemented;

– one in two integration solutions is not generalized.

This assessment is disconcerting. It underlies the relative disenchantment observed in the progress of the application integration market. It can hold certain enterprises back from a necessary evolution towards an IT that is oriented to processes and dataflow management. This loss of time is a source of decreased performance of the enterprise.

Do the results described above mean that the technologies selected were not the "right ones", or that the support ensured by software providers or integrators of integration solutions was not up to scratch? Sometimes, yes, but this is not the principal cause.

The most accomplished integration technology, the most pertinent business vision, the highest quality of technical teams and architects – none of these lead automatically to achieving the objective of IT reactivity faced with business developments. Far from it.

6.2. The technological approach

The essential cause of failure in application integration projects resides in a purely technical, and often, a purely tools-based response to a subject that is by its nature horizontal, mixing aspects of organization, business logic, functional needs and technical implementation.

6.2.1. *New technology or new packaging?*

The proliferation of technologies and acronyms is also a constant in the computing industry. Each new technology is often hailed by "specialists" as a revolution that will "remake the computing landscape from top to bottom, change the lives of users, IT staff, operators, in short, give a new vision of the business, the clients and the suppliers".

However, in most cases – with the notable exceptions of the micro-computer, the mouse, and the Internet – new technologies only prolong or generalize subjects already handled by previous technologies.

Consider the example of the architecture of services (SOA – see section 4.5). This new acronym is today flooding the entire application integration community. No forum – no specialized magazine fails to devote whole pages to this new paradigm. However, as we have already mentioned, the SOA approach only amplifies and generalizes – via tools and norms, we concede that point willingly – the ancient "call" in COBOL programming or the more recent use of Remote Procedure Calls (RPC) in structured and modular programming. The philosophy of segmentation into reusable services is not new.

6.2.2. *Technology confronts reality*

In fact, the emergence of a new technology requires an implementation cycle that comprises three phases (called EDM):

– **(E)nthusiasm**: revolution and replacement of old ways of doing things;

– **(D)isillusion:** contributes little, and hard to implement;

– **(M)aturity**: it can help in specific cases, and yield respectable ROI.

Applied to integration solutions, the various technologies designated with acronyms (such as XML, HTTP, SOA, EAI, ETL, FTP, MOM, BROKER, BAM, BPM, etc.) can make it difficult to choose integration solutions. In fact, the real interest in these solutions for an enterprise depends on the business context and on the technical state of its IT:

– without analyzing the real integration needs of the enterprise concerned;

– without shared definition of target objectives, some of which are accessible in the short/medium term;

– without precise definition of the responsibilities and tasks of each participant (project execution teams, business requirement teams, architects, "urbanists", operators, etc.);

– without directly connecting the project to the business issues of the enterprise;

– without analyzing all costs in relation to the benefits (the well known ROI which comes up later);

– without knowing the keys for internal allocation of implementation workloads for the integration project.

It is a good bet that *the real usage will often be scarcely larger than the scope of the mockup or prototype that was completed during the acquisition of the integration solution.*

Since the technological approach is often the only approach constructed between the potential client and the supplier during the pre-sales phase of the solution, the other potential problems that we just indicated will only reveal themselves during the completion phase, lengthening implementation delays and thus increasing the workload, blurring both objectives and results.

To ensure the maximum chance for the integration project, a strategy for integration project success must be implemented. Subsequent chapters describe the essential points in this strategy.

Chapter 7

Integration Myths

Drawing on our practical operational experience in application integration projects, we have been able to inventory a well stocked catalog of conventional wisdom on the subject.

The preoccupations that underlie these ideas are generally legitimate. But sometimes – often – the responses to them are "cookie cutter" responses, and can lead to more or less camouflaged failures. This is why it seems important to us to shed some light on them.

7.1. The mirage of the single tool

How many times have we heard or read the following statement: "one single tool responds to all requirements"!

When an IT director (often the Chief Information Officer) takes a long, hard look at the technical architecture of his or her IT department with the goal of technical component evolution, it is not uncommon that a consulting firm, generally after careful study of the different technologies on the market, selects a single technology to treat the entire problem addressed.

The choice is performed by favoring:

– *innovative* technology – after all, architectural consulting firms are also paid for integrating innovation inside IT – otherwise, what use are they?

– or perhaps just the technologies that the architects are aware of. What good does it do to change, since the architects in question are fully conversant with the technology? At least they will be fairly certain that their competence will still be required when the technology of today is also the technology of tomorrow.

With regards to application integration, this type of behavior can bring about the failure of the integration solution.

Some examples given below will illustrate the idea.

7.1.1. *A conservative choice: example and consequences*

For several years, the enterprise ENERGY ONE, positioned in the corporate services market, has been using an ETL tool to input its data warehouse repository. Data is extracted regularly (once per day is functionally sufficient) from production databases, validated and cleaned (with a check on functional doubles), then injected into databases of the data warehouse repository. With the success of this technology in mind, ENERGY ONE decided to generalize the use of the ETL to cover the whole of the application integration problem, specifically for:

– managing intra-enterprise business flows (real-time and "batch file");

– exchanging with its partners.

As one result, a generalized use of an ETL tool pushes the limits of a commercialized product that was never designed:

– to manage exchanges with a frequency greater than one session per hour. This is normal; this was not its initial objective;

– to pilot file flows with partners at an adequate level of quality of service. The use of FTP upstream and downstream from the ETL does not always allow the integrity of those files to be ensured;

– to verify the quality of services supplied to or received from the partners. The ETL tool provides no function for dataflow supervision;

– to offer real-time exchanges to the departmental applications which had signaled their need for them. The ETL tool functioned only by extracting/integrating files that use databases.

Faced with the lack of enthusiasm raised by the large-scale deployment of this technology, ENERGY ONE found that it had to:

– refocus the use of the ETL tool around its standard function of updating the data warehouse;

– restore the choices around application integration back to the different business departments – the CIO no longer had the credibility necessary to put a solution together.

On balance, the feeling inside the enterprise about application integration was negative. ENERGY ONE will not be restructuring its integration strategy anytime soon. The *status quo* and the principle of "every man (or every department) for himself" will be engraved there for a long time to come.

7.1.2. *"Modern" architectural choice: example and consequences*

Refer here to the concrete example presented in section 11.2.

7.2. XML: miracle format

Another statement we have often read or heard: "all formats must be XML formats – this guarantees the use of standards"!

Taking nothing away from the relevance of XML-type format (see sections 3.2.1.1 and 4.3.2), it is however important to recognize that its success among analysts, architects, software providers, and also among users, has resulted in the construction of a kind of Tower of Babel, perhaps with the same tools, but with bricks of completely different shapes, sizes and colors.

Several hundred and perhaps thousands of business "standards" use the XML format, though no general standardization has yet been defined by a "United Norms" organization, or has been publicly accepted by all stakeholders, even on attributes as universal as names and addresses, for example. A certain number of endeavors are however underway, for example, at OASIS around UBL (see section 4.3.2).

However, in the view of many decision-makers responsible for integration choices, XML offers a certain guarantee of simplification. If this is true for computing applications (which can indeed capitalize on a single grammar for writing or reading the dataflows for which they are responsible), it is inexact if not utterly false in everything that concerns the supposed uniqueness of the formats produced.

There has never been a greater need to for integration engines to transform XML formats to *other* XML formats.

Why should this be a problem? Is this not precisely what integration engines are for?

This is a problem because these transformations have a high cost in terms of performance (see section 3.2.1.1).

Like variable type formats – of which they are only a particular type – XML formats require dataflows to be parsed on input to search for the information to be checked or to be transformed in an integration.

As for transforming a format of the fixed length/position type (where, by definition there is no need to "parse" the information, since each type of data is in the same place in the record or the message), it requires on average *five to ten times as much time to process the same business event in an XML-type format as in a fixed format.* That ratio can vary slightly depending on the commercially available tools.

By way of illustration, an integration engine specialized in fixed position/length formats was able to process *100 million events in four hours on a mainframe CPU.* That performance level is simply not currently accessible to XML formats, even after associating functions of parallelism, multithreading, and scalability proper to a significant number of integration engines on the market.

The "all-XML" approach therefore has a cost that will make a lot of people happy... so long as they are among the providers of the hardware and software resources required to process the required volumes!

The concrete example presented in section 11.2 provides an excellent illustration of this problem.

7.3. Business adapters: simplifying the implementation

We often hear or read the peremptory statement: "the more business adapters in the solution, the simpler it is to implement"!

One of the selection criteria admitted by the entire community consists of searching for market solutions that include the largest possible number of thick (business) adapters.

Let us recall that a business or "thick" adapter (see section 3.1.3.3) is a component – placed between the business application and the integration engine – which provides connectivity functions (notably communication protocol) and which guarantees that the format sent or received conforms to the specifications expected by the business application. Information about the wrong or right integration (in the business meaning of the words) is also part of the package.

Common sense leads then to the idea that the more business adapters that are available, the simpler the integration between the applications.

Faced with these good sense arguments, providers of integration solutions step into the breach by presenting in their commercial brochures the largest possible number of thick (business) adapters. One such software provider – since absorbed by a market heavyweight – went so far as to make that its principal sales argument.

Indeed, this criterion is easy to understand and quantify, initially by potential clients, but also by the sales force for a software vendor, where anything that looks like routinizing the sales cycle is manna from heaven.

How does it happen then that in the real world, application integration based on solutions that comprise a large number of business adapters has produced *no significant benefit* compared to a solution which uses technical adapters – *not in delays, not in implementation workload*?

In a significant number of cases, *the deployment objectives for this type of solution were lowered.* Why?

First of all, by definition, there is no business adapter available on the market for specific applications developed for a given client.

In the case where the integration need is strongly centered on existing, often specific applications, the presence of business adapters in software providers' catalogs has therefore strictly no interest.

However, what about the case of integrating commercial software packages, such as solutions for managing customer relations or production, or the accounting and financial modules at the core of ERP (Enterprise Resource Planning)?

As the real-life example below illustrates, disillusion here can be sharp.

7.3.1. *Business adapter: implementation – maintenance – problem*

As part of our consultancy missions, we were called on by the CIO of a large French industrial manufacturing group who had:

– acquired an EAI solution with a good market reputation;

– chosen a commercial ERP to manage its financial back-office;

– purchased the adapter corresponding to the selected ERP and offered by the provider of the EAI solution.

Concerned with verifying the operational side of the said adapter, the CIO's team were given a convincing demonstration in the software provider's offices.

Once the solution was chosen, the project was implemented – and it is at that point that the problems started.

Extracts from our interview with the CIO:

"First of all, we chose the ERP version that conforms to our business needs. In addition, since part of the interest of ERP is that we can specialize it using its capacity to accept our specific additional parameters and business objects, we did not distrust the adapter. We thought that, in spite of adaptations, it would always function."

"However, when the provider of the EAI solution delivered the corresponding business connector to us, we were incapable of connecting it to the ERP as configured. After consultation, the supplier indicated the following precisions to us."

Response of the provider to the CIO:

"This connector is certified on the version X of the corresponding ERP.

"Its native operation with a different version is perhaps technically possible but does not commit us (which was in fact indicated in the contract, but not emphasized in discussion).

"The ERP parameters which your teams have specialized probably mean that you will have to adapt the adapter.

"We [the provider] *could undertake this adaptation, under the conditions described in your service contract.*

"We remind you that this adaptation does not fall under maintenance clauses of the corresponding software packages, but that it could be the subject of a 'services+' contract, whose measures could be communicated to you."

It therefore became necessary to ... "adapt the adapter"!

Rapidly, a meeting was convened between the provider and the integrator responsible for the EAI solution. It became apparent that the adapter had to be modified to serve the needs of the client. The solution provider accepted that the integrator would ensure the necessary modifications, because the provider did not have the local resources to provide this service. Maintenance conditions for the adapter (ensured by the provider or by the integrator) remained fuzzy.

Results assessment for the enterprise

We advised the enterprise to deploy and use technical adapters as much as possible (files, messages, DBMS, etc.). These adapters are by definition more stable than thick (business) adapters.

The enterprise, which had acquired a significant number of business adapters, reduced their use.

7.3.2. *By way of a conclusion on business adapters*

Too many business adapters can ultimately damage the adaptability of the solution, since the cost of their maintenance becomes very steep with respect to the parameter definitions carried out inside the EAI solution.

We end up then with the paradox that searching for a significant number of business adapters during the Request for Proposal (RFP) phase can in fact often delay later solution deployment.

Even so, when business adapters are stable with respect to changes in the EAI solution and in the ERP, then they ensure relevant connectivity for application integration solutions, in particular by ensuring more advanced tracking for updates to events inside the concerned application.

7.4. Java: the proof of a modern solution

"A modern application integration solution must be constructed in Java!"

Without in any way wishing to undercut the interest of Java either as a language or a development platform, we are forced to observe that, in the domain of application integration, the use of Java should be marked "handle with care".

7.4.1. *The real reason for Java*

As with C, C++ or even COBOL, Java is a development language. Its level of abstraction remains that of a third-generation language. Its readability and maintainability are not easy – in any case, not better than if Java was used natively in the specifically developed applications.

However, part of the interest in an integration solution resides in the simple and "auditable" nature of the parameter settings ensured by the integration broker. The language or "mappings" of the broker must be rapidly adaptable around business developments.

Massive use of a language such as Java entails no significant benefit in terms of maintenance between an integration broker and specific interfaces also written in Java. In this case, bypassing the broker in favor of specific development would save the cost of the licenses.

On the other hand, when significant language power is required, then recourse to third-generation languages – including Java – inside the integration broker is useful.

Java or any other third-generation language can then ensure generic functions such as:

– accessing business repositories;

– performing complex calculations;

– proceeding to global checks and generic types on the events that are checked and transformed.

In the real world, one of the conditions for the success of an integration broker in an enterprise requires a balanced proportion between the use of a third-generation language such as Java, and the parameterization of the broker as such, which should be high-level. Ideally, 80% of the functions for checking, transforming, and content-based routing must be processed by mapping functions or with a high-level[18] language. The remaining 20% falls in the domain of a third-generation language such as Java.

7.4.2. *Limitations of an all-Java integration solution*

The interest of Java as a development platform no longer needs to be demonstrated. Its capacities in deployment, its "natural" scalability for executing processes and its "once-only" development make Java one of the most interesting standard platforms on the market.

For all of that, if integration solutions are "all-Java", then what about applications that execute on other platforms?

Why should the integration needs of a technical universe such as Windows and above all IBM z/OS simply be ignored?[19]

Here again, it can be useful to analyze the real need of the enterprise in terms of the classification of different operating systems, in order to decide whether or not to depend solely on a Java platform.

7.5. Files: the "poor cousins" of application integration

"File dataflows are a side issue in application integration!"

As we saw in Chapter 3, in the majority of cases, application integration relies on an asynchronous exchange pattern. The application sends information to the application integration solution, not waiting for the response before continuing with other work. The information will be distributed to the different partners at an opportune moment.

MOM tools (see section 3.1.2.3) are natural candidates for "supporting" the dataflows that transit an application integration solution.

There is but a single step between considering file exchanges as outside the spectrum of application integration, and seeing it as the "poor cousin" of dataflow

18 On the other hand, nothing stops this high-level language from being constructed on the basis of macro-functions written in Java.

19 Even if today, Java virtual machines exist for z/OS, their connection with native z/OS applications is not yet entirely operational.

messaging. The step is often taken, because the majority of the offerings on the market were designed to process dataflows in message mode and not in files.

However, the studies on the subject all point in the same direction: *in inter- and intra-enterprise exchanges, file dataflows are in the majority, and represent between 65 and 80% of the total.* Not taking them into account ends up taking care of only about one-third of the needs – at best.

Implementing an application integration solution that must process file dataflows is a response to particular problems, that the simple implementation of file adapters upstream and downstream the integration solution does not resolve:

– Is the file a carrier of one or more functional integrities?

– In case of error detected by the application integration solution on one or more records in the file, should the whole file be blocked, or should all or part of it be allowed through?

– In case of error in processing by the sending application, how is it possible to be sure that sending the application did not re-send the file, including all the initial records that were not in error? And in that case, how is it possible to be certain that the same records are not processed twice?

– The volume of files to be processed is generally much more voluminous than messages. How then can we be certain that the integration engine was designed to handle such volumes?

Certain elements in the response are indicated as part of the concrete example presented in section 11.2.

7.6. Process and services are everything

"Goodbye application integration. Hello processes and services – everywhere!"

As we have previously underlined, the computing industry is perfectly content to stage its own revolutions. A new technology must drive out other, older ones because they are not adapted to the new issues that confront enterprises.

In fact, in the real world, application integration is a good deal more complex and multi-form subject.

It is commonly noted that EAI is mature technology, and that Business Process Management and SOA should now be installed everywhere "in double-quick time". This type of profession of faith has the advantage of simplifying the discourse from suppliers, making sure that potential clients can hear and understand it. It has only two drawbacks: it is dangerous and costly.

It is dangerous to lead business requirement teams to believe that just modeling a process will easily lead to aligning the information system with the business of the enterprise (see section 4.4). If the existing IT applications are not designed with services in mind from the outset, it will be difficult, perhaps impossible, to adapt them. Consequently, new SOAs will have to be developed from scratch, with all the associated delays and costs. It will not make matters better to use the same "design" workstation for setting the parameters in the application integration solutions and modeling the business processes. Indeed, the pace of modification to a business process is different from that of an integration layer. In addition, neither the user populations nor the preoccupations of the two approaches are the same.

It is dangerous to spread the idea that all the business processes in the enterprise must be orchestrated. For example, in an energy company, what is the use of handling the purchase of office supplies in process mode? What business benefits exist when the simple implementation of a B2B platform for management of the orders is quite sufficient?

It is costly to launch a broad-spectrum approach to modeling the processes of the enterprise, without questioning the link between this modeling and the underlying functional and technical models for the applications in the corresponding information system.

As was expressed recently by an architect responsible for large-scale deployment of processes inside his service delivery enterprise: "We underestimated the problems of aligning the business models with the execution models in the information system", a coyly roundabout way of indicating that at the end of four years, only five operational processes had been deployed, and the modeling of 150 others had been committed, after spending hundreds of person-years on the entire project.

We want to be quite clear: we are a long way from the idea of hollowing out the genuine interest in making BPM and SOA solutions available. Still, they must be used advisedly, i.e., on processes and service approaches with high added value that "deserve" spending the necessary means.

7.6.1. *BPM and SOA: top-down approach – from business to IT*

In this approach, processes that create value in the enterprise must be identified to make sure that they are eligible for process industrialization. Then the adaptations required in the information system must be committed to. This top-down approach proceeds from business to IT.

Organizationally in this case, we would expect to find business managers in the front line. They are they ones who necessarily must impose constraints in adapting existing applications that are typically implemented by the project execution teams.

7.6.2. *EAI and B2B: bottom-up approach – from IT to business*

The other processes of the enterprise will not be treated as such but implemented in a context of exchange platforms and/or of the flow manager[20] that implements services for:

– securing the transport layers for the information;

– ensuring functions of information distribution;

– offering services for transformation, routing and control of dataflows.

Organizationally, it is the project execution teams that deploy the required exchange platforms or dataflow managers. The business managers are generally called on to ensure the transformation functions and the business checks.

7.6.3. *Complementary approaches*

Far from being contradictory, the two approaches are in fact complementary. Each approach supplies supervision services that are pertinent for the enterprise:

– technical supervision of the transport layers;

– supervision of the dataflows exchanged in A2A or B2B;

– supervision and audit of technical and business transformations;

– process supervision;

– quality of service supervision;

– business supervision.

20 Or again, the exchange process sub-level.

Chapter 8

Integration and IT Urbanization

Discussing application integration without linking it to the problem of IT urbanization would be to miss much of the goal that we have set ourselves in this book.

"IT urbanization" is an approach and a discipline in its own right, whose methodological advances have made possible sustainable development of the information system based on segmentation into business blocks, and the implementation of rules for constructing these blocks (for more information see section 4.2 and the work of Jacques Sassoon [SAS 98]).

Our idea here is less to develop the themes behind the urbanization of information systems than to use its concepts and its operational realities for indicating how an approach that links application integration with IT urbanization can multiply benefits and return on investment, making IT more reactive to business developments.

8.1. IT urbanization review

The term "IT urbanization" clearly refers to the range of problems in "urban (or "city") planning":

– each district has its own characteristics (residences, offices, shops, recreation, etc.). An information system can similarly be divided into zones;

– each application can plug into and use a certain number of shared services (messaging system, file transfer, translators, etc.);

– each application can be renovated or rewritten without leading to disturbances in other IT applications (at least, this is the target objective);

– IT urbanism therefore consists of defining the different business components and their modes of assembly.

Since the business of the enterprise has a longer lifespan than the technologies in computing, segmentation into blocks favors, for reasons of stability, the larger functions of the enterprise and their interaction with the outside world: clients, suppliers, production of goods and services, orders, deliveries, billing, management internal, supervision, etc.

IT urbanism strives to create a global plan for the various blocks comprising the enterprise information system and the interactions between those blocks (see section 4.2.1).

Standardized rules for the construction of blocks[21] and for exchange management between them[22] constitute the core of IT urbanism, bringing a cross-department standardization to all domains of the enterprise, and therefore, reduced cost and increased IT reactivity in the face of technological and business developments.

Even if they start from different points of departure, the convergence between urbanism and application integration jumps off the page:

– application integration seeks to standardize modes of information exchange between applications in the information system;

– IT urbanism recommends using a "flow manager" that responds to standard rules;

– IT urbanism counsels a framework for construction of applications, for which many rules are the same as those of application integration (events, asynchronism, autonomy).

Curiously little methodological work has been conducted into getting the most out of the two approaches. Below, we indicate the principal lines.

---

21 Rules of membership, autonomy, asynchronism, anchor points, properties of data and normalization of results.

22 Rule of "dataflow management".

8.2. Limits of urbanization without an integration solution

Policies of IT urbanization have been deployed principally in large enterprises throughout Europe[23]. Essentially they have consisted of incorporating the development model for computing applications into the rules of urbanism. Norms and methods have been published to this end: it remains only for development teams to apply them, which does not always happen. Business managers can sometimes, if not often, consider these norms as constraints that weigh down the development workload and cause schedules to drift.

It should be clearly understood that, viewed by the department heads, the urbanization of computing applications does not seem at first glance to be of much help. The reactivity, flexibility and adaptability of urbanized applications is only observable over the long haul.

What good does it do to spend more time and money, while the business side is often demanding short-term results?

IT urbanism rests in fact on the good will of both business and IT actors, or the sustained vision of certain key players in the enterprise. There is no operational necessity to implementing it.

8.3. How do integration solutions support IT urbanization?

The implementation of application integration solutions can change the situation, by making most of the rules of urbanization operational or even mandatory:

– the use of an exchange platform or of a flow manager drives the applications to publish information under a structured form that represents a business event, hence the requirement for events published or subscribed to by the applications;

– the asynchronism of integration solutions prompts applications to be able to receive the business events at any moment, and in any order, which in turn requires the application of asynchronous rules and standardization of the results;

– the orchestration of processes obliges applications to be able to send and receive events in unitary form, and therefore to apply the rules of autonomy and anchor points;

23 To a lesser degree in the USA and Canada since North American culture has more of a tendency to wipe the slate clean then reconstruct, than to alter the existing system little by little.

– the provision of an exchange platform favors the distribution and the functional coherence of repositories in the application network and corresponds to the application of rules of membership and data properties.

The integration solution will not only handle applying the rules of urbanization proper to exchange management between applications, but it will also have a consequent effect on the rules of urbanization proper to the intra-application construction.

8.4. Limits of integration solutions without IT urbanization

It is entirely technically possible to implement integration solutions without applying the particular rules of urbanization.

It is true that, over time, these solutions have integrated certain functionalities precisely to make it possible not to be overly concerned with certain rules of urbanization:

– the provision of technical connectors that can "navigate" in the databases, in order to reconstruct a business event;

– the possibility of creating, inside "integrations", rules that are so complex that they would tend to be substituted for certain application processes, to the detriment of maintainability and performance.

The implementation of integration solutions without relying on all or some of the rules of urbanization can lead back to a purely technical enterprise, with the risk of recreating precisely the complexity of exchanges inside the solution that we had sought to simplify by applying the solution.

8.5. How does IT urbanization support integration solutions?

In fact the application of the urbanization rules facilitates the more general use of integration solutions, notably on the following points:

– rapid implementation of SOAs and orchestration of processes via the event-based approach and the rules of asynchronism;

– maximal use of the flow managers via the event-based approach, asynchronism rules, and data ownership;

– readability and ease of maintenance of parameter settings for integration engines via the event-based approach.

8.6. The need to correlate integration solutions and urbanization

There remains therefore a methodological project that aims to correlate the two approaches:

– in governance terms, by seeking to group both urbanization and the integration solution inside the same organization of cells or departments;

– in coherence terms, by coupling and aligning models of urbanization on the one hand, and design and execution of the integration solutions on the other hand.

– finally, in human terms, by helping staff with predominantly research and methodology profiles collaborate – and not simply cohabitate – with the operational teams in development and parameter definition, as well as with teams that use the data.

Chapter 9

Choosing an Application Integration Solution

9.1. General approach

Application integration is an approach which both imposes and helps to produce structure, an approach that commits the enterprise for many years. These justify an organized approach to finding the solution and the partner that assist in implementation.

The present chapter does not have the ambition of treating in detail the approach to choosing a software solution for enterprises. We will focus only on the elements related to application integration. Figure 9.1 illustrates the global approach to this choice.

9.2. Methodology for calculating return on investment (ROI)

9.2.1. *Introduction to the method*

When it comes to application integration, calculations of return on investment (ROI) are not simple to determine. In the absence of credibility, a number of approaches to choosing a solution do not incorporate such calculations. Such calculations can, however, be useful, because they objectify the perceptions and intuitions of decision-makers, and lead the approach to choosing the solution. They may also help convince decision-makers to free up the necessary budgets.

ROI can be represented by the following equation:

$$\mathbf{ROI} = \Sigma_{\mathbf{1\ to\ N}}\ \mathbf{\Delta(GAINS - LOAD)\ n}$$

where:

– **GAINS (n)** is the sum of the benefits of integration for year n;

– **LOAD (n)** is the sum of the workload in integration for year n;

– $\Sigma_{\mathbf{1\ to\ N}}$ the algebraic sum of the delta Δ(Gains – Load) in each year.

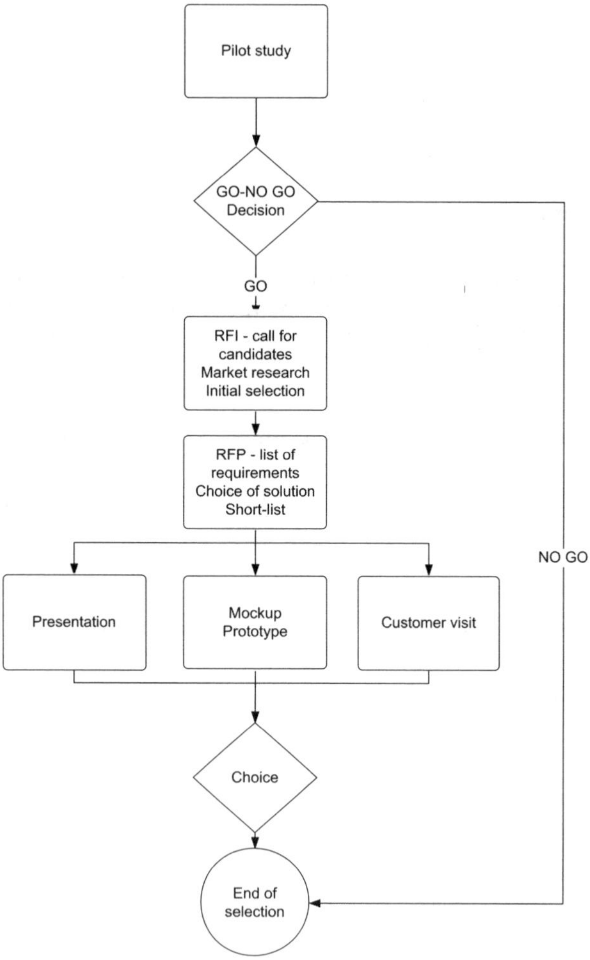

Figure 9.1. *Application integration: choice of solution*

In general, there are no particular difficulties in measuring work and other loads.[24] Nothing important should be omitted.

Here we find the following costs:

– initial usage rights for the solution (license of the software packages);

– annual usage rights including maintenance/evolution and support of the solution (maintenance);

– charges for training users on the solution;

– charges for designing and setting parameters of the solution;

– charges for implementing the solution:

- purchasing and hosting of hardware and basic software;

- technical operation;

- training the operators;

- adapting operating procedures;

- industrializing solution deployment;

– change management, organizational adaptation:

- management, operational coordination;

- alignment of the integration service with the projects that use it.

On the other hand, the benefits of the application integration solution are not easy to measure. They are expressed either in terms of load reduction, or in terms of benefit in revenues.

It is usual to look for the benefits of productivity in the workstation where the parameters for the integration engine ensure functions for checking, enriching and transforming the dataflows.

Numerous providers of application integration solutions announce average benefits of the order of 40% with respect to classic development solutions.[25]

The fact that many application integration solutions in fact utilize third-generation languages such as Java does not make it easy to achieve the advertised

24 For the budgetary allocation of charges, see section 10.4.

25 We will see that this value is in fact situated in the upper range of possible benefits with respect to classic solutions.

benefit (even if we could suppose that the integration tool avoids coding all the algorithmic portion).

Our experience in the implementation of application integration solutions allows us to define and quantify the benefits with respect to a classic solution on the three following focus points:

– development/maintenance workload;

– operating workload;

– improvement in the quality of service.

9.2.2. *Equations: maintaining the language of integration*

The annual benefit to the workload of development/maintenance with respect to classic development can be expressed initially by the Equation for Gains in Maintenance:

EGM = Gmin + (Gvar *ModRate * (100 -%3GL)/100)

where:

– **Gmin** is the minimum benefit observed compared to classic development (due to the common approach of interface parameterization which an application integration solution provides). Its average value is 0.2 or 20%. Its maximum value is 0.4.

– **Gvar** is the "plate" on which are poised the benefits linked to the type of language used and to the annual percentage of modification to the parameter settings. *Gvar = (1 - Gmin)*. Its average value is then 0.8.

– **ModRate** specifies the percentage of annual modification to the parameter settings of the application integration solution.

– **%3GL** is the percentage of use of a third-generation language (C, Java, COBOL, etc.) set in the solution parameter settings.

By directly applying the average values of Gmin and therefore Gvar, the EGM resulted in the following Equation for Gains in Maintenance: Simplified version:

EGMS = 0.2 + (0.8 *ModRate * (100 -%3GL)/100)

9.2.2.1. *Value of the EGMS with a high-level parameter language*

Where 20% of the parameter settings are modified each year, and where a third-generation language is used for only 20% of the total parameter settings in the application integration solution, the benefit is as follows:

EGMS = 0.2 + (0.8 *0.2 * (100 - 20)/100) = 0.33 or **33%**

9.2.2.2. *Value of EGMS with a 3GL for parameters*

For a rate of modification to parameter settings of 20% per year, and the use of a third-generation language to ensure 80% of the total parameter settings in the application integration solution, the benefit is as follows:

EGMS = 0.2 + (0.8 *0.2 * (100 - 80)/100) = 0.23 or **23%**

The EGMS gives indicative values, providing orders of magnitude that can sometimes be used to compare specific application integration solutions.

At the same time, if we wanted to be more specific, we cling to using the full EGM instead, and produce a specific value for Gmin. This value oscillates between 10% and 40% (0.1 to 0.4).

Its value is principally a function of:

– the number of applications and the daily dataflows to be processed;

– the degree of "dispersal" of the applications within the infrastructure;

– the degree of duplication of parameter settings in the integration solution.

It takes its optimal value, i.e., 0.4 or 40%, in the case of the generalized use of an application integration solution applied to the information systems of large enterprises, for one of:

– a number of applications greater than 150;

– a distribution of the applications over more than 50 machines;

– a number of dataflows to be processed daily in excess of 2,000 files or 100,000 messages modification;

– a degree of reuse of parameter settings of at least 20%.

In this case, the EGM is equal to:

EGM = 0.4 + (0.6 *0.2 * (100 - 20)/100) = roughly 0.5 or **50%**

9.2.3. *Operational workload gains through centralized supervision*

Benefits in terms of operation should not be looked for in functions for routing, checking, transforming and enriching, but rather in the contributions around technical supervision of the application integration solution, reducing the manual workload by verifying that dataflows have correctly been made available.[26]

The more dataflows that must be managed between applications, the more those applications will be "dispersed" inside the extended enterprise on heterogenous and remote machines, and the greater the benefits conferred by centralized supervision of the dataflows.

We can use the following equation to quantify the number of person/days of operation freed (NbDF) by the integration solution:

$$\mathbf{NbDF = NbPD * (f(NbSites) + f' (NbDataflows))}$$

where:

– **NbPD**: number of person/days dedicated to manual surveillance of flows;[27]

– **NbSites**: number of machines supervised by the integration solution;

– **NbDataflows**: number of flows exchanged daily by the integration solution.

The functions f and f' applied respectively to the parameters NbSites and NbDataflows are exponential (x) then logarithmic (x), where x represents respectively NbSites or NbDataflows.

Some discrete values of these functions – product of our experience – are indicated below and allow the calculation of the number of days of operation freed up.

---

26 We presuppose here that we mostly have to supervise file dataflows.

27 In some large enterprises, thousands of person/days each year can be dedicated to tracking dataflows.

Value of NbSites between	**Value of F (NbSites)**	**Value of NbDataflows range**	**Value of f '(NbDataflows)**
1	0.1	Less than 100	0.1
> 2 and <= 5	0.2	> 100 and <= 200	0.2
> 5 and <= 10	0.3	> 200 and <= 500	0.3
> 10 and <= 20	0.35	> 500 and <= 1,200	0.35
> 20	0.40	> 1,200	0.40

Table 9.1. *Table of values for f(NbSites) and f'(NbDataflows)*

Thus, the implementation of centralized dataflow supervision on a single computing machine for fewer than 100 file dataflows per day will show a benefit of 20% of the number of days of operation dedicated to manual surveillance of the dataflows.

Turning that around, centralized supervision of dataflows that transit more than 20 machines and more than 1,200 file flows per day leads to a benefit of 80% in the number of days of operation dedicated to manual surveillance of the dataflows.

Here again this equation gives indicative values – compared, we should remember, to manual supervision – for evaluating the return on investment of the solution in this area.

9.2.4. *Quality of service improvements*

Of the three major criteria used to measure the ROI from an application integration solution, improvement to quality of service is probably the one that brings the most significant benefits. However, it is also the most difficult to measure generically, independently of the business context for the enterprise and of the characteristics of the service contracts that it sets up internally or with clients.

One of the objectives in the implementation of an application integration solution is the improvement in the quality of service supplied by the information system:

– the solution has functions for supervising dataflows and processes that let the enterprise react to malfunctions of the system in a shorter time;

– the solution increases the quality – technical and functional – of the data exchanged between the applications of the information system.

As the two examples below illustrate, this increased reactivity can manifest itself by a reduction in loss of revenues or an increase of respect for quality of service.

9.2.4.1. *Reduction of the direct loss of revenues*

An international enterprise in the domain of telecommunications sees its revenues hinge on "collection tickets" recovered through its telecom network.

At the level of the information system, these tickets are found in the form of files that are created, then transported within the network.

With the approach to application integration which was in place at the time, a low percentage of these files (but significant when converted into equivalent revenues) could not be handled using normal billing techniques:

– files saved but not sent (bad "timing" in certain cases);

– files sent to an incorrect address, therefore not processed;

– files corrupted following transmission problems;

– etc.

The implementation of an application integration solution on a more secured protocol layer conjoined with the implementation of dataflow supervision with alert management made it possible to divide the percentage of files in error by 10.

In other words, the enterprise recovered 90% of previously lost revenues.

The corresponding investment was amortized in two months.

The opportunity study had projected that the rate of files in error would fall by a factor of 5.

9.2.4.2. *Respect of Quality of Service*

A bank executes an order from one of its large clients concerning a large transfer of funds between the parent company of the enterprise and one of its subsidiaries. For reasons linked to the switch to the Euro currency, this order is not executed on time and in time. Since the subsidiary's account is not sufficiently funded, a large overdraft risk occurs, which the bank in question would have to cover, since it must respect its quality of service agreement. The bank will therefore bear the cost of the overdraft during the 24 hours needed to regularize the account.

Fortunately for the bank, some months beforehand, they had put in place a supervision system over sensitive dataflows with the help of an application integration solution. A system of alerting is triggered before “cut off” that allows the bank to react before it is too late. The account is therefore correctly credited on time and in time.

Taking account of the sums involved, the investment in an application integration solution was covered by detecting this single alert before it was too late.

9.3. Opportunity study

Setting up one or more application integration solutions inside an enterprise is neither trivial nor easy.

The business managers, who are also frequently the ones with the investment budgets, may not necessarily see the interest. They can (wrongly) view application integration as a purely technical approach which will, at best, optimize the workload involved in developing interfaces between applications.

Few business managers naturally suggest implementing application integration solutions, though regulatory obligations in auditing are behind the notable exception of domains such as inputting accounting and financial back-office systems.

For project execution teams, and for operational computing services, the need is often perceived as a structuring response to increase the reactivity of the information system in the face of business developments. For all of that, it is not always easy to step back from the daily grind to structure an approach to choosing a solution.

In the majority of cases, an opportunity study is to be carried out.

To increase the chances for success, i.e., to reach a decision about whether or not subsequently to appeal to the market, several conditions need to be brought together:

– search for a business “sponsor” interested in the approach (possibly even the reader);

– identify at least one business or technical domain that seems “naturally” to call for an application integration solution;

– go into some detail on the subject via specialized reading, participation in conferences or seminars on the theme;

– present the approach to management and obtain a budget for this opportunity study (which in our opinion will require a range of from 10 to 20 person/days).

The opportunity study must absolutely be directed by an employee of the enterprise, identified and recognized as such and assisted if necessary by external consultants.

We will not describe a standardized "boilerplate" study. We know that all consultancy firms offer one of their own, more or less derived from their previous experience in this domain. Instead, we indicate below questions and points for processing that seem key to us, even it means subsequently going into more detail during the RFP phase.

9.3.1. *Analyzing the real needs of the enterprise*

For this, targeted interviews must be conducted with key collaborators who confront integration problems, ideally one employee each from operations, from R&D, and from the business side.

These interviews should reveal which requirements must be handled "right away", and which form part of an ideal target vision that the collaborator would put on a wish-list.

The objective is to extract "obvious" improvement points. It is not uncommon that at the end of the interviews, basic needs such as the secured exchange of dataflows (files, messages, HTTP, SMTP) constitute the major desired axis for short term improvement.

9.3.2. *Real needs and the "state of the art"*

The goal of reading the specialized press or seeking the help of external consultants is to rapidly find an initial match between internal needs and offerings on the market.

Discernment is required when reading the messages of software providers, most of whom prefer to present avant-garde technologies, such as SOA-type solutions for example, while most of their clients' projects will be based on EAI solutions or a B2B platform.

We recommend updating an initial matrix of Need and Service Level with the Software Provider, clearing the view to an initial orientation in terms of potential suppliers.

9.3.3. *Identifying possible business benefits*

This analysis is paramount if we want subsequently to proceed to acquiring a solution.

The ideal situation calculates potential benefits that can be directly measured in terms of gain – or at least of non-loss – either of revenues, or of quality of service failures leading to penalties for clients (as we illustrate in section 9.2).

9.4. Go/NoGo from General Management

This meeting is to be convened if:

– the opportunity study attracted interest in the implementation of an application integration solution;

– commercial solutions were rapidly identified, and seem at first glance to correspond to the requirements;

– an internal “sponsor” is ready to lend support to choosing a solution.

The main input to the meeting is the prior distribution of the *Conclusions* document from the opportunity study.

The meeting must be conducted with a deliverable presentation (typically slide show or video) that:

– summarizes the expectations and conclusions of the study, in particular expected costs and ROI;

– suggests a way to continue the study;

– indicates the principal logics in future cost allocation (see section 10.4).

General Management decides whether to continue via a Request for Information (RFI) or a Request for Proposal (RFP).

At the conclusion of the study phase, if the choice to acquire was made, then the Go/NoGo meeting of General Management has the further advantage of sensitizing the department heads to the implementation of an application integration project from the beginning. This could turn out to be useful later.

9.5. The search for a candidate: Request for Information (RFI)

9.5.1. *Why issue an RFI?*

The RFI, an address to candidate providers, is not a mandatory step. It generates work and delay. It is however necessary in European RFP approaches. And, it can be useful, particularly in cases where the opportunity study has brought the following requirements to light:

– a multiplicity of needs that require clarification in the types of offerings available;

– need for better knowledge of commercial providers;

– the identified providers are not already known by the enterprise.

9.5.2. *Key points in an integration RFI*

The objective is to learn more about the state of the art of the application integration offerings and their providers, then to preselect providers who can subsequently respond to the RFP in the next phase.

Types of suppliers who could be addressed include:

– a software provider able to provide integration solutions in the form of software package components;

– an associated integrator to offer prepackaged integration solutions;

– a global provider, combining provider with integrator, reducing the number of external contacts for the project to just one.

There is no "typical" answer. At the same time, since the RFI tends to center on the state of the art, we recommend sending it to software providers and global providers.

We also recommend fairly wide distribution for the RFI:

– top worldwide or European[28] suppliers;

28 The list of top providers in Europe is often different from the worldwide list.

– national or local suppliers who are already known and referenced by the enterprise.

The content of an RFI should show up at least the following points:

– synopsis of the problem to be processed;

– request for information about the solution(s) put forward by the provider;

– information about the corporation, in particular:

- type of support in your geographical domain(s);[29]

- resources for delivering services;

- partnerships with integrator(s);

– similar references and possibly client contacts.

9.6. Request for Proposal (RFP) or specifications document

9.6.1. *Interest and spirit of an RFP*

The RFP, or *specifications* document, comprises the central document for choosing an application integration solution partner. Following the results of the RFI, or the orientation flowing from the requirements, different types of partners could be considered:

– providers of integration software packages;

– integrators, who provide a prepackaged solution of component products;

– global providers.

The RFP document must try to characterize the specific enterprise requirements, and the specific solution expectations, including assistance from and vendor commitment to completing the project.

9.6.2. *Myths: standard questionnaire + one-stop supplier*

One of the mandatory steps in the RFP process involves providing a questionnaire that asks the provider to position their solution in terms of service levels and conditions of implementation and operation.

29 And worldwide for enterprises whose activity is also worldwide.

A significant number of consulting firms in the area of choosing application integration solutions offer typical questionnaires, enriched over the course of their successive experience. The reuse of these questionnaires can help accelerate the process of writing the RFP, and ensure that nothing important is forgotten.

However, they are often too general for specific enterprise requirements.

In addition, by using standard questionnaires originally from a particular consulting firm, it is not uncommon that providers already have the corresponding standard answers.

How then can we be sure that the provider will understand the real need of the enterprise if that need is "drowned" in a questionnaire that is too rich in requirements and questions?

To be efficient, the RFP requirements and questions absolutely must be prioritized around the principal functions needed in the enterprise. Without this, it will not be possible to discern which service levels are essential and which are ultimately accessory.

It is more worthwhile to select the questions that are important to the context of the enterprise, and put the emphasis on how the provider responds to those questions.

9.6.3. *Key points in an RFP for application integration*

Let us recall that our objective is not to provide a complete treatise on finalizing IT specifications, but rather to indicate the points in the context of application integration that appear key to us.

9.6.3.1. *Enterprise interest in an application integration solution*

Reminders:

– take account of general issues for the enterprise (departments, perspectives);

– recall how the implementation of an application integration solution is strategic for the enterprise.

9.6.3.2. *Expression of need*

– Recall the business objectives, both initial and target.

– Indicate the technical constraints, initial and target.

– Indicate the organizational context, initial and target.

9.6.3.3. *Expectations from the provider*

Depending on individual cases, the enterprise is looking for a provider:

– of component software packages;

– of a prepackaged application integration solution;

– of a complete turnkey solution with implementation services;

– to be a partner who can help with enterprise needs in the medium- and long-term.

9.6.3.4. *Standardized responses and selection criteria*

To get straight to the point but still be sure that important aspects are correctly emphasized, a standardized response form is required.

From our point of view, this form should incorporate at a minimum:

– comprehension of the need;

– presentation of the solution;

  - logical architecture;

  - physical architecture;

– key points for the success of the project;

– content and modes of access to support services;

– services of support;

– level of commitment;

– financial proposition;

– similar references;

– presentation of the provider;

  - key figures,

  - the weight of application integration in its market,

  - sales force, services, R&D in Europe – around the world.

9.7. Presentations from the candidates

The delivery of a concise response dossier is an important step. However, the rather formal character of written responses must be clarified by a kind of "thesis defense" where the tenderers present their response.

This presentation should reuse the same framework as the standardized form. It will be completed by questions asked in Q&A after the response dossier is read by the enterprise. Sometimes, an illustration of the solution will be supplied. The objective is not to demonstrate the solution or ensure a lightning-fast training course, but rather to contribute to a better understanding of the response.

The presentation is a special moment where a relationships level can be established beyond the purely objective aspects. Certainly, such a presentation makes it easier to gauge the tenderer's real commitment to long-term support for the enterprise in its approach to integration.

Chapter 10

Deployment Methodology

10.1. Introduction to the method

The deployment of an application integration solution must respond to sometimes contradictory objectives:

– deploying the solution at the earliest time, to serve the first project that will use it;

– setting up an exchange infrastructure that is stable enough over time that it does not have to be modified every time a new project wants to use it;

– producing norms and rules for using the solution in order to maintain overall coherence and adjust the possible incompatibilities between projects;

– giving each project sufficient autonomy of implementation so that solution use is pertinent in its context;

– capitalizing on project experience to generalize rules for follow-up projects.

The task is not easy. It is therefore particularly important to suggest a method for deploying application integration solutions whose principal objective will be to bring project constraints, infrastructural norms, capitalization and acquired experience into harmonious coexistence.

Below, we present the principal lines.

10.2. Deployment methodology: general principles

The implementation of an application integration solution must align with a program that is only launched (initialized) after selecting the solution. This program involves permanent resource elements (the competency center) as well as tasks to be ensured (quality assurance, communication, support, capitalization). It also calls on ad-hoc resources during the implementation of projects between this or that application.

The method proposes a global approach that, from the outset, includes a long-term vision and stepped deployments (Figure 10.1).

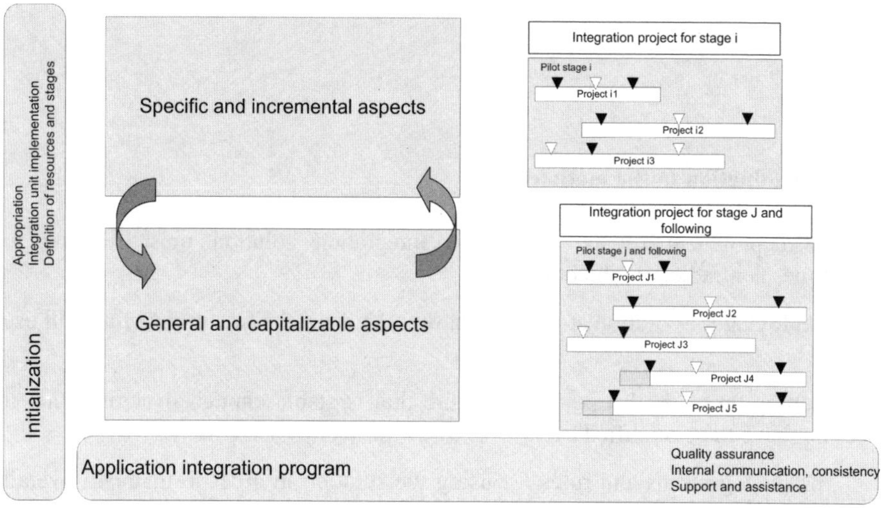

Figure 10.1. *Deployment methodology*

These deployments will be of two orders:

– at the level of the application integration infrastructure, successive versions of this infrastructure are implemented at different levels:

- Project ⇒ Department ⇒ Enterprise ⇒ Extended enterprise;

- per operating system;

- per level of application integration service;

- etc.;

– at the level of each integration project, between applications that are selected according to departmental needs.

Some recommendations can be made:

– deploying a version of the integration infrastructure involves much more than just taking account of the constraints of projects that will use it;

– the frequency of infrastructure versions must be lower than the frequency of project implementations;

– it is important to look for incremental "edges" between successive versions, so as not to put the whole of a previous version in question, and thus require a complete re-test;

– at the same time the application integration solution is launched, a capitalization program must be put in place;

– this capitalization program is input from development activities carried out during projects, by determining what will be useful in subsequent projects;

– the project launch phase can involve generic aspects that have already been capitalized on;

– the project assessment phase can involve looking for developments that could be capitalized;

– the project initialization phase must immediately define objectives, quantifying the means to establish scheduling;

– an application integration competency center is recommended at the same time as the initialization phase;

– the generic (capitalizable) aspects most often encountered include:

- technical or business connectors;

- access to enterprise repositories to check the dataflows;

- definitions of pivot formats;

- industrialization of parameter settings for transformations;

- solution integration tests;

- audit trails and supervision of the dataflows;

- best practice recommendations for integration components;

- frequently asked questions ("FAQ").

– the long-term vision specified during the initialization phase can be adjusted over time, as long as the new vision changes only incrementally from the previous one.

10.3. Special case: deploying BPM and SOA

The recommendations indicated above are just as valid for application integration solutions that use BPM tools and SOA.

At the same time, given that these approaches are naturally horizontal, cross-domain and event-based, we must also focus on the following points:

– knowing how to identify processes that really create value for the enterprise and exhibit rapid ROI (above all for the initial projects);

– assessing the "service oriented" character of applications that interact with the process;

– extracting the necessary adaptations and know-how from the application to evaluate the impact on costs and delays;

– ensuring benchmarks and measuring the scalability capacities of the solution;

– including the necessary preproduction site in the projections;

– modeling all combinations of recycling and rollback within processes.

10.4. Economic models of cost allocation

As soon as the use of application integration solutions exceeds the frame of a single organizational domain – which is often the case – then objective rules for sharing costs must be established. If this step is omitted, then the rule of the strongest or cleverest is applied. The predictable consequence will drag down the generalization of the use of the integration solution.

Different models can be put forward to distribute the cost of investments and operation.

10.4.1. *Cost allocation linked to usage*

The easiest economic model for allocating recurring costs in an application integration solution allocates costs by system use.

10.4.1.1. *Cost allocation linked to traffic*

As a variable, we will use a simple indicator: the number of dataflows emitted by one application.

This presupposes the availability of consolidated statistics on dataflow activity transiting the solution, which can then be used to set up a cost allocation table.

However, it can be useful to distinguish two types of projects:

– projects that address a specific enterprise domain, with its own operating budget;

– projects referred to as "horizontal", that concern a group of domains;

Depending on the project type, and on the activity of the measured dataflows, the rule for cost allocation will be as follows:

Domain Project

%CsDo = NbDataflowsDo/NbDataflowsT

where:

– **%CsDo** is the percentage of consumption of the domain;

– **NbDataflowsDo** is the number of dataflows measured for the domain;

– **NbDataflowsT** is the number of total dataflows measured for all domains.

The calculated percentage is applied to the total amount of the costs to be distributed, then billed back to the domain.

Horizontal Project

%CsCD = NbDataflowsCD/NbDataflowsT

where:

– **%CsCD** is the percentage of consumption of the horizontal project (Cross-Department);

– **NbDataflowsCD** is the number of dataflows measured for the horizontal project;

– **NbDataflowsT** is the total number of dataflows measured for all domains.

The calculated percentage is applied to the total amount of the costs, and depending on allocation keys (such as revenues of the domain, number of users, number of computing sites or production centers), distributed over the complete set of eligible domains.

Allocating costs in horizontal (cross-department) projects *to the complete set of eligible domains and not just to the domains in operation at the instant T* is an incentive model that favors the use of the application integration solution.

As for new projects, estimations of recurring costs can be based on projections supplied by the domains, in a way that rapidly communicates the future costs that must be accounted for.

10.4.1.2. *Cost allocation linked to processes*

Here again, as for our variable, we will use a simple indicator: the number of task instances executed by the solution.

Once again, we distinguish the same two types of projects:

– projects that address a specific enterprise domain, with its own operating budget;

– projects referred to as "horizontal", that concern a group of domains;

– depending on the project type, and on the number of process instances that are measured, the rule for cost allocation is as follows.

Domain Project

%CsDo = NbInstceDo/NbInstceT

where:

– **%CsDo** is the percentage of consumption of the domain;

– **NbInstceDo** is the number of instances measured for the domain;

– **NbInstceT** is the number of instances total measured for all domains.

The calculated percentage is applied to the total amount of the costs to be distributed, then billed back to the domain.

Horizontal Project

%CsCD = NbInstceCD/NbInstceT

where:

– **%CsCD** is the percentage of consumption of the horizontal project;

– **NbInstceCD is** the number of instances measured for the cross-department (horizontal) project;

– **NbInstceT** is the number of instances total measured for all domains.

The percentage calculated is applied to the total amount of the costs, and, depending on allocation keys (such as revenues of the domain, number of users, number of computing sites or production centers), distributed over the complete set of eligible domains.

Allocating costs in horizontal (cross-department) projects *to the complete set of eligible domains and not just to the domains in operation at the instant T* is an incentive model that favors the use of the application integration solution.

Concerning new projects, estimations of recurring costs can be based on projections provided by the domains, in a way that rapidly communicates the future costs to account for.

10.4.2. *Cost allocation linked to usage and services (developed model)*

The economic model presented above can be enriched to take account of new factors that influence recurring solution costs. Two new factors appear pertinent.

10.4.2.1. *Level of service requested by the domains*

A domain which uses the solution solely for transporting dataflows generates lower recurring costs than a domain which uses the solution for transport, transformation and routing. Cost allocation could therefore be calculated taking account of the service levels called on by a domain.

10.4.2.2. *Service contract or "Service Level Agreement" (SLA)*

Non-stop service coverage is more costly than "5/7" service coverage during traditional business hours. Cost allocation could therefore also be calculated taking the SLA into consideration.

10.4.2.3. *Principles of calculation*

Taking account of these two supplemental factors, this model for calculating cost allocation can be completed with a notation principle that evaluates each of the factors that must be considered.

As illustrative examples, we provide below the following notations for selected factors.

Notation linked to traffic

The notation can be based on a grid that shows different ranges for the number of dataflows. The following table presents a case in point.

Flow range	Note
1 to 100	1
100 to 500	2
500 to 1,000	3
> 1,000	4

Table 10.1. *Grid bracketing the number of dataflows*

Notation linked to processes

The following grid, also given as a case in point, presents a scoring based on the number of task instances.

Number of task instances	Note
< 5,000	1
Between 5,000 and 50,000	2
Between 50,000 and 500,000	3
> 500,000	4

Table 10.2. *Grid bracketing the number of task instances*

Notation linked to service levels

The notation grid for service levels could be as follows.

Services used	Note
Transport	1
Transport Transformation	3
Transport Transformation BAM Supervision	5
Transport Transformation BAM Supervision BPM Orchestration	8

Table 10.3. *Notation grid for service levels*

Notation linked to the SLA

The notation grid for the service level agreement could show the following.

SLA	Note
5-day Coverage (8:00 to 18:00)	1
7-day Coverage (8:00 to 18:00)	3
Non-stop Coverage	5

Table 10.4. *Notation grid for SLA*

10.4.2.4. *Equation for Restricted Allocation (ERA)*

For each domain, an evaluation of each factor must be established that applies the notation grids. The rule for calculating the percentage for billing recurring costs back to the domain is then the following:

$$Percentage_{Domain} = \frac{\left(\dfrac{Score_{Traffic}}{ScoreMax_{Traffic}} + \dfrac{Score_{Process}}{ScoreMax_{Process}} + \dfrac{Score_{Services}}{ScoreMax_{Services}} + \dfrac{Score_{SLA}}{ScoreMax_{SLA}}\right) * 100}{\sum_{Total} Score_{Domain}}$$

10.4.2.5. *Equation of General Allocation (EGA)*

To be even more specific, the notation principle could take account of weighting that gives precedence to one factor or another. For example, because the SLA is an important factor in evaluating recurring costs, it would weigh more strongly in the notation principle.

The rule of calculation thus becomes the following:

$$Percentage_{Domain} = \frac{\left(\dfrac{Score_{Trafic}}{ScoreMax_{Trafic}} * Weight_{Trafic} + \dfrac{Score_{Process}}{ScoreMax_{Process}} * Weight_{Process} + \dfrac{Score_{Services}}{ScoreMax_{Services}} * Weight_{Services} + \dfrac{Score_{SLA}}{ScoreMax_{SLA}} * Weight_{SLA}\right) * 100}{\sum_{Total} Scores * Weight_{Domain}}$$

The value of the weights, as well as of the notation grids, must be set judiciously by observing recurring costs depending on the factors applied to structure those costs.

10.4.2.6. *Impact of allocation types: case of an automobile manufacturer*

Context

With more than 20,000 connected partners, the integration focus for this automobile manufacturer is on its B2B problem. The reactivity required to process the demand definitely presupposes a high, practically non-stop coverage rate.

Moreover, an important criterion involves knowing what the traffic is in a number of dataflows to or from these partners, given that the manufacturer uses this traffic to bill its partners for services.

On the other hand, in this case, business transformation functions are unimportant, involving only technical transformations to the format (EDI, XML).

Selected parameters

The following parameters were defined to take account of traffic, service levels, timeslots for opening or SLA and balancing weights.

Traffic: flow bracket	Note
1 to 1,000	1
1,000 to 5,000	3
5,000 to 10,000	5
> 10,000	7

Table 10.5. *Notation on traffic*

Note: the daily volume of dataflows is on average 21,000, exclusively in the form of files.

Services used	Note
Transport	1
Transport Transformation	1.5
Transport Transformation Technical Supervision	2

Table 10.6. *Notation on services*

SLA	Note
5-day Coverage (9:00 to 18:00)	1
7-day Coverage (9:00 to 18:00)	3
Non-stop Coverage	5

Table 10.7. *Notation on SLA*

Weighting factor	Grade
Traffic	0.1
Services	0.3
SLA	0.6

Table 10.8. *Weighted*

Simulation and calculations for allocation types (ETA, ERA, EGA)

Supposing only three application domains, with no "horizontal" dataflows, the following table gives the percentages for traffic-based allocation (ETA), restricted allocation (ERA) or general allocation (EGA).

Domain	Number of dataflows	Services used	SLA	ETA	ERA	EGA
1	12,000	1.5	1	57.14%	31.49%	22.60%
2	7,000	1	3	33.33%	29.30%	29.52%
3	2,000	2	5	9.52%	39.22%	47.88%
Total	21,000			100%	100%	100%

Table 10.9. *Table for calculating allocation*

The diagrams below present allocation by traffic, restricted allocation and general allocation.

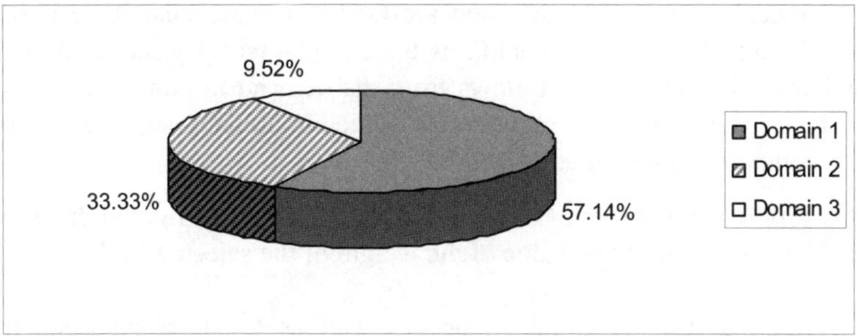

Figure 10.2. *Allocation by traffic*

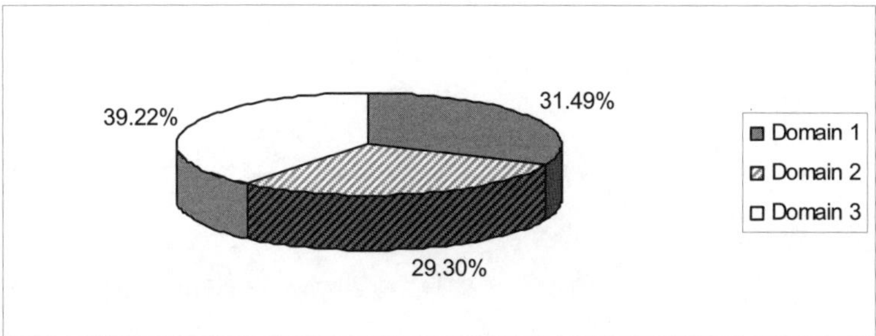

Figure 10.3. *Restricted allocation*

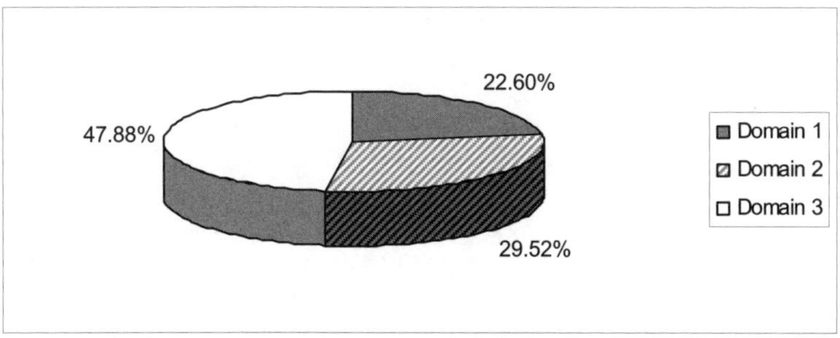

Figure 10.4. *General allocation*

Notes:

– calculations were performed with rounding;

– the choices in terms of allocation are far from innocuous, since if we apply ERA or still more EGA, then domain 3 is the one that will pay the most, despite its low number of dataflows. This follows from the demand in domain 3 for non-stop availability of the service, a requirement which mobilizes significant operating resources compared to the other domains;

– the difference between ERA and EGA is well highlighted here between domains 1 and 3, owing to the value of the weight of the selected SLA.

We recall that the weighting values as well as the notation grids must be established depending on the objectives that the enterprise sets for itself in terms of deploying the application integration solution, as well as the contribution of each domain. A prior study, using simulations, is therefore strongly recommended.

Chapter 11

Operational Examples of Implementation

The examples that follow are all taken from genuine, observed facts. For reasons of confidentiality, the business lines and some elements have been changed.

11.1 Rationalizing bond purchase order management (banking)

11.1.1. *The context*

Bermano Bank, a subsidiary of a large European bank, negotiates financial and derivative instrument products in different markets, ranging from highly regulated domestic markets, and extending to unquoted and international markets.

This diversity of instruments and markets is reflected in the diversity of the IT applications required in both the front-office and back-office to manage a variety of bonds. For historical reasons, as in all information systems, integration between these applications was carried out one step at a time, by creating point-to-point links, with all the consequences already mentioned in this work: frequent manual intervention to process errors, high maintenance costs throughout the system, technical touchups to make up for missing functions and correct breakdowns in processing purchase orders. Moreover, integration between certain applications relies on batches, which add complementary delays to the process of purchasing bonds.

The existing system is summarized by Figure 11.1.

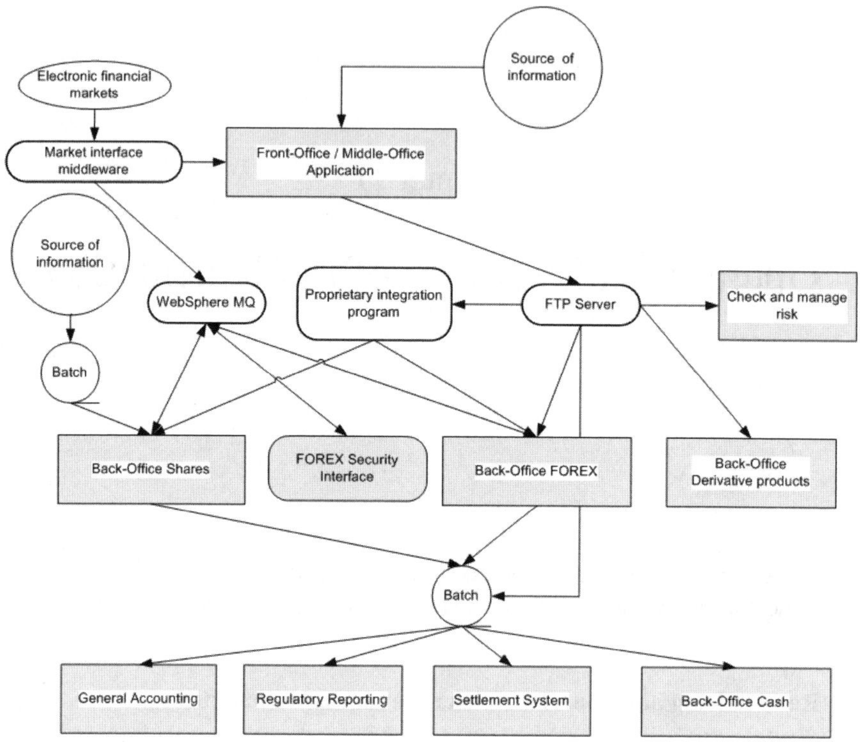

Figure 11.1. *Rationalization of bond purchase order management in a bank: "before"*

To improve the global functioning of *Bermano Bank*, an integration solution implementation study was therefore launched.

11.1.2. *The choices*

The project was conducted under the driving impulse of General Management and the CIO, who became deeply involved as it progressed. The study was entrusted to a consulting and systems integration firm that worked in concert with business users and IT staff.

Taking account of the hoped-for business objectives, it was decided to adopt an approach using processes, with the particular goals of eliminating human intervention whenever possible, and constructing interfaces that allowed operations to be aligned in time. In particular, the contemplated solution involved six of the fundamental applications of the enterprise and four different organizational entities.

For *Bermano Bank*, the integrator recommended the choice of an integration solution supplied by a commercial software provider, one which could respond to the needs and constraints of the project, including:

– a complete exchange infrastructure that integrates file mode and message mode;

– operation of this infrastructure on heterogenous platforms (z/OS, Unix, etc.);

– management of different formats, including XML, explaining the need for advanced and high-performance transformation functions;

– business process manager for modeling using the BPMN standard;

– complete system of supervision and Business Activity Monitoring.

A provider of an application integration solution which exhibited the desired characteristics was selected. The solution provider also supplied the specialists to help with implementation: training systems integrator and client personnel, installing and parameterizing components, defining global architecture of the system, etc.

To validate the approach and the functioning of the solution a prototype for managing foreign currency deposits was defined and launched. The problem of these deposits genuinely constituted a representative subset of the functionalities and the expected volumes that had to be processed.

When this prototype proved satisfactory, the solution was deployed.

11.1.3. *The solution*

To resolve the traditional problem of spaghetti architecture, the project put a complete integration solution in place. This solution relies on basic integration layers (transport, transformation, routing, etc.) but was extended to the layers for managing and automating the underlying business processes in handling purchase orders, by transparently orchestrating and combining the complete set of operations required to integrate the value chain. Figure 11.2 illustrates the project.

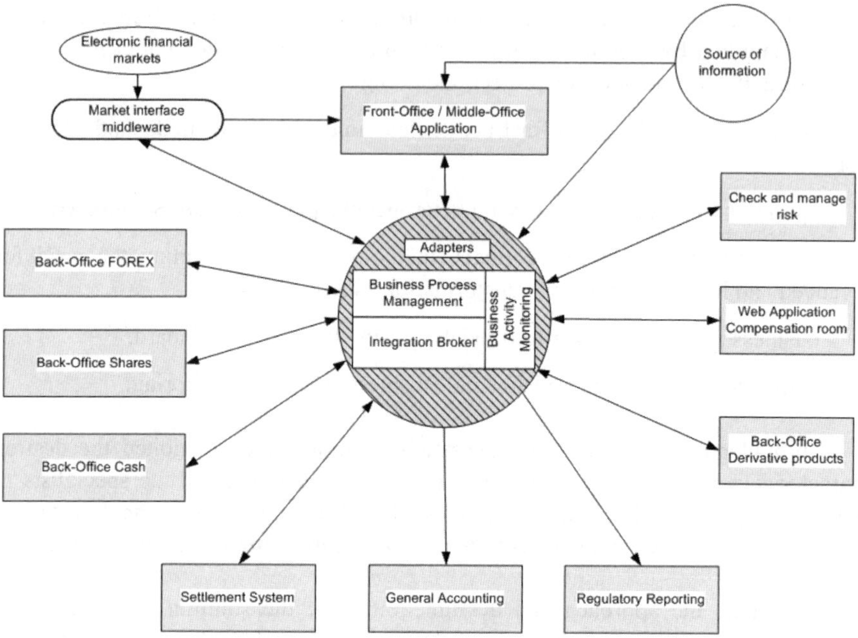

Figure 11.2. *Rationalization of bond purchase order management in a bank – "after" (Target Architecture)*

11.1.4. *The results*

With the implementation of this solution following a progressive and continually optimized deployment, *Bermano Bank* can now:

– execute its processes in real or near real time, removing the long pauses from execution times that were previously imposed by overnight batch processing requirements;

– automate most of the value chain, thus significantly reducing the costly human interventions that both generate errors and consume time;

– process greater volumes of orders at the least cost;

– reduce its exposure to financial risk by reducing the delays for handling and processing purchase orders;

– dispose of end-to-end, business-oriented tracking of processes, considerably improving the quality of customer service;

– benefit from greater visibility over operations via total traceability and reinforced operational security.

Beyond even purely business benefits, implementing the solution drastically reduced maintenance costs throughout the system, while conferring a new agility that made it easy to adapt business processes from end to end at the least cost.

The success of the project was principally due to:

– solid involvement of upper management;

– global, combined process/integration approach;

– judicious choice of prototype;

– use of a readable standard for modeling the processes (BPMN);

– work in common between the teams from *Bermano Bank*, the integrator and the solution provider.

In short, an almost ideal approach – and therefore a success.

11.2. An EAI hub (telecommunications)

11.2.1. *The context*

The enterprise *2M Telecom* is present in the world of telecommunications. The key word in this market is reactivity – to the competition, in flexible offerings and in anticipating the expectations of various customer categories.

True to this "high tech" image, *2M Telecom* decided to put in place an intra-enterprise EAI hub, whose fundamental points were the reliance on a message-type technology and an enhanced set of transformation functions. Mindful of the need for standards, the architecture department of the enterprise laid down the rule that all the applications must send and receive dataflows in "standard" XML.

11.2.2. *The choice*

The prototype proceeded entirely correctly. Questions about performance only came to light with the first results obtained from the transformation part of integration. However, since the "scalability" of the product had been checked, the possibility of simply adding machine power using open system infrastructures guaranteed both the necessary power, and therefore, success. Or so it was thought.

11.2.3. *Implementing the pilot: first difficulties*

When the choice of vendor was confirmed, an initial, pilot project was selected. At a functional level, very few concerns emerged; parameters for the transformation functions were easily set using the tool.

A first obstacle: the chosen applications were in fact exchanging information in files. In the time available, it was neither functionally necessary nor technically possible to modify them to produce and/or receive messages. In addition, the EAI vendor provided a "file adapter" (see section 3.1.3.2) that could read or write the file upstream/downstream from its integration engine.

Then, a second concern: for the slightly older existing applications, most file record formats used fixed position/length, though some used a variable format of "indicator ⇒ mnemonic ⇒ value". To respect the architectural rule imposing the use of XML, the following "simple" steps were required:

– for each application, use a specialized business adapter (see section 3.1.3.3) that can perform an initial transformation of fixed or variable format from the application to an XML format representing the format of the sending application and described in the EAI tool;

– ensure transformation via the EAI tool of the said XML format to a canonical XML format (this rule had also been imposed);

– ensure the transformation via the EAI tool of canonical XML format to the representative XML format for the receiving application, described in the EAI tool;

– use another specialized adapter so the receiving application can transform the initial XML format into the fixed format that it requires.

Result: simply transforming two fixed or variable formats required four steps, while at a technical level, we would have been happier with just one.

Then functional implementation began. No problem arose in transforming XML to XML; this is the domain of predilection for the EAI tool. On the other hand, adapters had to be completed, since by definition, no adapter on the market knows the format of the existing applications. Their completion took time – using two types of languages C and Java.

A question arose. How and when to adapt the adapter when the format required by the application shifted from fixed to variable, or vice versa?

The response from the architects was clear: all subsequent adaptation to the format of the existing applications required the application to natively produce the XML format described in the EAI hub.

The managers of the concerned applications viewed this as a additional burden asked of them with no business justification.

Who would pay the additional costs, the application's management team – who had the budget – or the CIO – who did not? For the pilot, the question remained unresolved, but it was obvious that this was a keystone for the generalization phase.

Functional tests could start after the necessary application adapters were developed, after the file adapters supplied by the provider were used, and after the correct parameters were set in the implemented EAI tool.

Functional reception was pronounced fairly rapidly, given that the transformation functions were relatively simple; the first pilot essentially had to validate the robustness and performance of the solution.

11.2.4. *Integration tests: disturbing results*

Tests for robustness are carried out jointly by R&D, who are responsible for the pilot project, and the operations team. The results are judged disturbing:

– *application adapters*: average results – in the case of operational problems, information was not always transmitted. If an item of information was posted, who processes it, and who decides the integrity of the processed file (keep the entire file? only allow correct records through?)?

– *file adapter*: not correct for the operation – for the needs of the EAI tool, the file was divided into messages. If an error arises during the transformation phase, the EAI tool does not natively know the integrity context for the records in what *used to be* the file. In other words, integrity has to be managed in the parameter settings of the EAI tool. This was an extra load for the integration tool;

– *transformation function, narrowly defined* – no particular problem encountered, other than the previous point.

11.2.5. *How did we end up here? Consequences of architectural choices*

The problems of integration and more still, the problems of performance, were the direct consequence of architectural choices:

– By favoring message mode for applications that deliver information in files, even by requesting a file connector – very significantly decreasing the performance of the EAI tool in a minimum ratio of 1 to 10 – since the EAI tool was working in message mode, it had to save the execution context with each message.

– An EAI tool that worked natively in file mode did not save its context in each message (each record) but rather in each file (or at most, in each collection of logically integrated records). Moreover, other things being equal, this explained the large differences in performance.

– By requiring the assurance of the four steps of adapters and transformers instead of just one (refer above), the architecture did not seek to optimize performance. In addition, the potential benefit from an EAI tool that directly transforms fixed formats into fixed or variable formats with respect to an architecture that relies on XML formats was estimated in a ratio of 1 to 5. The essential reason was due to the time required to parse an XML document, while by definition, there was no need for parsing fixed format, since the same information was always in the same place.

11.2.6. *Performance tests: catastrophic results*

– *Application adapters*: correct result. The developments requested subsequent to integration tests should not fundamentally change the data.

– *File adapter and transformation functions*: these results were judged catastrophic, in a ratio from 1 to 50 compared to the performance elements observed during the mockup. The experts from the provider were called in. After analysis of the parameter settings and application of the recommendations, the global observed benefit was an improvement by a factor of 1.5 – which meant the results went from 1 to 30. Taking the selected architecture into account, that was as far as it could go.

Managers on the enterprise side and on the integrator/provider side met. Initially, a conservation action contemplated an upgrade to the machines that supported the production hub. The financial consequences were not negligible. Technical managers on the enterprise side wondered how to announce the news to their management.

11.2.7. *Report card: final decision*

Faced with the final results and taking into account all of the investment that the enterprise had already agreed to, the pilot project achieved production with volume levels that created no particular problem.

As for generalizing to other projects, more or less explicit directives were issued, aimed at reserving the use of the EAI only during major application rebuilds (which cleared the problem of adaptation costs), favoring EAI only for exchanges that justified message mode.

When these elements were taken into account, generalization did not really take place. After four years of operation, EAI was only implemented on some 15 applications (the enterprise application base exceeds 150).

The vision of the business requirement team and those responsible for the project execution teams remain an elitist view of EAI: the tool may be functionally rich, but it was poorly adapted to mass generalization.

11.2.8. *The lesson: what we could have done*

Before taking decisions, the focus should have been on the principal requirement: transformation in file mode, searching for commercial tools that natively use the file channel, with all the associated performance.

At least temporarily following the choice of the EAI technology, the requirement was for XML ⇔ XML transformation, using EAI to natively process the fixed type formats sent and received by the applications. This led to a sharp increase in performance.

If the benefits turn out to be insufficient, then search for a new, commercially available tool that better conformed to the needs of the enterprise.

11.3. A2A and B2B (retail)

11.3.1. *The context*

With its network of more than 280 points-of-sale, *Union Distributors* offers household and leisure goods to the general public.

Its upstream activity was directly concerned with the product catalog (references and pricing) but also downstream by the tracking of the sales activity (payment of settlements). This context highlights the paramount importance of managing information dataflows between the points-of-sale and head office, since it was this that makes it possible to track the activity, determine the needs to be served and then launch delivery orders.

Problems were observed with the previous solution, both functionally (no integrity management on the dataflows) and technically (loss of data during dataflow transfers).

Since activity continued to increase, it became imperative to introduce security into the management of the dataflows between head office and the points-of-sale.

11.3.2. *The choice*

An audit had to be ensured when implementing an EAI exchange platform, to manage dataflows to all points-of-sale, logisticians and partners.

An EAI vendor was selected, initially on the basis of the vendor's solution but also for the vendor's capacity to implement the project.

11.3.3. *The solution*

The EAI platform was at the core of the information system for which it ensured all exchanges in real time:

– with points-of-sale in the form of file exchanges scheduled and performed using the protocols PeSIT or FTP;

– with central systems to an ERP, updating the processing center database via JDBC;

– with logisticians, who are integrated using file exchanges performed using the PeSIT protocol;

– with other providers, who use a secured access portal and exchange files on an HTTP link.

The platform was supervised using a tool for monitoring dataflows and posting alerts.

A component for technical and business transformation was also implemented.

The solution ensured data propagation and imposes data consistency.

11.3.4. *The results*

"Daily information exchanges between departmental applications and out to partners such as logisticians, were made dependable, secured and optimized."

"Supervision provides the expected level of visibility, exceptions are signaled without delay and problems can even be anticipated."

Thanks to the implementation of the platform, *Union Distributors* was able to deal with the Christmas peak in activity with no holdups, reducing the error rates usually recorded on the dataflows by a factor of three.

From that point on, *Union Distributors* disposed of a genuine supervision tool for its activity, and could function with flows held close to the level of its inventory.

Union Distributors was able to benefit from up to one half-day on the resupply of points-of-sale, leading to direct benefit on revenues, linked to the drastic drop in the number of out-of-stocks.

Every day, 2,500 exchanges and treatments of files were and are taken into account.

The platform is operational 24/7.

11.4. BPM and SOA in service delivery

11.4.1. *The context*

As a group with worldwide scope and "high tech" offerings for both enterprises and the general public, the *MenTech* corporation was confronted with an explosion in demand in its market. It needed to sharply optimize its processes for ordering and delivering goods and services. At the same time, the greater part of its information system was being rebuilt.

In the beginning, the process of going from order to delivery was ensured in large part manually, resulting in an average processing time measured in dozens of days, incompatible with the new demand from the market.

Not only was the number of orders increasing, but the marketing teams were being highly creative, presenting new offerings to a wider public in very short timeframes – weeks at the most – before the offerings were operational. For this reason, a traditional development approach around a dedicated application was not suitable.

11.4.2. *The choice*

MenTech's upper management decided to functionally optimize company processes,[30] implementing an innovative approach of "automated management of horizontal processes".

This took concrete form through the use of a BPM solution coupled with a services approach.[31]

11.4.3. *The solutions*

11.4.3.1. *Initial solution*

The first implementation based on a commercial BPM tool was satisfactory, right up to the point where the volume of orders to be processed became too large. Since the BPM tool operated synchronously with the applications, services or tasks that it called, there was therefore no possibility of processing in parallel. In the short term, it was therefore decided to parallelize the processing servers, with an allocation logic based on large geographical worldwide zones.

During that time, *MenTech* also produced specifications to send to the suppliers of BPM solutions. We summarize those specifications next.

11.4.3.2. *Needs*

"A powerful BPM tool that supports scalability, which can not only serve the existing process but also respond more generally to other needs in business process automation within the group."

"Technical and commercial production of mass ordering in short timeframes."

"Faster go-to-market for new offerings by utilizing existing applications and services."

"Process supervision to guarantee quality of service to the client."

---

30 While looking to reduce human interventions whenever possible.

31 Utilizing existing applications notably via an EAI-type integration layer.

"Support for manual tasks dedicated to the business players as part of automated processing."

"Grouped production servers to achieve economies of scale."

11.4.3.3. *Implementation of the target solution*

A BPM solution vendor, with a functionally and technically innovative product, was selected. Since the product was relatively young, it was subject to successive developments and optimizations during the implementation of the project.

Moreover, the solution relied on a MOM, an application server, an EAI tool, a DBMS, a tool for supervision and application services. This was a composite application using a services architecture.

11.4.4. *The results*

More than 95% of order processing currently uses tasks or activities that are automated. On average, the first task is activated 20 minutes after the application takes the order.

The average time for handling an order went down to less than three days.

The solution is capable of processing between 2 and 3 million orders monthly, i.e., 100,000 orders per day, with daily spikes of 150,000 to 200,000 orders. In point of fact, this was one of the largest implementations of BPM and SOA in the world today.

Direct ROI:

– reduction of costs following the grouping of the production servers;

– capacity to augment the number of orders processed without significant increase in resources.

Indirect ROI:

– innovative offerings go into production much faster;

– parts of the infrastructure are reused to handle other processes.

11.4.5. *Points to watch for this type of solution*

The project debriefing brought out key points to survey for this type of solution:

– to detect possible bottlenecks, implement tools to measure the performance and activity on each component in the solution;

– prepare a preproduction site equipped with all applications and business services;

– ensure progressive increase in workloads, functionally and technically;

– solution component experts should be called in without hesitation as soon as necessary for purposes of diagnosis or optimization propositions;

– use internal competences mastering the global architecture of the solution.

Conclusion

"Organizing the application territory and the communications between applications renders business process 'music' audible and harmonious. Metaphorically but genuinely, then, these are the issues in application integration."

This extract from Chapter 2 of this book highlights our concern of placing application integration at the heart of strategic thinking about the evolution – none speak of governance – of the corporate information system.

The objective of this book was to organize thinking about the subject, to explore new trails, and to position the subject in all its dimensions, whether technical, organizational or business. It does not have the ambition of constituting the detailed operations guide to the procedures to be implemented to make the information system permanently reactive to business developments.

These subjects are not therefore closed, and merit ongoing exploration. As consultants, trainers, project directors and designers of software packages for application integration, we are participating in that exploration along with teams from Axway, particularly in the principal themes that we have developed in this book, such as:

– propagating data advisedly, via the data or the events;

– knowing how to distinguish inter-application problems from intra-application problems;

– finding the right balance between integration through dataflows and integration through processes;

– using business adapters correctly;

– the interest in supervising the business as soon as the infrastructure was dependable;

– using the different types of format advisedly, including XML;

– static routing and dynamic routing – how (and if) to choose;

– striking the right balance between setting parameters and writing code;

– coherence and complementarity of models for processes and for integration;

– making service-oriented approaches and infrastructures into concrete realities;

– impact of SOA approaches on the existing applications;

– advantages and drawbacks of hub and bus architectures;

– articulating the service levels inside an integration platform;

– familiarity with the types of application integration tools;

– application integration: a product, yes, but also a project to be constructed;

– avoiding obstacles and accepted wisdom in application integration;

– urbanization and application integration: a winning duo;

– judiciously choosing an integration solution and a provider;

– calculating ROI and method of cost allocation;

– industrializing the production of the parameter settings of an integration solution;

We are therefore conscious of the road that remains to be traveled, and hope that this work helps to found an exhaustive and global approach to the subject of application integration, whose essential and strategic character for enterprises Aline Bec underlines in her preface.

Your remarks, critiques and suggestions are welcome. Please do not hesitate to send them to us via our publisher.

Bibliography

[ALT 99] ALTMAN R., HILL J., KLEIN J., LHEUREUX B., NATIS Y., PEZZINI M., SCHULTE R., VARMA S., "Middleware: The Glue for Modern Applications", *GartnerGroup, Strategic Analysis Report*, 26 July 1999.

[BER 99] BERNADAC J.C. and KNAB F., *Construire une application XML*, Eyrolles, 1999.

[BPM 04] BUSINESS PROCESS MANAGEMENT INITIATIVE (BPMI), *Business Process Modeling Notation (BPMN) Version 1.0*, BPMI.org, 3 May 2004.

[COR 00] CORDIER I., "Intégration d'applications – Des métiers au cœur du puzzle informatique", *Informatiques Magazine no. 99*, 18 February 2000.

[DEB 04] DEBAUCHE B. and MEGARD P., *BPM Business Process Management: Pilotage métier de l'entreprise*, Hermes, 2004.

[GIL 99] GILPIN M., "Bank Mergers in France Highlight City Planning: Lessons Learned for Enterprise Architecture", *Giga Information Group, Ideabyte*, 12 March 1999.

[MAN 95] MANOUVRIER B., "Organiser les échanges inter-applications", *Le temps des Ordinateurs*, 25 June 1995.

[MAN 01] MANOUVRIER B., *EAI Intégration des applications d'entreprise*, Hermes Science, 2001.

[ORM 06] OASIS, *Reference Model for Service Oriented Architecture 1.0*, Committee Specification 1, 19 July 2006.

[R33 05] ECONOMIC COMMISSION FOR EUROPE, United Nations Centre for Trade Facilitation and Electronic Business (UN/CEFACT), "Recommendation and Guidelines on establishing a Single Window to enhance the efficient exchange of information between trade and government", *Recommendation No 33, United Nations*, July 2005.

[SAS 98] SASSOON J., *Urbanisation des systèmes d'informations*, Hermes, 1998.

[SCH 97] SCHULTE R., "Architecture and Planning for Modern Application Styles", *GartnerGroup, Strategic Analysis Report*, 28 April 1997.

[WFM 99] WORKFLOW MANAGEMENT COALITION *Terminology & Glossary*, The Workflow Management Coalition Specification, February 1999.

[WMC 99] WORKFLOW MANAGEMENT COALITION, *Interface 1: Process Definition Interchange: Process Model*, The Workflow Management Coalition Specification, 29 October 1999.

Index

V, W

X